Microcredit as a Poverty Alleviation Strategy, Women's Empowerment and Gender Relations

(A Study of SHG Households in Visakhapatnam District, A.P., India)

MICROCREDIT AS A POVERTY ALLEVIATION STRATEGY, WOMEN'S EMPOWERMENT AND GENDER RELATIONS

(A Study of SHG Households in Visakhapatnam District, A.P., India)

KUNDI HARIKA

Research Director
R. RAMAKRISHNA
Department of Economics Andhra University
Visakhapatnam

SWASTIK

SWASTIK PUBLICATIONS

New Delhi-1100 02, India

SWASTIK PUBLICATIONS
213, Vardan House 7/28, Ansari Road
Darya Ganj, New Delhi- 110002
Phones: 9968482939, 9899462604
E-mail: *swastik_books@yahoo.com*

Regd. Office
31 Gali No. 1, A Block, Pocket 5, CRP Water Tank,
Sonia Vihar, Delhi-110094
Phones: 9968482939

MICROCREDIT AS A POVERTY ALLEVIATION STRATEGY, WOMEN'S EMPOWERMENT AND GENDER RELATIONS

First Published 2019

ISBN : 978-93-87367-01-2

Published in India by Indra Mani Pandey for Swastik Publications, and printed at **Global Printing Services**, Delhi.

Acknowledgements

First and the foremost, I express my deep sense of gratitude to my Research Director, Professor R. Ramakrishna, Department of Economics, Andhra University for his kind encouragement, valuable time spent, timely suggestions and able guidance at different stages of my research work.

I owe a great deal to Prof. P. Tara Kumari Head of the Department, Department of Economics, Prof. L. D. Sudhakar Babu, Chairman, Board of Studies and Director, School of Distance Education and to Prof. D. Prabhakar Rao, Principal A.U. College of Arts and Commerce, for my success in this endeavour. I express my sincere thanks to all my teachers in the Department for their cooperation, help and support extended during my research work. I would like to thank Mr. R. Appa Rao, Lecturer (Retd.), Govt. Degree College, Srikakulam for his help in correcting the manuscript.

I am thankful to the staff members of Dr. V.S. Krishna memorial library, Andhra University for providing me with all the necessary facilities. I am thankful to Librarian, School of Economics, Andhra University, for readily supplying me any information required for my work. I am also thankful to the office staff of the Department of Economics, for their help in the completion of my work. I am very much impressed by the generous help rendered by Dr. Padma Narayana, Dr. Jayaseela Prakash, Dr. B. Kanna Rao and Dr. M. Subbaiah for their cooperation in collecting the data and the help extended at various stages of my work. I express my sincere thanks to my friend, Ch. Chiranjeevi for his help in completing my work.

I would be failing in my duty, if I do not place on record my deep sense of gratitude to my mother in law K. Suryanarayanamma, Smt. R. Bharathi, Advocate and all my family members and friends for their cooperation in completion of my research work.

KUNDI HARIKA

Contents

List of Tables

List of Figures

List of Appendixs

1

Introduction

1.1 Background Information

Poverty is a major challenge to the South Asian country of India, the largest democracy in the world. With its accelerated economic growth since the last decade, India has emerged as a global player and as the world's fourth largest economy in terms of purchasing power parity and has advanced on most of the Millennium Development Goals (World Bank - 2010, India Country Overview). The rise of the new Indian middle class as a social group that advocates economic liberalization has received great scholarly attention (Fernandes, 2006). However, as the World Bank - 2010, India Country Overview points out, poverty remains as a major challenge. A focus on the poor assumes heightened salience especially in the face of criticism of the impact of globalization on labour sector of developing countries. Jhabvala and Sinha (2002) point out that while the employment opportunities for women have decreased in certain sectors it has improved in certain others. Yet, as they reiterate, gender based wage differentials cutting across sectors and occupations, coupled with increasing actualization and in formalization continue to haunt the employment scenario.

In the wake of the precarious labour position in the context of globalization, a good portion of wealth generated by the recent growth of the country is invested to deliver services to poor. For instance, massive number of women is being mobilized to form Self Help Groups (SHGs) in order to discover new livelihood opportunities. Microcredit through SHGs is one such attempt directed at different social groups of people who fall under the broad rubric of "the poor". Initiatives by both the state and non-state actors have actively promoted the mobilization of the poor, especially poor women, into SHGs as an attempt at a countervailing force against actualization and exclusion from the formal sectors of the economy. The small loans (microcredit) given to poor women empower them in several ways. Apart from aiding in extricating themselves from loans sharks, microcredit empowers poor women financially to meet certain emergencies without relying on others or even their own men folk. In addition to catering to material requirements, the women become empowered psychologically too thorough a sense of security generated from belonging to a collective identity, through different kinds of knowledge ranging from banking operations to legal literacy, through acquisition of confidence to travel alone as well as in groups, and to meet and discuss without fear, serious issues of concern with statist agents, through enhanced communication skills and ability for public speech, through development of self-esteem (Kumar Bhargavi Valsala Kumari, 2011).

The Microcredit by itself does not rescue a woman from chronic poverty unless it is backed up by a remunerative activity. Further, the microcredit by itself is not the appropriate instrument for poverty alleviation of the most vulnerable segments among

the category "poor" and that they need more structural solutions to the problem of their vulnerability and sense of insecurity (Kumar Bhargavi Valsala Kumari, 2011). The two key sets of debates viz., (i) Gender and Development and (ii) Role of State in Microcredit as a tool for Development are drawn attention in the present study.

(i) Gender and Development:

The gender dimension of development has received considerable attention since the time of Esther (Boserup, 1970) who has been highly critical of development programs that bypass women. Since Boserup pointed out the need for integrating women into all development initiatives, feminists of various persuasions have shown empirically the unrecognized, unremunerated contribution of women to the economy. The world of political economy is a gendered one. Men and women are positioned differently in society and have differential access to resources which makes them articulate their responses differently (Rai, 2002). Traditionally, development has been equated in the West with economic growth. But Ester (Boserup, 1970) had highlighted the gendered world of development and pointed out how development sidetracked women. Others have critiqued development for impoverishing women (Dutta, 2002) and for disempowering them (Rai, 2002). The "Women in Development" theorists placed a heavy emphasis on rights-especially reproductive and educational rights.

On the other hand, the basic needs theorists Sen (1999), Nussbaum (2000) held that poverty was a manifestation of the inability of people to meet their basic needs, which included both tangible and intangible needs like "agency achievements" of participation, empowerment, community life etc. The basic needs theorists focused on the quality of life, and this is reflected in the Human Development Index of the United Nations Development Programme. For Sen, poverty is "capability deprivation". The capability theory not only engaged concerns of the marginalized groups like the old, children and women, it was sensitive to gender relations as well. Moving beyond capabilities, Sen discussed the entitlements which are required for developing capabilities. Capability theorists like Dreze and Sen argued that due to women's restricted access to the world of paid labour and control over family income their position in the family is negatively impacted.

But since women in the paid labour sector are also subordinated, access to paid labour and control over family income will not account completely for a just gender relation. Something more is required. Agarwal (1994) and Mearns (1999) have drawn attention to the significant role played by independent property rights in the improvement in socio-economic conditions of women in rural South Asia. Means and Sinha (1999) pointing out the huge obstacles faced by the poor and marginalized in India in accessing land maintain that women's access to and control over land and their bargaining power vis-à-vis their husbands can be enhanced through joint land titling. Although academics and feminists make the distinction between Women in Development and Gender and Development both are used interchangeably by development agencies as pointed out by Rai (2002). Development agencies and NGOs have long been votaries of development whose explicit objective has been women's empowerment. But there seems to be no consensus on what constitutes empowerment.

The word "empowerment" has come to signify a range of meanings from economic independence, and access to resources, to intangibles like autonomy, and self- confidence. Although economic activities may enlarge options for marginalized people that do not lead them to take charge of creating the options from which they may choose. For that to happen, what is needed is a "combination of confidence and self-esteem, information, analytical skills, ability to identify and tap into available resources, political and social influence, and so on". Feminist scholars have critiqued conventional understanding of development at least on four counts (Verma, 2004). First, is the critique of the liberal conception of the public/private dichotomy as a normative principle and an institutional arrangement (Pateman, 1987) and (Okin, 1989). This view calls for demolishing the false dichotomy between the two spheres as they are intimately intertwined and as such separation of the public and the private is one of the major causative factors of women's subordination.

Further it leads to asymmetrical distribution of benefits and burdens among members of the household with serious implications for women. Second, the critique of the assumption underpinning both modernization and Marxist theories that women's labour force participation will automatically lead to their enhanced status. Third, the feminist critique of the notion of culture that serves to distinguish the modern from the traditional and the representation of the complex, diverse, and multilayered. Third World Countries (Parpart et al, 2000) as homogenous, "primitive" and static. Finally, feminist critiques have been directed at the methodological issue of knowledge production. The rejection of a development paradigm based on economic growth has led feminists to conceptualize development in inclusive and participatory terms and with respect for nature that is so vital in sustainable development (Shiva, 1988) and (Agarwal, 1992, 1997).

Thus, it is obvious that development discourse is not monolithic but comprises of multiple and competing discourses (Ebrahim, 2001). Any attempt at exploring women's subordination needs to employ a bifocal lens of critical scrutiny at both the private and the public spheres, including the family on the one hand, and the civil society and the state on the other, in order to understand how all these institutions work at tandem to structure women's subordinate position in society. In the current context of neoliberal policies of world powers, some are pessimistic about the future of the field of Gender and Development. But scholars like Marchand (2009) believe that it provides the space for critical and innovative thinking about development issues in a transformed world. Two strands of feminist thought provide valuable insight in dealing with gender and development. The first is Post-colonial Feminism with its emphasis on representation, "mothering" and silencing the voice of Third World Women and second is Transnational Feminism that gives us a better appreciation of the current realities of the world we live in like migration and construction of transnational communities (Marchand, 2009). One critique of Gender and Development field is the instrumental use women are put to, in order to meet wider development objectives. For instance, microcredit programs treat women as efficient economic actors.

(ii) Role of State in Microcredit as a tool for Development:

The group based approach to lending small amounts of money (microcredit) to the poor saw a rapid expansion during the early 1970s (Thierry van Baseliner, 2000). The 1970s and early 1980s are credited as the years of discovery of microcredit as a poverty alleviation program and the 1990s as the year of legitimizations of the microcredit sector (Mahout, 2001). Some of the early generation scholarship focused on the impact of microcredit on the health and education of children of parents who were members of microcredit. Thus Todd (1996) using the three criteria to measure the health of children, viz., of height, weight for height and weight for age, found the children of Graeme Bank groups healthier than the children of control group. The study conducted by UNICEF (1997) in Nepal found that when microcredit was delivered in conjunction

with other social services it empowered women and girl children. In eighties and nineties when the role of the state was reduced drastically especially in the sectors of welfare and development by the World Bank and IMF conditionality resulting in the deepening and expansion of poverty, many civil society organizations/NGOs stepped in to help meet the challenge. The extent of outreach of microcredit to the poorest by these organizations has been a matter of great scholarly attention.

Microcredit's capacity to successfully reduce poverty through community mobilization along with the Diasporas has been documented in the Nigerian city of Lebo-Ode, where an estimated 90 per cent of the population lived below the poverty line of US $1.00 per person per day. Poverty in the city has been reduced significantly. Such stories of reduction of poverty and other benefits of microcredit from around the globe abound the microcredit literature. Changes have been brought in the non-economic aspects as well. The notion of the "male breadwinner" has been dismantled by the coming of microcredit (Kalka, Nathan, Johan, 2004). While some scholars eulogize the empowering capacity of microcredit, there is an equally forceful voice challenging those assumptions of empowerment and control that microcredit gives to women. Goetz and Gupta (1996) contest such assumptions. Close scrutiny of loan histories in five villages of Bangladesh revealed that in close to 63 per cent of cases women had either partial, very little or no control over the loans they took. Scholars have pointed out the low intake of credit among the poorest and also that the poorest are making repayment by reducing their consumption or borrowing from other informal sources of credit thus worsening their condition (Galba and Rae, 2003). Microcredit has to augment other programs to address the concerns of the poorest.

Scholars have shown the positive impacts of microcredit in Bangladesh, like greater decision making power in household, freedom of mobility and bargaining power (Pitt, Chandler and Cartwright, 2003), positive differential health impacts (Pitt, Khandhker, Chowkhury, and Millimet, 2003), enhancing cash income and ownership of non-land assets, and greater intra household resource allocation (Khandker, 1998), greater anthropometric measurements of children of loaners (Todd, 1996 and UNICEF 1997), greater use of contraceptives (Schuler and Hashemi, 1994), and reduction of transitory poverty (McCulloch, Neil and Baulch Bob, 2000). Others have pointed out the inability of microcredit in targeting and altering the lives of the hardcore poor (Hashemi, 1997-2001, Rahman and Hossain, 1995), (Montgomery, Bhattacharya and Hulme, 1996), (Zaman, 1997), achieving sustainability at the cost of impoverishing the poor (Rahman, 1999 and Khandker, 1998), inappropriateness of microcredit in certain kinds of circumstances (Parker and Pearce, 2001), and inability to address all the problems of poverty (Wright, 2000).

The relationship between microcredit and gender has received great scholarly attention globally (Lamia Karim, 2008). Linda Mayoux (2002) shows how microcredit increases women's access to and control over income and assets. Jacka (2010) on the other hand found in her study of poor households in Xinpu, China that although the small loans made significant contribution to the domestic economies it did not generate other forms of empowerment like increased respect or status in the community or a greater degree of control over resources. Without broad community wide changes in gender norms and expectations microcredit can be disempowering because men take control over the loans women borrow and transfer the burden of repayment to women (Jacka, 2010 and Goetz and Gupta, 1996). Vonderlack-Navarro (2010) in her ethnographic study of women participants in microcredit program in Tegucigalpa, Honduras, found that male partner's behavior can both facilitate and restrict the use and repayment of loans.

Chari-Wagh (2009) in her analysis of a microcredit program run by a rural feminist group of Maharashtra examines the linkages between citizenship, gender and development and concludes that we cannot empower women purely by focusing on economic factors without factoring in their inter related dimensions of nutrition, health, violence, insecurity etc. Shetty (2003) in her comparison of microcredit programs in three communities in India and the USA argues that if empowerment is the objective of microcredit rather than poverty alleviation, then more broad based interventions are required. Further, in her study she found that although women have been able to negotiate some changes at the household level, microcredit has not been able to dismantle the gendered division of labour. As a development model, microcredit is viewed as a poverty alleviation strategy, an economic development and an empowerment tool. That microcredit has made positive difference in the lives of a large number of poor women by way of enlargement of role for women in household decision making, greater accessibility to loan, social networking, bargaining power and freedom of mobility is widely acknowledged (Pitt, Khandker, and Cartwright, 2003). The collateral benefits on other members of the family have also been documented (Pitt, Khandker, Cartwright, and Millimet, 2003).

The UNICEF (1997) study also highlights the lower infant mortality rate and higher school attendance for girls as positive outcomes of microcredit in the hands of women. Other positive results include use of contraceptives (Schuler and Hashemi, 1994), reduction in income poverty, especially transitory poverty (McCulloch, Neil and Baulch, Bob, 2002), better per capita income, per capita expenditure, and household net worth (Khandker, 2001), better household resource allocation by way of increased investment in human capital as opposed to increased investment in physical capital by men (Khandker, 1998). Scholars have pointed out that very few evaluations have studied the impact of microcredit on power relations of gender within the household and the community (Goetz and Sen Gupta, 1996). Since most studies take the household as the unit of analysis, scholars have challenged the assumption that greater access to microcredit gives women greater control and empowerment since research has revealed that a significant portion of the loan taken by poor women are controlled by male relatives.

1.2 Statement of the Problem:

An attempt to review those studies that examine the impact of microcredit on women empowerment and gender relations has been limited. The effect of microcredit intervention through SHG concept on employment, income and poverty to understand the benefits of group lending to small borrowers is important. Further, certain issues like loan repayment performance of rural poor to formal, informal and microcredit sources have not received wide attention. The present study therefore, contributes to the debate on how microcredit influences women empowerment and gender relations.

1.3 Objectives:

I. To examine the effect of Microcredit on employment, income and poverty among rural households

II. To analyze the overview of rural indebtedness

III. To identify the factors influencing borrowing and repayment of loans

IV. To study the economic and social impact of microfinance in empowering women

V. To suggest policy initiatives for empowering women

1.4 Organization of the Study:

This study has been organized into eight chapters. The Introductory Chapter deals with problem, objectives and organization of the Study. The Second Chapter focused on the review of literature on credit market with special reference to microfinance. In the Third Chapter, an attempt is made to analyze the methodology used in the study. The Forth Chapter examined the effect of microcredit on employment, income and poverty. The Fifth Chapter presented the indebtedness of households and the factors influencing borrowing and repayment of loans. The economic impact of microfinance in empowering women and gender relations has been presented in the Sixth Chapter. The social impact of microfinance in empowering women has been presented in the Seventh Chapter. The last Chapter provides conclusions of the study.

References:

Agarwal, B. (1994), "Gender and Command Over Property: A Critical Gap in Economic Analysis and Policy in South Asia", World Development, 22(10): 1455-78.

Agarwal, B. (1997), "Environmental Action, Gender Equity and Women's participation", Development and Change, 28(1): 1-44.

Agarwal, B. (1992), "The Gender and Environment Debate: Lessons from India", Feminist Studies, 18(1): 119-58.

Boserup, E. (1970), Women's Role in Economic Development. Earthscan, London.

Chari-Wagh, A. (2009), "Raising Citizenship Rights for Women through Microcredit Programs: An Analysis of MASUM, Maharashtra, India", Community Development Journal, 44(3): 403-414.

Dutta, I. (2002), "Knowledge and Skills in a Global Economy: A Dialectic of Inclusion and Exclusion", Indian Journal of Lobour Economics, 45(4): 1121-28.

Ebrahim, A. (2001), "NGO Behaviour and Development Discourse: Cases from Western India", International Journal of Voluntary and Nonprofit Organizations, 12(2): 79-101.

Fernandes, L. (2006), India's New Middle Class: Democratic Politics in an Era of Economics Reform. U of Minnesota Press.

Galab, S., & Rao, N. C. (2003), "Women's self-help groups, poverty alleviation and empowerment", Economic and Political weekly, 38 (12/13): 1274-1283.

Goetz, A. M., & Gupta, R. S. (1996), "Who takes the Credit? Gender, Power, and Control over Loan Use in Rural Credit Programs in Bangladesh", World Development, 24(1): 45-63.

Hashemi, Syed M. (1997), "Those Left Behind: A Note on Targeting the Hardcore Poor", In Wood Geoffrey D and Sharif, Iffath A (Eds), Who Needs Credit; Poverty and Finance in Bangladesh, Zed Books, London and New York.

Jacka, T. (2010), "Women's Activism, Overseas Funded Participatory Development, and Governance: A Case Study from China", Women's Studies International Forum, 33 (2): 99-112.

Jhabvala, R., & Sinha, S. (2002), "Liberalization and the Woman Worker", Economic and Political Weekly, 37(21): 2037-2044.

Karim, L. (2008), "Demystifying Microcredit: The Grameen Bank, NGOs, and Neoliberalism in Bangladesh", Cultural Dynamics, 20(1): 5-29.

Kelkar, G., Nathan, D., & Jahan, R. (2004), "Redefining Women's "Samman": Microcredit and Gender Relations in Rural Bangladesh", Economic and Political Weekly, 39(32): 3627-3640.

Khandker, S. (2001), "Does micro-finance really benefit the poor? Evidence from Bangladesh", In ponencia presentada a Asia and Pacific Forum on Poverty: Reforming Policies and Institutions for Poverty Reduction, The Asian Development Bank, Manila (pp. 5-9).

Khandker, S. R. (1998), Fighting poverty with microcredit: experience in Bangladesh, Oxford University Press.

Kumari, K. B. V. (2011), Microcredit as a poverty alleviation strategy, women's empowerment and gender relations (Doctoral dissertation, Rutgers University- GraduateSchool-New Brunswick). See alsoat HYPERLINK http://rucore.libraries.rutgers.edu/rutgers-lib/33894/PDF/1/http://rucore.libraries.rutgers.edu/rutgers-lib/33894/PDF/1/

Marchand, M. H. (2009), "The Future of gender and Development After 9/11: Insights from Postcolonial Feminism and Transnationalism", Third World Quarterly, 30(5): 921-935.

Mayoux, L. (2001), "Tackling the Down Side: Social Capital, Women's Empowerment and Micro-Finance in Cameroon" Development and Change, 32 (3): 435-64.

Mayoux, L. (2002), "Micro Finance and Women's Empowerment: Rethinking "best practice", Development Bulletin, 57: 76-81.

McCulloch, N., & Baulch, B. (2000), "Simulating the Impact of Policy upon Chronic and Transitory Poverty in Rural Pakistan" Journal of Development Studies, 36(6): 100-130.

Mearns, R., & Sinha, S. (1999), Social exclusion and land administration in Orissa, India, Working paper no: 2124, World Bank.

Mearns, R. (1999), Access to land in rural India: policy issues and options, Working paper no: 2123, World Bank.

Montgomery, R., Bhattacharya, D., Hulme, D., & Mosley, P. (1996), Credit for the poor in Bangladesh, The BRAC Rural Development Programme and the Government Thana Resource Development and Employment Programme, Finance against poverty, 2: 94-176.

Nussbaum, Martha C. (2000), Women and Human Development: The Capabilities Approach, Vol. 3, Cambridge University Press, Cambridge. Okin, S. M. (2008), Justice, gender, and the family, Basic books, USA.

Parker, J. and Pearce, D. (2001), Microfinance, Grants, and Non-Financial Responses to Poverty Reduction: Where does Microcredit fit? Consultative Group Focus

Note number 20, Washington D.C, See also at HYPERLINK http://ntl.ids.ac.uk/cgap/wnewlib.htm http://ntl.ids.ac.uk/cgap/wnewlib.htm.

Parpart, J. L., Connelly, P., & Barriteau, V. E. (Eds.). (2000), Theoretical perspectives on gender and development, IDRC.

Pateman, C. (1987), "Feminist Critiques of the Public/Private Dichotomy", In Anne Phillips (ed) Feminism and equality, Basil Blacwell, Oxford.

Hashemi, S. (2001), Including the poorest: linking microfinance and safety net programs, CGAP, Occasional Paper no: 20.

Pitt, M. M., Khandker, S. R., Chowdhury, O. H., & Millimet, D. L.(2003), "Credit Programs for the Poor and the Health Status of Children in Rural Bangladesh", International Economic Review, 44 (1): 87-118.

Pitt, M., Khandker, S., & Cartwright, J. (2004), "Does micro-credit empower women? Evidence from Bangladesh", Evidence from Bangladesh), World Bank Policy Research Working Papers, No: 2998.

Rahman, A. (1999), "Micro-credit Initiatives for Equitable and Sustainable Development: Who Pays?", World development, 27(1): 67-82.

Rahman, H. Z., & Hossain, M. (1995), Rethinking rural poverty: Bangladesh as a case study, Sage Publications Pvt Ltd, India.

Rai, S. M. (2002), Gender and the political economy of development, Polity Press, UK. Schuler, S. R., & Hashemi, S. M. (1994), "Credit programs, women's empowerment, and contraceptive use in rural Bangladesh", Studies in family planning, 65-76.

Sen, A. (1999), Development as freedom. Oxford University Press, Oxford.

Shetty, S. (2003), Gender, Poverty, Empowerment and the Promise of Microcredit in India and the United States, Dissertation Abstracts International. Section A: Humanities and Social Sciences, 63(10): 3758.

Shiva, V. (1988), Staying Alive, Women, Ecology and Survival in India, Kali, New Dilhi. Todd, Helen (1996), Women at the Center. Westview Press. New York.

Unicef. (1997), Give us credit, Division of Evaluation, Policy and Planning, Available online: http:// www. unicef. org/credit/-credit. pdf

Van Bastelaer, T. (2000), "Imperfect information, social capital and the poor's access to credit", Center for Institutional Reform and the Informal Sector (IRIS), University of Maryland.

Verma, V. (2004), "Engendering Development: Limits of Ferminist Theories and Justice", Economics and Political Weekly, 39(49): 5246-5252.

Vonderlack-Navarro, R. (2010), "Targeting women versus addressing gender in microcredit: Lessons from Honduras". Affilia, 25(2): 123-134.

World Bank (2010), World Development Report 2002, Oxford University Press, Oxford. Wright, G. A. (2000), Microfinance systems: Designing quality financial services for the poor, Zed books, London.

Zaman, H. (1997), "Micro-credit Programs: Who Participated and to What Extent?", In Wood Geoffrey D and Sharif, Fifth A (Ends), Who Needs Credit; Poverty and Finance in Bangladesh, Zed Books London.

2

Review of Literature

2.1 Introduction

Since beginning the developments in agricultural sector have resulted in changes, which had both beneficial and adverse effects on the conditions of rural households. For instance, developments in bio-chemical technology resulting in a spectacular rise in agricultural output, institutional reforms such as land reforms and policy measures like minimum wage legislation have had a positive impact on the economic welfare of rural poor. On the other side, which may off-set the advantages of bio-technology viz., increasing adoption of labour-displacing machinery in high growth regions and demographic factors like increase in proportions of rural labour in the total work-force, may even-out the marginal benefits that emanated from the spectacular growth in the agricultural sector. The effect of these variables on the conditions of the rural poor households has been widely discussed with reference to employment, real wages and other related issues by the academics. It is inferred that though the incomes of this class have been on the increase, the real income is on the decline and they are forced to borrowfor both production and consumption. This chapter has been divided into two sections. Section-I presented the review of Credit Policy for the poor. In Section-II, the review of empirical studies on the impact of Microfinance on rural households is analysed.

SECTION – I
REVIEW OF THE CREDIT POLICY

2.2.1 Review of the Credit Policy

Generally, there is an excess of expenditure over income among the poor and to bridge the gap credit is important. The poor do not have sufficient and reliable access to credit from the formal banking system for a number of reasons. These relate to the inability of the poor to provide adequate physical collateral and transaction costs due to cumbersome banking procedures while dealing with large number of small borrowers and risk costs of lending institutions associated with timely repayment of the loans. The risks or uncertainties in the credit market often arise from the problem of information asymmetry. The problem of information asymmetry can be solved but it is costly for the lending institutions. The microfinance groups, based on the principle of joint liability, have the potential to solve the problem of information asymmetry and improve access to credit for the poor. In this context, the following questions become relevant: How do imperfections emerge in the rural credit markets? How can these imperfections be reduced in microfinance groups? What factors play an important role in ensuring collective action at the group level while selecting the creditworthy borrowers, monitoring the utilization of the loan and ensuring repayment under microfinance groups? What are the different mechanisms and incentives incorporated to bring about collective action among microfinance group members? (Emil Mathew, 2006).

Instead of improving the credit availability, members have widened the existing inequality in the distribution of credit. In this context, the group approach of microfinance assumes significance. Since collective responsibility is a public good, it is quite possible that the members may free ride. Therefore, members should be provided with adequate incentives and mechanisms, which constitute the major focus of the present study. An attempt has been made in this chapter to review the theoretical and empirical literature to answer these questions. Unlike goods market, credit market transactions have future implications. A credit transaction involves a relationship between the lender and the borrower, in the context of uncertainty. A credit transaction is said to be complete only when the borrower repays the amount borrowed and there is no certainty about this repayment (Bhatt, 1987). This implies that both lenders and borrowers face risks about the completion of a credit transaction. Borrowers face the risk that the expected increase in income from an investment project for repayment may or may not materialize. On the other hand, lenders risks have two elements: one relates to the same risks which the borrowers face, and the other relates to the borrowers' commitment to repay; even if she/ he is able to repay, she/ he may not be willing to repay (Hoff and Stiglitz, 1990).

Asymmetry of information in the rural credit market results in a situation similar to (Akerlof's, 1970) market for lemons. In these markets, the sellers of good quality products withdraw from the sale as their products are ranked equivalent to bad quality products. Therefore, the difficulty to gather information on risks that are faced by the borrowers forces the lenders not to extend credit to large number of borrowers with varied risks. When the lenders cannot obtain information on risks of the borrowers and assume that they are all the same in terms of risks, adverse selection arises. The second problem of information relates to the difficulty in gathering information regarding the utilization of the money borrowed. The lenders have to monitor the purposes for which the borrowers have invested and hence, it examines whether the investment leads to repayment (Emil Mathew, 2006).

In short, the information problems in the credit market impose certain costs on the lenders and they are ex-ante costs of adverse selection and ex-post costs of moral hazard (Lin and Nugent, 1995). The former relates to the imperfections on the information regarding the creditworthiness of the borrower or his/her willingness to make repayment, whereas the latter relates to his/her ability to make repayments. As it is costly to gather information on these two major aspects of credit transactions, the rural credit markets deviate from the classical assumption of perfect competition and therefore, these markets are imperfect. The imperfect credit markets bring down the total volume of the loan able funds transacted. The costs involved in acquiring information about these two aspects often lead to a market failure and constrained Pareto efficiency (Besley, 1994). However, credit market failure of such kind in the institutional sources of credit can be brought down once information about the transactions is obtained.

As it is difficult to gather information on creditworthiness of large numbers of small borrowers without adequate collateral, formal lenders finds it difficult to lend in the rural areas. Moreover, the credit markets of these rural areas are characterized by covariant risks, especially in the absence of portfolio diversification and segmented markets (Beasley, 1994). As in the case of lenders, the borrowers too face problems in rural credit markets. The poor lack adequate physical capital to provide as collateral. Moreover, they face certain imperfections in the banking system such as complicated procedures, political interference, cultural gap between the officials and borrowers and short banking hours etc., which restrict their access to credit (Rajasekhar, 1996).

According to Hoff and Stiglitz, (1990), lenders are entrusted to examine imperfect information problems of three kinds in the rural credit markets. They are problems of screening, incentive and enforcement. The first one relates to the problem of ensuring the likelihood of default of the borrowers and it looks into the willingness of the borrowers to make repayment. The incentive problem relates to the problem of borrowers to take actions, which makes repayment more likely. The third problem relates to the problem of ensuring repayment. The information costs involved for both lenders and borrowers for bringing about the transactions are called transaction costs. The rural credit demands of the poor are being met by informal sources of credit even though they are charging high rates of interests. But, their higher rates of interests can be justified in terms of the transaction costs for gathering information about the creditworthiness of the borrowers.

According to Braver man and Gush (1986), the informal sources of credit were better in reaching the poor through their informal linkages to output market and also through the information acquired about the creditworthiness of the borrowers through their prior credit dealings. With this objective, the lenders generally lend to those borrowers with whom they have a longer duration of credit dealings. In short, the imperfections in the rural credit market impose costs for both lenders and borrowers. The explicit transaction costs experienced by the rural poor from the formal credit market and the implicit transaction costs in terms of higher rates of interests charged by the informal sources of credit put a stumbling block on the rural poor to access credit.

2.2.2 Innovations in Rural Credit Market:

Realizing the problem of inadequate access to credit to the rural poor, governments have been introducing specialized banks and rural development programmers from time to time. Without giving due attention to the costs of administration and default risks in the credit market, these specialized banks were instructed to impose interest rate ceilings for their transactions. But, such an action resulted in an increased demand for credit and led to credit rationing, whereby non- rationed rich borrowers received larger amounts of the loan (Vega, 1984; Adams et. al., 1984; Sadhu and Rajasekhar, 2005). Consequently, the rich received higher amounts and larger number of loans at the cost of the poor. Thus interest rate ceilings also widened the already existing inequality in the distribution of wealth. The policies of administered interest rates were criticized by the economists of Ohio School (Adams et. al., 1984; Vega, 1984; Cuevas and Douglas, 1984). These economists were of the opinion that the market forces of demand and supply should be left free in determining the interest rates in the credit market. The rate of interest determined by the market should cover the costs of administration, in addition to the risks of default (Emil Mathew, 2006).

According to the proponents of Ohio School, the rate of interest charged by the informal sources of credit are market determined as it covers the transaction costs of acquiring information about the creditworthiness of the borrowers. As the interest rate ceilings widened the already existing inequality in the distribution of wealth, the Ohio School criticized the professed objective of outreach of the specialized banks. Because, instead of reaching the needy, these deliberately constituted institutional credit mechanisms taxed the poor while subsidizing the rich (Vega, 1984). Subsidized credit programmes encouraged corruption, capital flight and unproductive investment. Many of the financial institutions created to channel and allocate credit to the rural sector lacked accountability, fostered arbitrary practices and allocated credit more on political rather than on economic grounds (Braverman and Gusach, 1993). Another significant criticism revelled against the interest rate ceilings of the specialized banks relate to the long run sustainability of the financial institutions. The proponents of the Ohio School questioned the financial sustainability of the lending institutions in the context of subsidized rates of interests and they argued that institutional sustainability could not be realized under interest rate ceilings. The lower interest rates could not only cover the costs of administration and risks of default but also failed to stimulate savings of the rural poor.

In the regime of administered rates of interest the propensity to save was low. Moreover, lending institutions assumed that the poor were unbankable as they could not make regular saving contributions due to their fluctuating income. However, the Ohio School strongly recommended that savings contributed by the poor, even if they were small, gave information about their creditworthiness (Vogel, 1984). Inability of the formal institutions to mobilize savings in the context of interest ceilings leads to inadequate loan able funds. In the absence of adequate loan able funds, banks were forced to depend on internal and external sources of funds for lending and it created dependent. Thus, the proponents of Ohio School argued that the specialized banks could not achieve the twin objectives of financial sustainability of the lending institution and the targeting of the programme to the most desirable.

The poverty alleviation programmes introduced in the developing countries suffered from problems of targeting, poor utilization of loans, misappropriation of funds and poor recovery (Gaisha, et. al., 2001). As noted earlier, informal lending agencies were observed to be better in bringing down the costs of interest rate ceilings, as they had good information about the credit dealings of their clients. They could charge differential rates of interest. Moreover, they reduced the risk by inter-linkages or by diversifying into product, input and processing markets (Bouman, 1984). Even though the arguments put forth by the Ohio School are worthwhile, it should be noted that the School has not given adequate attention to the implicit gains, which the specialized development banks could generate. However, it is essential to look into the points raised by the Ohio school, especially those relating to the sustainability of the financial institution. It is significant to note that the savings on the part of the members provided information about the creditworthiness of the borrowers and capital for lending (Desai, 1983; Vogel, 1984; Rutherford, 2001; Adams, et. al., 1984). A freely determined market rate of interest is viable to cover the transaction costs of the lenders. But, a higher rate of interest charged by the moneylenders, even though justifiable from the point of acquiring information on creditworthiness of the borrowers, is not desirable. Therefore, both the formal and informal lending institutions have merits and demerits. This necessitated the creation of a new credit institution, which combined good features of formal and informal institutions.

Microfinance as an Innovation in the Credit Market

Recently, developing countries have adopted microfinance programmes as financial innovations aimed at poverty alleviation. Generally, women participate in these programmes and thereby, improving their standard of living. (Mayoux, 1998, 2001; Hashemi et. al., 1996; Khandker, 1998) have stated that the participation in the microfinance programmes empowered the women socially, politically and economically and hence, improved their status within the household and outside. Women are engaged in activities of lending and savings besides engaging in matters of social significance. These groups incorporate good features of reduced transaction costs and improved targeting. Under these groups, large number of small borrowers without adequate collateral can access credit by using social collateral. Under these groups, lenders issue loans to groups rather than to individuals and the group undertakes the responsibility of repaying back the loan. Thus the transaction costs of the lenders while exercising the functions of selecting, monitoring and enforcing repayment are brought down. Since the individual borrowers find it difficult to access credit from formal institutions, they can make use of the social networks, social connections and mutual trust for bringing down the asymmetry of information and achieve a better outcome (Reinke, 1998).

The social networks and the mutual trust among the members of the groups bring down transaction costs of both the lenders and borrowers. As against formal institutions, these groups do not require physical collateral from the poor borrowers and hence, a large number of small borrowers without physical collateral can access credit (Huppi and Feder, 1990; Godquin, 2004). Lenders select group members, based on their familiarity and personal contacts. Self-selection of the members into the group has the advantage that it exploits local information about the borrowers. By making use of this intangible resource, that is, information about creditworthiness of the members through social networks, they can alleviate credit market failures (Ghatak, 1999). Intimate knowledge of each other's activities facilitates mutual monitoring and the joint liability principle creates peer pressure for repayment. Besides ensuring repayment of the co-partners, the principle of joint liability influences the members to undertake the responsibility to repay the share of the loan of their partners in case of their default.

As the members are familiar to each other, the application of other social control mechanisms based on custom and social norms are effective (Schneider, 1996). While formal lenders have only limited options to compel repayment from delinquent borrowers, group members can employ social sanctions (Sharma and Zeller, 1997). According to (Reinke, 1998), solidaristic structure imposes high costs on the group members in terms of costs of formation of the groups, obligations for fortnightly meetings and mutual screening and risks of joint liability. However, such costs are observed to be less in rural areas where social stability and flow of information are more as members interact in small numbers and often, they belong to similar socio-economic characteristics (Braverman and Gusach, 1993).

Unlike the earlier subsidized credit programmes that neglected the capacity of the poor to make savings, the savings contributed by the members under Microfinance programmes has many advantages. The regular saving contributions made by the members to the group strengthen the perceptions that members have a stake in the institution. Groups rely on such savings of members as a reliable source of loanable fund. Such savings also help to know the creditworthiness of the borrowers and provide an incentive to make timely repayments (Bhatt, 1988; Vogel, 1984; Bouman, 1984; Hulme and Mosley, 1996). The periodic savings contributed by the members act as checks and balances (Morduch, 1999a, 1999b; Hulme and Mosley, 1996).

Joint liability principle asserts that all the members in a group are equally responsible to timely repayment. The principle of joint liability among the members in a group provides incentives to its members to undertake those actions, which reduce uncertainty in the credit market (Bhatt and Tang, 1998; Morduch, 1999b). This collective responsibility among the members in a group is the key aspect of Microfinance groups whereby the transaction costs relating to the enforcement of the contract can be brought down. Such lower costs increase the volume of transactions in the credit market and in the process, lead to an improved access to credit for large number of members.

It is, observed that in remote communities where the poorest are less mobile and do not have alternative sources of credit, the Microfinance programmes work effectively (Sharma and Zeller, 1998; Morduch, 1999b).

Additional non-financial services offered by the group such as training programmes, provision of inputs for project initiation and marketing facilities, etc., have positive impact on the performance of the group in terms of repayment (Mosly and Dhal, 1985; Godquin, 2004). These together with dynamic incentives such as second and higher amount of loan will be provided only after the repayments of the first loan have improved their performance. Collective action is the force behind the success of microfinance groups while bringing down transaction costs. Thus, it is pertinent to examine the concept of collective action and how it is applicable among the microfinance group members.

Concept of Collective Action

The concept of collective action has been taken from New Institutional Economics to understand the sharing of collective responsibility and the exercise of peer pressure among the Microfinance group members. Collective action represents the group of individuals with common interest tending to act to further those common interests. If rational and self-interested individuals realize that they gained from particular collective action, then they could be expected to engage in such an action (Olson, 1965), (Buchanan and Tullock, 1965) have supported the same argument by stating that a group would choose a collective mode of action, when each of its individual members found it profitable to act collectively rather than individually. But, those individuals with higher perceived private costs of co-operating over the perceived private benefit of co-operating might not attempt for collective action. This raises a question of what incentives were provided to group members to participate in collective action. The Prisoner's Dilemma game of (Campbell, 1985) reveals the benefits from collective action by the members in a group. Since collective sharing of responsibility brings down transaction costs, there should be free flow of information so that there should not be any free riding on the part of the members. Moreover, there should be a norm that one should forgo self-interest and act according to the collective interest of the group (Coleman, 1988). Most important aspect is that the members should feel the significance of acting collectively rather than individually (Emil Mathew, 2006).

The game theorists have proposed various conditions under which collective action will become a workable solution. In Olson's (1965) static analysis, non-co-operative outcome is the equilibrium solution. But, the repetition of the game into the future brings out a co-operative solution. Under situations of repetitive game, the fear of non-co-operative action from the participants of the game in future and the introduction of penalties for violating arrangements can be a powerful incentive for collective behaviour. If the players in a Prisoners Dilemma know that the game will be played repeatedly, the chances are that they will co-operate today in the hope that others will then do so are much higher than where the game is played only once (Axelord, 1981). If we assume that the players are able to negotiate changes in the rules of the game among themselves, then one likely change is the introduction of penalties for violating agreements. The effect of such penalties is to reinforce the tendency towards co- operation. Generally, if the individuals in a group share a common interest, the furtherance of common interest will automatically benefit each individual in the group, whether or not he/she has borne any of the costs of collective action to further the common interest.

In most of the studies, it is argued that certain preconditions are necessary for the collective enforcement of group norms, while in some other studies it is argued that these conditions can be developed in due course of time through their interactions. According to (Olson, 1965), two conditions were required to make collective action possible. One condition was that the number of individuals acting collectively to further their common interest should be sufficiently small. The other condition was that the groups should have access to 'selective incentives'. The number of members in a group was an important factor determining the incentive for collective action. For him, larger groups had a lower incentive for collective action, as an additional member added heterogeneity to the group in some or the other dimension and hence, the chances of free riding. Small groups might prevent the incentives for cooperation getting diluted. He has stated that partnership could be a workable solution, when the number of partners was quite small. When the number of partners increased, the incentive for each partner to work for the welfare of the enterprise lessened. Moreover, small group was more durable and the degree of consensus was easily workable as they had close and continuous interactions.

Various scholars have looked into the issue of number of members involved in a cooperative effort. According to (Stiglitz, 1990), small size increased the risk from a single member's default but increased the incentive for peer monitoring. The gains from the latter were likely to exceed the losses from the former. Larger groups had free rider problems, as each would expect others to expend the energy required to monitor and incur the ill-will that would result from reporting offenders who had misused the funds lent to them. Moreover, the cost to each member as a result of a default by one member might be sufficiently small that incentives to monitor were minimal in large groups. In short, as the size of the group increased, the time spent for monitoring also increased. Even though the costs of supervision increased for larger groups, the costs of mobilizing resources could be brought down for larger groups (Poteete and Ostrom, 2004). (Ghatak and Guinnane, 1999) have brought out that smaller groups could effectively cope up with free rider and mass co-ordination problems.

Homogeneity of the members involved in a cooperative effort was another most important precondition often discussed and debated by the scholars. It is argued that the socio-economic homogeneity of the members could ensure collective action (Lin and Nugent, 1995). Homogeneous groups emerged as those with lower default risk recognized their mutual interest in grouping together and the process would continue until the individuals with the highest risk were forced to group together (Stiglitz, 1990). Social norms, rules and conventions present in the society can influence the cooperative behaviour (Putnam, 1993). Historical experiences and traditional mores help the people to shape their preferences and degree of trust in their mutual relationship (Baland and Platteau, 1996). A study on the Malawian group credit has brought out that the pre- existing groups had a significant impact on collective outcomes, as it was easy for them to join the groups (Schaefer-Kehnert, 1983). Moreover, groups formed without any external influences would sustain for long, as they were formed voluntarily.

The effectiveness of the cooperative outcome depends to a large extent on the effectiveness of the repeated interactions with lower alternative opportunities and effective implementation of the incentives in the cooperatives. In order to stimulate cooperative action or to avoid non-cooperative outcome, the members in a group should be provided with both the positive and negative incentives (Olson, 1965). Social sanction or social ostracism was often used as the negative incentive or sticks for the members to avoid non-co-operative behaviour. Moreover positive incentives like higher amounts of loans in successive lending were provided to the members to encourage co-operation. (Young, 1998) has argued that expectation of the gains from repeated interactions into the future could be considered as an incentive for co-operation. The patterns of interaction, presence or absence of reciprocity among the members and decision-making arrangements determined whether a group would succeed or not (Oakerson, 1986).

Reciprocity required that members of the group contributed positively to each other's welfare.

Microfinance Groups as Institutions of Collective Action:

Stiglitz (1990) Morduch (1999) Floro and Yotopolous (1991) have advocated the significance of group lending programmes in bringing down the transaction costs. These studies have highlighted the welfare enhancing features of group lending programmes, either for the borrowers or for the lenders or for both. The linkage between formal banking institutions and microfinance groups leads to improved access to bank credit and financial discipline among borrowers. This is made possible by way of generating information about the bank ability of the rural borrowers, providing a guarantee cover to loans in order to encourage rural lending and allocating resources to upgrade the creditworthiness of the rural borrowers (Llanto, 1990). Under group lending mechanisms, welfare could be improved by transferring the risks from the lenders to the borrowers (Stiglitz, 1990), (Varian, 1990) has stated that if group members insured against one another across states of nature, it was advantageous for the lender. Some of the studies have emphasized the significance of the process through which group lending attained efficiency. These studies have brought out the significance of joint liability under group lending and how it enforced successful repayment of the loans borrowed through social ties among members (Floro and Yotopolous, 1991; Besley and Coate, 1995; Wydick, 1999).

In order to ensure bonding and timely repayment of loans, group lending needs to promote certain rules and at the same time, it should provide incentives to the members. The social ties among members in a group have the potential to promote solidarity in the group. Here, the interactions among the group members are structured within the lending group. The social relations among the individuals can help the entire group rather than a single individual. Without high degree of trustworthiness among the members in a group, the institution cannot exist. Thus, social relations among the group members can provide information, which facilitate collective action.

While group borrowing is advantageous on account of its capacity to reduce transaction costs, it has disadvantages also on account of the common ownership and team production. It is likely to emerge as a non-co-operative outcome, as the liability is fully shared among members under group lending. (Huppi and Feder, 1990) have stated that under the joint liability "the risk is borne by the group, whereas the benefit is reaped by individual. Group members have little incentive to repay if the majority of their peers default". A non-co-operative outcome leads to over-borrowing and under-supply of effort or of other individually costly production activities. In order to control the occurrences of such unhealthy practices, the members have to be provided with a system of incentives and rules (Braverman and Gusach, 1993).

According to (Huppi and Feder, 1990), group lending had both advantages as well as disadvantages. On the one hand, they brought down the transaction costs of credit market dealings by providing information about the creditworthiness of the borrowers, ensured timely repayment of the borrowers and improved their bargaining position. On the other hand, these programmes suffered from portfolio diversification and reduced the incentives of the members to make repayment if a majority of the members were found defaulted. It had the disadvantage of successful borrowers to default because of the burden of repaying for their partners. According to Devereux and Fishe (1993), joint liability was a useful solution under group lending, if the members of the group gained individually by the misfortune of another member or if the other members avoided the costs from repaying another member's loan. The element of individual gain or cost avoidance was the external factor exploited by the joint liability clause. When this element was not present, the default of one member tended to encourage the group as a whole to default, thus, exacerbating the delinquency problem.

The social sanction ensured through joint liability could be misguided in societies where homogeneous group members with covariate risks faced adversities (Braverman and Gusach, 1993). During good harvest, group lending worked well. Group lending failed during poor harvests when the successful members did not show any interest in repaying their co-partners as a majority of them were defaulting and the gains from repaying were less (Bratton, 1986). Another problem which might emerge in these collective entities was that the members would have the incentive to undertake risky project. Since the group was liable to repay for the share of the defaulters, it would generate a negative incentive among the members to undertake risky projects and ultimately this might increase the probability of default (Sharma and Zeller, 1997). But, such things could be circumvented, if the group cohesion was strong and the members felt responsible for the effect of the actions of others (Huppi and Feder, 1990). However, in these groups with high social connectedness or social cohesion or social capital repayment could be ensured through the use of negative incentives of loss of social reputation.

The social pressure among members had its own place in Microfinance programmes (Hulme and Mosley, 1996). If the social penalty of not repaying the loans was greater than the value of financial penalty imposed for non-repayment, peer pressure would be effective. Greater the homogeneity, stronger was the social pressure to repay. On the other hand, (Ghatak and Guinnane, 1999) have argued that the availability of alternative sources of credit determined the success of group lending. The competition among various joint liability institutions excluded people from the threat of denial of credit, since they had alternative credit institutions. Moreover, the existence and the cost of dynamic incentives decided whether joint liability would work or not. If a group was having heterogeneous characteristics, the burden of group formation and solidarity would be high. Similarly, if the social ties were weak, the mechanism of joint liability would not work.

Challenges before Microfinance Groups:

Various studies on Microfinance programmes have looked into the ability of the institutions to reduce asymmetry of information and its capacity to ensure access to credit for the rural poor based on the principle of joint liability (Besley and Coate, 1995; Bhatt and Tang, 1998; Desai, 1983; Godquin, 2004; Huppi and Feder, 1990; Jain and Mansuri, 2002; Schaefer-Kehnert, 1983; Sharma and Zeller, 1997; Wenner, 1995 Wydick, 1999; Zeller, 1994 and 1998;). All these studies have considered repayment achieved by the groups as a measure of success. This was because timely repayment of the loans reduced their dependence on subsidies and improved institutional sustainability. In other words, these studies were of the opinion that higher repayment ensured financial sustainability of the credit institution. But, they had not considered the problem of borrowers at the time of repayment and the processes behind repayment of the loans.

An important mechanism for ensuring loan repayment was the presence of tightly structured installment repayments, which enabled microfinance groups to overcome informational hurdles they faced while enforcing repayment and also reduced the burden of repayment on a lump sum basis (Hulme and Mosley, 1996). But, such a repayment pattern imposed certain costs onto the borrowers. Since members were required to make repayment immediately after their borrowing, it was difficult for them to repay the loan from the income generated from the investment made on the project. Moreover, they had to limit the type of projects they financed and there were transaction costs of making regular instalment repayments.

A study by Jain and Mansuri (2002) has brought out that this mechanism of installments repayment constituted by social sanction created dependence on informal credit markets at the time of repayment by borrowers. According to them, dependence on informal sources of credit was more among microfinance group members than non- members. As the principle of joint liability was strictly followed by the members to ensure repayment, the strong social pressure and the fear of social ostracism from the community associated with the peer pressure forced members to borrow from moneylenders at the time of repayment (Chavan and Ramakumar, 2002). If members were repaying the loans from the income generated from the activities undertaken with the microfinance loans, the risks of inability to make repayment and unwillingness to repay would have been brought down or would be made negligible. But, if the members in a group were very poor to make investments in productive projects or could not generate remunerative income from the invested activity, microfinance programmes, in fact, worsened the financial condition of the poor women.

The idea of giving loans to women who do not have physical collateral may seem attractive. But, it has a hidden transcript that since women have limited physical mobility and culturally imposed restrictions, often, the positional vulnerability of women is used at the time of repayment (Rahman, 1999). The bankers select women borrowers, as it is easier for them to ensure repayment. But, often, their husbands and other family members put pressure on them to join the programme to get loans for their own use. Rahman's study (1999) on Grameen Bank model of microfinance programme in Bangladesh reveals that at the time of repayment women experienced tensions and violence from within the household and from the members in a group and also from the bankers (Goetz and Gupta, 1996).

It is significant to note that often their male relatives controlled a large proportion of the women's loans. The peer pressure exerted by microfinance programmes at the time of repayment, often strained the social relation between group members and the staff (Woolcock, 1999). Woolcock's (1999) study reveals that in Bangladesh, the country where the programme had received wide popularity, the poorest members were forced to leave the programme and the attitude of the officials pressurizing the members to make timely repayments forced them to borrow money from the moneylenders. The principle of joint liability forced those members who repaid on time to bear the burden of willful default of their counterparts.

The rural credit markets are imperfect as it is difficult for the lenders to gather information about the creditworthiness of borrowers. The imperfect information about credit transactions imposes transaction costs for both the lenders and borrowers and thereby, it brings down the volume of the goods transacted. However, the asymmetry of information can be brought down through group based Microfinance programmes. Under these groups, the poor who do not have any physical collateral, can access credit through social collateral. Microfinance groups bring down the transaction costs by providing information about the creditworthiness of borrowers. They bring down the asymmetric information through social collateral offered by the members and improve access to credit to the poor who do not have any physical collateral. The principle of joint liability ensures repayment of the loans borrowed. Various mechanisms have been incorporated for the selection of the creditworthy borrowers for monitoring the utilization of the loan; and to ensure timely repayment or to avoid the problem of default in repayment. We have discussed both the positive and negative incentives, which play major roles while ensuring collective action among the members. Before going into the details of these issues, it is relevant to examine the evolution and growth of microfinance programmes in India.

2.2.3 Progress and Performance of SHGs: Concept of Self Help Groups:

Microfinance groups in India are called Self-Help Groups (SHGs). In addition to the usual functions of microfinance groups such as savings, credit and insurance, SHGs engage in issues of social significance. These are small groups of 10-20 members. In India, almost 90 per cent of the groups comprise of only women. The SHG provides the poor with alternative means of obtaining economic and social entitlement to resources through their active participation. SHGs are formed on voluntary basis, perceived appropriately as people's institution, providing the poor with the space and support necessary to take effective steps towards greater control over their lives in private and in society. Each group acts like a bank, and decides the internal operations of the group in the distribution of loans, monitors the utilization of loan amount and enforces repayment. Generally, the group disburses the loan amount among the members according to the criteria arrived at by the members. The members borrow both for consumption and productive purposes. As the group attains maturity in due course of time and the common pool of resources of the group, i.e., savings become insufficient for meeting the varied credit demands of the members, the group applies for external assistance mostly from banks under the NABARD bank linkage programme although other avenues are also emerging of late.

Differences between Grameen Bank Groups of Bangladesh and SHGs of India:

There are differences between Grameen Bank groups of Bangladesh and SHGs in India. Grameen groups are relatively smaller in size as they consist of five members whereas membership of SHGs is 10 to 20. Unlike Grameen Bank of Bangladesh, SHG has its own credit fund for relending and the initial lendings are made through internal savings contributed by the members. Moreover, SHG is considered as the ultimate lender and can be perceived as a microfinance Institution, whereas Grameen Bank groups do not normally have resources at their disposal. Members' thrift is deposited in the financial institution which has a federating structure and which is lent to the members of Grameen Banks. As a result, after some time, SHG may have enough capital to meet the financial requirements of its members and may not require any borrowing from financial institutions. Therefore, SHGs can be considered as independent institutions, if they mobilize sufficient funds for disbursal among members. On the other hand, Grameen Bank group members have to depend on an outside financial institution for credit, as long as they maintain thrift in the federation.

The NABARD's involvement with SHGs came about in 1986 when the NABARD supported and funded an action research project on "savings and credit management of SHGs of MYRADA (Mysore Resettlement and Development Association)". In 1988-89 the NABARD undertook a survey of 43 NGOs to study the functioning of SHGs in the mobilization of rural savings and improving the delivery of credit to the poor (NABARD 1995). In order to operationalise this concept, the NABARD launched a pilot project in February 1992 to link 500 SHGs with banks across the country (Jayaraman, 2001). To formalize the mechanism further, the RBI constituted a working group in Nov- 1994 to review the functioning of NGOs and SHGs. Accepting the recommendations of the working group, the RBI had set up a Microcredit Cell in April 1999 (Jagadish Capoor, 2001). The GOI bestowed national priority to the programme through its recognition in the Union Budget, 1999. Bank linkage is prominent in terms of outreach, recovery and meeting the credit needs of the rural poor.

There are three models of SHG bank linkage. In the Model-I, banks themselves take up the work of forming and nurturing the groups, opening their savings accounts and providing them with loans. In the Model-II, NGOs and formal agencies in the field of Microfinance act only as facilitators. They facilitate organizing, forming and nurturing of groups, and train them in thrift and credit management. Banks give loans directly to these SHGs. In the Model-III NGOs take an additional role of financial intermediation. In areas where the formal banking system faces constraints, the NGOs are encouraged to approach a suitable bank for bulk loan assistance. This, in turn, is used by the NGO for on-lending to the SHGs. In areas where a very large number of SHGs have been financed by bank branches, intermediate agencies like Federations of SHGs are coming up as links between bank branch and member SHGs. These federations are financed by banks, which in turn finance their member- SHGs. Other agencies like NBFCs are also coming up to take up this role.

Model-wise per cent distribution of SHGs and SHG credit in 2010 shows that (Figures-2.2 & 2.3) 17% of total no. of SHGs were financed under Model-I, 75% under Model-II and only 8% under Model-III but in years to come, Model-III is expected to become a major delivery model. As on March 2013 about 11.31 million SHGs (cumulative) spread all over India have been linked with banks (Tables-2.1, Fig-2.1).

Further, the cumulative refinance disbursed under SHG bank linkage programme by NABARD to Banks upto 31 March 2013 stood at Rs 22,396 crore. Cumulatively 11.31 million SHGs held savings bank accounts with total saving of Rs.8,21,725 crore. As on March 31, 2013, 4.45 million SHGs had outstanding (cumulative) bank loans of Rs. 39,37,530 crore. Commercial banks have the maximum share of around 59 percent of outstanding bank loans to SHGs followed by RRBs with a share of 30 percent and cooperative banks with the balance (Table 2.4C). Region-wise, Southern Region plays a dominating role in physical and financial progress of SHG-bank linkage programme (Tables-2.2 ABCD and Table-2.3). States selected under this programme in Southern Region upto March 2010 were Andhra Pradesh (14.48 lakhs), followed by Tamil Nadu (8.26 lakhs), Karnataka (5.34 lakhs) and so on.

Table- 2.1 SHG-Bank Linkage- Highlights March 2001 to March 2013

Items	2000 -2001	2001 -2002	2002 -2003	2003 -2004	2004 -2005	2005 -2006	2006 -2007	2007 -2008	2008 -2009	2009 -2010	2010 -2011	2011 -2012	2012 -2013
No of new SHGs provided with bank loan during the year (in millions)	0.15	0.20	0.25	0.36	0.54	0.62	1.10	1.22	1.60	1.59	1.20	1.15	1.22
No of SHGs provided with bank loan(cumulative) in millions	0.26	0.46	0.72	1.0	1.6	2.23	3.33	4.55	6.15	7.74	8.94	10.09	11.31
% of women Groups	90	90	90	90	90	90	90	90	90	90	90	90	90
No of participating Banks	314	444	505	560	545	545	498	-	-	446	-	-	-
Comm. Banks	43	44	48	48	47	47	50	-	-	47	-	-	-
RRBs	177	191	192	196	158	158	96	-	-	81	-	-	-
Co-op Banks	94	209	265	316	340	340	352	-		318	-	-	-
No. of States / Uts	27	30	30	31	31	31	31	31	31	31	31	31	31
No. of district Covered	412	488	502	563	N.A	583	587	-	-	-	-	-	-
No. of NGOs	1,030	2155	2800	3024	N.A	4896	-	-	-	-	-	-	-
Bank Loan (Cumulative) (in crores)	4,809	1,026	2,049	3,904	6,898	11,398	18,040	26,889	39,143	53,596	68,144	84,679	1,05,264
Bank loan Disbursed during year(crore)	-	545	1,023	1,855	2,994	4,499	6,570	8,849	12,254	14,453	14,548	16,535	20,585
Of which disbursed to new groups(crore)	-	453	691	1,158	1,727	2,330	3,044	-	-	-	-	-	-
Of which disbursed as repeat loans (crore)	-	92	332	698	1,268	2,169	3,599	-	-	-	-	-	-
Refinance(Cumulative) (in Crore)	400	796	1,419	2,124	3,086	4,157	5,459	-	-	12,862	15,407	18,480	22,396
No. of families Assisted (in million)	4.5	7.8	11.6	16.7	N.A	32.98	40.95	42.24	48.51	97.00	97.00	103.00	95.00
Average loan / SHGs (Rs)	18,227	22,240	28,559	36,179	N.A	50,917	59,420	72,076	76,128	91,083	-	-	-
Model-wise linkage (Cumulative)													
Model – I	13 %	16 %	20 %	20 %	20%	20%	17%	-	-	17%	-	-	-
Model – II	76 %	75 %	72 %	72 %	74%	74%	75%	-	-	75%	-	-	-
Model – III	11 %	9 %	8 %	8 %	6%	6%	08%	-	-	08%	-	-	-

Source: Status of Microfinance in India- various issues, NABARD, Mumbai.

Table – 2.2A Progress under Microfinance Savings of SHGs with Banks Region/State Wise

(Amount Rs. lakh)

Region	Total 2009		Total 2010		Total 2011		Total 2012		Total 2013	
	No of SHGs	Savings Amount	No of SHGs	Savings Amount	No of SHGs	Savings Amount	No of SHGs	Savings Amount	No of SHGs	Savings Amount
Northern Region	3,10,998	22,704	3,51,801	34,207	3,72,772	32,857	4,09,326	25,277	3,72,837	29,119
North Eastern Region	2,40,093	10,210	2,92,188	12,167	3,24,739	13,104	3,66,718	15,252	3,23,896	13,011
Easter Region	12,33,635	1,59,688	13,74,242	1,12,015	15,27,618	1,40,837	16,25,714	94,726	14,71,099	1,39,326
Central Region	7,12,915	38,679	7,65,965	51,364	7,86,436	60,338	8,12,767	61,358	7,02,198	62,422
Western Region	7,96,262	66,428	9,45,620	92,667	9,60,921	82,901	10,62,087	87,194	9,06,016	69,586
Southern Region	28,27,244	2,56,852	32,23,434	3,17,451	34,89,460	3,71,592	36,83,737	3,71,335	35,41,505	5,08,263
Grand Total	61,21,147	5,54,562	69,53,250	6,19,871	74,61,946	7,01,630	79,60,349	6,55,141	73,17,551	8,21,725

Source: Status of Microfinance in India- various issues, NABARD, Mumbai.

State	Total 2009		Total 2010		Total 2011		Total 2012		Total 2013	
	No of SHGs	Savings Amount	No of SHGs	Savings Amount	No of SHGs	Savings Amount	No of SHGs	Savings Amount	No of SHGs	Savings Amount
Andhra Pradesh	12,80,900	1,19,193	14,48,216	1,25,529	14,66,225	1,30,780	14,95,904	1,49,016	14,21,393	2,54,179
Karnataka	4,57,389	56,687	5,34,588	62,705	5,64,545	96,503	6,28,643	1,00,213	6,45,695	1,15,619
Kerala	3,58,863	23,242	3,94,197	37,556	4,93,347	42,144	6,15,714	41,371	5,81,325	51,759
Lakshadweep	-	-	-	-	164	10	171	12	27	7
Tamil Nadu	7,30,092	57,731	8,26,710	90,373	9,43,098	99,724	9,25,392	1,683	8,73,012	84,967
Pondicherry			19723	1,287	22,081	2,431	17,913	79,040	20,053	1,732
Total	28,27,244	2,56,852	32,23,434	3,17,451	34,89,460	3,71,592	36,83,737	3,71,335	35,41,505	5,08,263

Source: Status of Microfinance in India- various issues, NABARD, Mumbai.

Table – 2.2B Progress under Microfinance-Bank loans disbursed of SHGs with Banks Region/State Wise

(Amount Rs. lakh)

Region	Total 2009		Total 2010		Total 2011		Total 2012		Total 2013	
	No of SHGs	Loans disbursed Amount	No of SHGs	Loans disbursed Amount	No of SHGs	Loans disbursed Amount	No of SHGs	Loans disbursed Amount	No of SHGs	Loans disbursed Amount
Northern Region	42,688	30,243	37,375	30,633	42,493	37,752	30,751	33,543	31,285	34,230
North Eastern Region	35,506	24,642	49,307	28,717	39,307	32,096	51,003	45,129	25,168	18,022
Easter Region	2,36,789	1,23,767	2,77,446	1,54,019	2,47,624	1,61,950	2,01,201	1,62,406	1,82,823	1,29,019
Central Region	1,01,060	78,141	77,846	63,210	48,734	60,755	58,460	70,937	64,180	69,889
Western Region	1,25,173	58,393	1,49,130	64,698	91,954	62,591	1,01,044	75,286	70,429	70,994
Southern Region	10,68,370	9,10,166	9,95,718	11,04,054	7,26,022	10,99,629	7,05,419	12,66,176	8,45,936	17,36,383
Grand Total	16,09,586	12,25,351	15,86,822	14,45,330	11,96,134	14,54,773	11,47,878	16,53,476	12,19,821	20,58,536

Source: Status of Microfinance in India- various issues, NABARD, Mumbai.

State	Total 2009		Total 2010		Total 2011		Total 2012		Total 2013	
	No of SHGs	Loans disbursed Amount	No of SHGs	Loans disbursed Amount	No of SHGs	Loans disbursed Amount	No of SHGs	Loans disbursed Amount	No of SHGs	Loans disbursed Amount
Andhra Pradesh	6,36,816	5,50,860	5,64,089	6,70,664	3,67,420	6,20,919	3,78,526	8,17,142	4,84,292	11,16,440
Karnataka	1,34,225	1,02,040	1,04,151	1,13,044	90,342	1,37,435	87,943	1,62,949	1,45,733	2,29,941
Kerala	60,376	51,674	62,058	50,745	72,761	77,769	55,242	85,415	60,830	89,892
Lakshadweep	-	-	-	-	14	7	8	1	1	1
Tamil Nadu			2,59,161	2,56,130	1,91,469	2,55,622	1,79,902	1,93,292	1,50,586	2,91,610
Pondicherry	2,36,953	2,05,592	6,259	13,470	4,016	7,877	3,798	7,377	4,490	8,499
Total	10,68,370	9,10,166	9,95,718	11,04,054	7,26,022	10,99,629	7,05,419	12,66,176	8,45,936	17,36,383

Source: Status of Microfinance in India- various issues, NABARD, Mumbai.

Table – 2.2C Progress under Microfinance Outstanding of SHGs with Banks Region/State Wise

(Amount Rs. lakh)

Region	Total 2009		Total 2010		Total 2011		Total 2012		Total 2013	
	No of SHGs	Loans O/S Amount	No of SHGs	Loans O/S Amount	No of SHGs	Loans O/S Amount	No of SHGs	Loans O/S Amount	No of SHGs	Loans O/S Amount
Northern Region	1,66,511	67,892	1,52,491	81,513	1,49,108	90,314	2,12,041	1,17,828	2,13,955	1,16,068
North Eastern Region	1,17,812	46,931	1,33,785	67,348	1,50,021	69,525	1,59,416	99,327	1,43,660	79,676
Easter Region	9,33,489	3,02,300	10,27,570	3,69,491	11,05,533	4,20,255	9,85,329	4,62,980	10,20,656	5,53,813
Central Region	3,32,116	2,04,533	4,97,922	2,46,240	3,58,872	2,36,540	3,52,452	2,78,029	3,62,521	2,77,685
Western Region	3,93,499	1,55,115	4,57,476	1,36,948	3,16,821	1,24,623	2,89,472	1,36,378	2,95,451	1,46,752
Southern Region	22,80,911	14,91,214	25,82,112	19,02,288	27,06,408	21,80,859	23,55,732	25,39,459	24,15,191	27,63,536
Grand Total	42,24,338	22,67,984	48,51,356	28,03,828	47,86,763	31,22,117	43,54,442	36,34,000	44,51,434	39,37,530

Source: Status of Microfinance in India- various issues, NABARD, Mumbai.

State	Total 2009		Total 2010		Total 2011		Total 2012		Total 2013	
	No of SHGs	Loans O/S Amount	No of SHGs	Loans O/S Amount	No of SHGs	Loans O/S Amount	No of SHGs	Loans O/S Amount	No of SHGs	Loans O/S Amount
Andhra Pradesh	12,19,311	8,90,217	14,71,284	11,73,954	16,93,792	13,36,912	14,00,995	15,34,172	13,56,720	17,48,105
Karnataka	3,09,097	1,61,362	3,00,738	2,05,530	2,52,613	2,24,612	2,66,978	3,46,988	3,79,305	3,29,358
Kerala	1,76,153	95,093	2,57,760	1,01,531	1,78,211	1,57,275	1,59,843	1,77,923	1,53,336	1,67,828
Lakshadweep	-	-	-	-	14	6	35	12	12	3
Tamil Nadu	5,76,350	3,44,542	5,38,867	4,05,943	5,74,385	4,52,624	5,14,203	4,63,927	5,11,859	5,04,018
Pondicherry			13,463	15,331	7,393	9,430	13,678	16,437	13,959	14,224
Total	22,80,911	14,91,214	25,82,112	19,02,288	27,06,408	21,80,859	23,55,732	25,39,459	24,15,191	27,63,536

Source: Status of Microfinance in India- various issues, NABARD, Mumbai.

Table – 2.3 Progress under Microfinance-Non-performing Assets (NPAs) against Bank Loans to SHGs Region wise

(Amount Rs. lakh)

Region	Total 2009			Total 2010			Total 2011			Total 2012			Total 2013		
	Amount of out standing loans to SHGs (Rs. Crore)	Amount of Gross NPAs	% age NPAs of out-standing Bank loans to SHGs	Amount of out standing loans to SHGs (Rs. Crore)	Amount of Gross NPAs	% age NPAs of outstand-ing Bank loans to SHGs	Amount of out standing loans to SHGs (Rs. Crore)	Amount of Gross NPAs	% age NPAs of outstand-ing Bank loans to SHGs	Amount of out standing loans to SHGs (Rs. Crore)	Amount of Gross NPAs	% age NPAs of out-stand-ing Bank loans to SHGs	Amount of out standing loans to SHGs (Rs. Crore)	Amount of Gross NPAs	% age NPAs of out-standing Bank loans to SHGs
Northern Region	64,426	4,256	6.6	81,513	5,391	6.61	90,314	6,366	7.05	1,17,828	8,155	6.92	1,16,068	12,987	11.19
North Eastern Region	44,346	3,775	8.5	67,348	3,713	5.51	69,525	5,856	8.42	99,327	5,133	5.17	79,676	6,824	8.56
Easter Region	2,75,469	9,291	3.4	3,69,491	11,874	3.21	4,20,255	18,107	4.31	4,62,980	33,708	7.28	5,53,813	57,056	10.30
Central Region	1,87,848	16,770	8.9	2,46,240	19,866	8.07	2,36,540	25,404	10.74	2,78,029	36,703	13.20	2,77,685	47,976	17.28
Western Region	1,45,962	8,141	5.6	1,36,948	6,106	4.46	1,24,623	9,042	7.26	1,36,378	11,214	8.22	1,46,752	12,657	8.63
Southern Region	14,38,053	20,353	1.4	19,02,288	35,653	1.87	21,80,859	82,636	3.79	25,39,459	1,26,359	4.98	27,63,536	1,41,193	5.11
Grand Total	21,56,104	62,587	2.9	28,03,828	82,304	2.94	31,22,117	1,47,411	4.72	36,34,000	2,21,273	6.09	39,37,530	2,78,693	7.08

Source: Status of Microfinance in India- various issues, NABARD, Mumbai.

<table>
<tr><th>State</th><th colspan="3">Total 2009</th><th colspan="3">Total 2010</th><th colspan="3">Total 2011</th><th colspan="3">Total 2012</th><th colspan="3">Total 2013</th></tr>
<tr><td>Andhra Pradesh</td><td>7,76,773</td><td>3,773</td><td>0.5</td><td>11,73,954</td><td>1,51,42</td><td>1.29</td><td>13,36,912</td><td>27,049</td><td>2.02</td><td>15,34,172</td><td>5,30,100</td><td>3.46</td><td>17,48,105</td><td>54,391</td><td>3.11</td></tr>
<tr><td>Karnataka</td><td>2,47,523</td><td>1,977</td><td>0.8</td><td>2,05,530</td><td>4,135</td><td>2.01</td><td>2,24,612</td><td>6,686</td><td>2.98</td><td>3,46,988</td><td>11,638</td><td>3.35</td><td>3,29,358</td><td>10,777</td><td>3.27</td></tr>
<tr><td>Kerala</td><td>89,515</td><td>3,171</td><td>3.5</td><td>1,01,531</td><td>2,557</td><td>2.52</td><td>1,57,275</td><td>13,547</td><td>8.61</td><td>1,77,923</td><td>16,081</td><td>9.04</td><td>1,67,828</td><td>20,779</td><td>12.38</td></tr>
<tr><td>Lakshadweep</td><td>-</td><td>-</td><td>-</td><td>-</td><td>-</td><td>-</td><td>6</td><td>-</td><td>-</td><td>12</td><td>-</td><td>0.00</td><td>3</td><td>-</td><td>0.00</td></tr>
<tr><td>Tamil Nadu</td><td rowspan="2">3,24,243</td><td rowspan="2">11,432</td><td rowspan="2">3.5</td><td>4,05,942</td><td>13,731</td><td>3.38</td><td>4,52,624</td><td>34,957</td><td>7.72</td><td>4,63,927</td><td>44,465</td><td>9.58</td><td>5,04,018</td><td>54,502</td><td>10.81</td></tr>
<tr><td>Pondicherry</td><td>15,331</td><td>88</td><td>0.57</td><td>9,430</td><td>397</td><td>4.21</td><td>16,437</td><td>1,075</td><td>NA</td><td>14,224</td><td>743</td><td>5.23</td></tr>
<tr><td>Total</td><td>14,38,053</td><td>20,353</td><td>1.4</td><td>19,02,288</td><td>35,653</td><td>1.87</td><td>21,80,859</td><td>82,636</td><td>3.79</td><td>25,39,459</td><td>12,6359</td><td>4.98</td><td>27,63,536</td><td>1,41,193</td><td>5.11</td></tr>
</table>

Source: Status of Microfinance in India- NABARD, Mumbai.

Table-2.4A Progress under Microfinance - Savings of SHGs with Banks Region- wise/ State- wise/Agency-wise position as on 31 March 2013

Region	Commercial Bank		Regional Rural Banks		Cooperative Bank		Total	
	No. of SHGs	Saving Amount	No. of SHGs	Saving Amount	No. of SHGs	Saving Amount	No. of SHGs	Saving Amount
Northern Region	1,68,471	15,044	90,322	7,224	1,14,044	6,851	3,72,837	29,119
North Eastern Region	1,16,784	8,016	1,72,423	4,602	34,689	393	3,23,896	13,011
Easter Region	6,70,875	62,356	5,99,084	60,538	2,01,140	16,432	14,71,099	1,39,326
Central Region	2,76,566	37,077	3,83,430	23,353	42,202	1,991	7,02,198	62,422
Western Region	4,22,238	36,447	1,47,729	10,386	3,36,049	22,753	9,06,016	6,95,86
Southern Region	24,22,052	3,94,317	6,45,020	46,607	4,74,433	67,338	35,41,505	5,08,261
Grand Total	40,76,986	5,53,257	20,38,008	1,52,710	12,02,557	1,15,758	73,17,551	8,21,725

Source: Status of Microfinance in India- various issues, NABARD, Mumbai.

State	Commercial Bank		Regional Rural Banks		Cooperative Bank		Total	
	No. of SHGs	Saving Amount	No. of SHGs	Saving Amount	No. of SHGs	Saving Amount	No. of SHGs	Saving Amount
Andhra Pradesh	10,00,156	2,22,038	4,04,600	30,082	16,637	2,059	14,21,393	2,54,179
Karnataka	3,07,657	66,929	1,28,645	10,467	2,09,393	38,223	6,45,695	1,15,619
Kerala	4,63,219	40,501	46,892	1,386	71,214	9,872	5,81,325	51,759
Lakshadweep	27	7	0	0	0	0	27	7
Pondicherry	12,861	1,110	3,468	280	3,724	341	20,053	1,732
Tamil Nadu	6,38,132	63,731	61,415	4,393	1,73,465	16,843	8,73,012	84,967
Total	24,22,052	3,94,317	6,45,020	46,607	4,74,433	67,338	35,41,505	5,08,261

Source: Status of Microfinance in India- various issues, NABARD, Mumbai.

Table-2.4B Progress under Microfinance -Bank Loans disbursed during the year Region- wise/ State- wise/Agency-wise position as on 31 March 2013

Region	Commercial Bank		Regional Rural Banks		Cooperative Bank		Total	
	No. of SHGs	Loans disbursed Amount	No. of SHGs	Loans disbursed Amount	No. of SHGs	Loans disbursed Amount	No. of SHGs	Loans disbursed Amount
Northern Region	13,114	17,116	8,722	8,768	9,449	8,346	31,285	34,230
North Eastern Region	9,391	7,906	14,956	9,233	821	883	25,168	18,022
Easter Region	75,973	64,261	56,796	46,152	50,054	18,606	1,82,823	1,29,019
Central Region	26,942	32,860	30,672	34,669	6,566	2,361	64,180	69,889
Western Region	42,320	47,475	12,142	12,150	15,967	11,369	70,429	70,994
Southern Region	5,67,837	11,68,883	1,88,722	4,51,681	89,377	1,15,819	8,45,936	17,36,383
Grand Total	73,55,77	1,33,8501	3,12,010	5,62,652	1,72,234	1,57,384	12,19,821	20,58,536

Source: Status of Microfinance in India- various issues, NABARD, Mumbai.

State	Commercial Bank		Regional Rural Banks		Cooperative Bank		Total	
	No. of SHGs	Loans disbursed Amount	No. of SHGs	Loans disbursed Amount	No. of SHGs	Loans disbursed Amount	No. of SHGs	Loans disbursed Amount t
Andhra Pradesh	3,30,750	7,45,307	1,48,356	3,67,713	5,186	3,419	4,84,292	11,16,440
Karnataka	87,325	1,30,331	24,677	50,335	33,731	49,274	1,45,733	2,29,941
Kerala	43,536	69,320	4,560	5,774	12,734	14,798	60,830	89,892
Lakshadweep	1	1	0	0	0	0	1	1
Pondicherry	3,455	6,004	767	1,548	272	945	4,494	8,499
Tamil Nadu	1,02,770	2,17,920	10,362	26,311	37,454	47,380	1,50,586	2,91,610
Total	5,67,837	11,68,883	1,88,722	4,51,681	89,377	1,15,819	8,45,936	17,36,383

Source: Status of Microfinance in India- various issues, NABARD, Mumbai.

Table-2.4C Progress under Microfinance - Bank Loans outstanding against SHGs Region- wise/ State- wise/Agency-wise position as on 31 March 2013

Region	Commercial Bank		Regional Rural Banks		Cooperative Bank		Total	
	No. of SHGs	Loans O/S Amount	No. of SHGs	Loans O/S Amount	No. of SHGs	Loans O/S Amount	No. of SHGs	Loans O/S Amount
Northern Region	1,27,472	69,463	40,219	28,332	46,264	18,273	2,13,955	1,16,068
North Eastern Region	77,625	44,575	57,532	30,572	8,503	4,528	1,43,660	79,676
Easter Region	5,05,205	2,95,943	4,05,482	2,23,839	1,09,969	34,032	10,20,656	5,53,813
Central Region	1,62,250	1,48,818	1,84,872	1,18,796	15,399	10,071	3,62,521	2,77,685
Western Region	1,71,185	1,02,243	57,080	27,685	67,186	16,825	2,95,451	1,46,752
Southern Region	16,00,234	20,02,903	5,82,182	6,22,899	2,32,775	1,37,734	24,15,191	27,63,536
Grand Total	26,43,971	26,63,944	13,27,367	10,52,123	4,80,096	2,21,462	44,51,434	39,37,530

Source: Status of Microfinance in India- various issues, NABARD, Mumbai.

State	Commercial Bank		Regional Rural Banks		Cooperative Bank		Total	
	No. of SHGs	Loans O/S Amount	No. of SHGs	Loans O/S Amount	No. of SHGs	Loans O/S Amount	No. of SHGs	Loans O/S Amount
Andhra Pradesh	9,35,510	12,50,875	4,06,615	4,91,336	14,595	5,893	13,56,720	17,48,105
Karnataka	1,66,642	1,95,486	1,15,864	91,679	96,799	42,193	3,79,305	3,29,358
Kerala	1,09,892	1,33,797	19,347	11,312	24,097	22,718	1,53,336	1,67,828
Lakshadweep	12	3	0	0	0	0	12	3
Pondicherry	11,576	11,509	1,456	1,329	927	1,386	13,959	13,224
Tamil Nadu	3,76,602	4,11,232	38,900	27,243	96,357	65,543	5,11,859	5,04,018
Total	16,00,234	20,02,903	5,82,182	6,22,899	2,32,775	1,37,734	24,15,191	27,63,536

Source: Status of Microfinance in India- various issues, NABARD, Mumbai.

Source: Status of Microfinance in India- NABARD, Mumbai

Table-2.5 Cumulative Growth in SHG-Linkage in Priority States (As on 31March) (Number of SHGs)

State	2004	2005	2006	2007	2008	2009	2010	2011
Assam	10,706	31,234	56,449	81,454	1,07,098	1,80,996	2,18,352	2,45,120
Bihar	16,246	28,015	46,221	72,339	93,410	1,30,005	1,40,824	24,8,197
Chhattisgarh	9796	18,569	31,391	41,703	60,763	1,12,982	1,13,982	1,18,167
Gujarat	15,974	24,712	34,160	43,572	46,526	1,05,046	1,68,180	1,92,834
H.P	13,228	17,798	22920	27,799	31,899	41,744	50,182	53,113
Jharkhand	12,647	21,531	30,819	37,317	42,605	49,753	79,424	87,205
Maharashtra	38,535	71,146	1,31,470	70,912	83,336	6,85,324	7,70,695	7,60,167
M.P	27,095	45,105	57,125	2,25,856	3,26,425	1,73,725	1,78,226	1,53,817
Orissa	77,588	1,23,256	1,80,896	2,34,451	3,07,591	4,41,960	5,03,172	5,21,152
Rajasthan	33,846	60,006	98,171	1,37,837	1,73,192	1,92,479	2,13,295	2,33,793
Uttar Pradesh	79,210	1,19,648	1,61,911	1,98,587	2,36,929	3,91,906	4,29,760	4,70,157
Uttaranchal	10,908	14,043	17,588	21,527	24,679	34,302	43,997	44,295
West Bengal	51,685	92,698	1,36,251	1,81,563	2,28,395	6,09,439	6,47,059	6,66,314
Total for 13 priority States	397,464 (36.8)	667,761 (41.2)	10,05,272 (44.9)	13,74,917	17,64,856 (35.22)	31,49,661	35,57,148 (51.15)	30,81,082
Southern States	674,356 (62.5)	938,941 (58.0)	12,14,431 (54.3)	15,22,144 (52)	18,61,373 (51.33)	28,27,244	32,23,434 (46.35)	34,89,460
BIMARU States	156,397 (14.5)	252,774 (15.6)	3,63,428 (16.2)	6,34,619	8,29,956	-	9,62,105 (13.83)	
All-India Total	1,079,091	1,618,456	22,38,565	-	50,09,794	61,21,147	69,53,250	74,61,946

Source: Status of Microfinance in India- various issues, NABARD, Mumbai.

Figure - 2.1

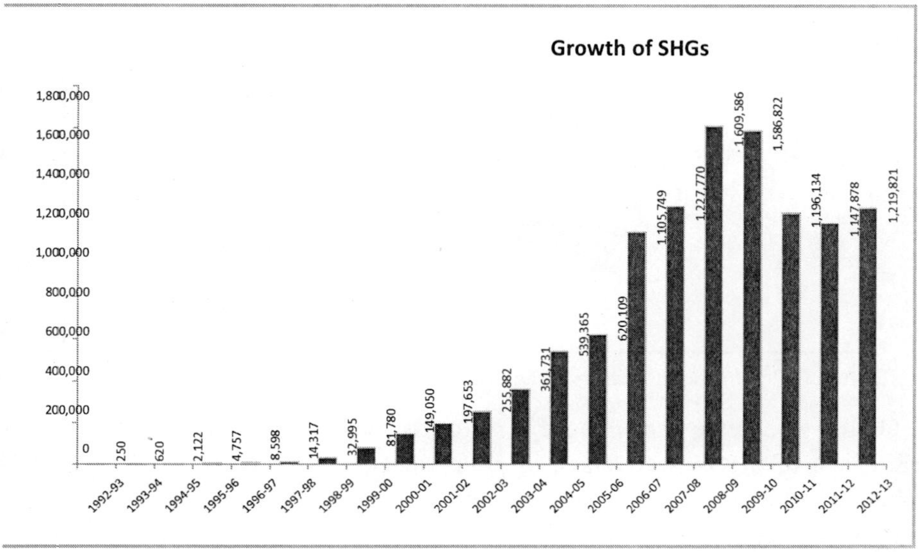

Figure - 2.2
Different Models of Linkages

Model I: - SHGs formed and financed by banks.

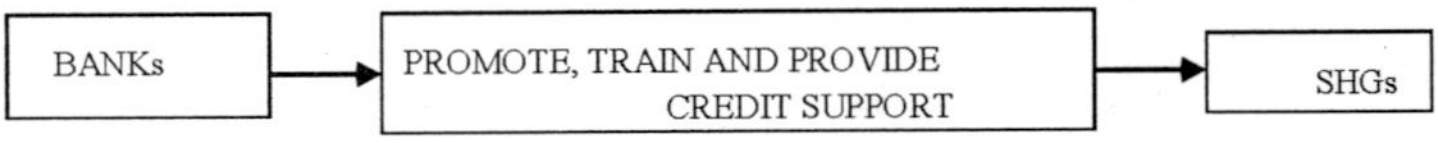

Model II: - SHGs formed by NGOs and formal agencies, but directly financed by banks

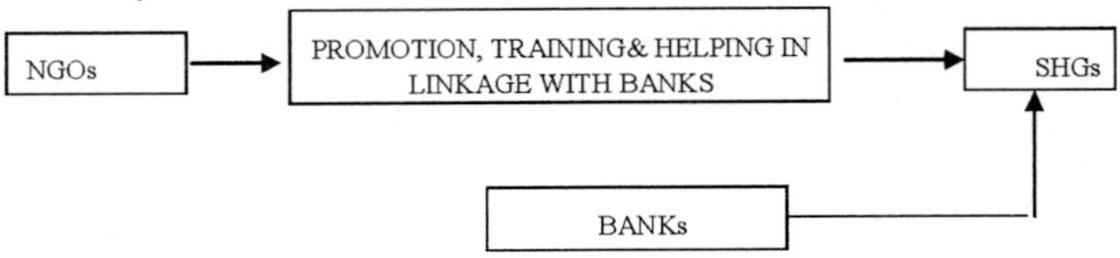

Model III:-SHGs financed by banks using NGOs and other agencies as finance Intermediaries

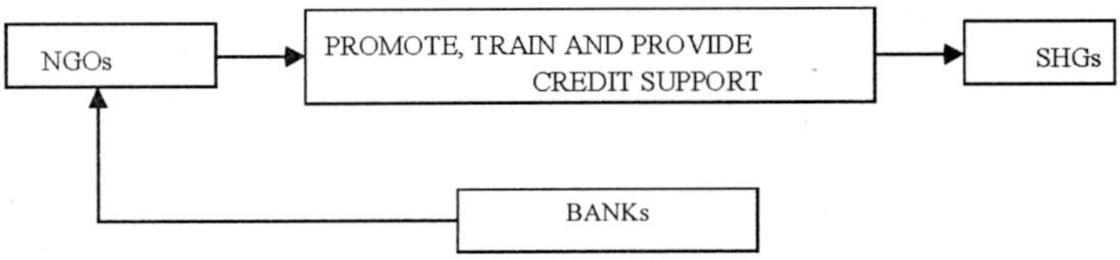

Figure - 2.3

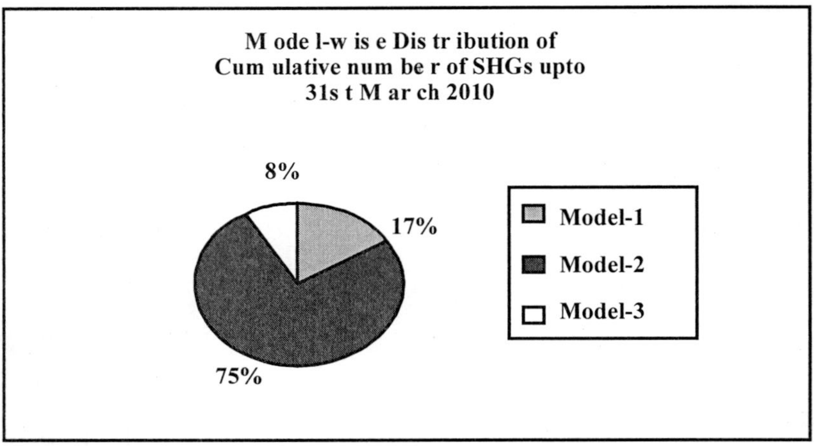

Source: Status of Microfinance in India- various issues, NABARD, New Delhi.

On the whole, the performance of SHGs is satisfactory. A major feature of the performance of SHGs is coverage of poor especially women (Rajasekhar, 1994). Secondly, most of the SHGs have been able to successfully promote regular savings among the poor (Fernandez, 1994). Thirdly, with funds mobilized through savings and borrowings from banks, the SHGs, are able to meet diverse loan demand of the members. Fourthly, despite not following collateral-based lending, the SHGs have been able to register high loan recoveries (Rajasekhar, 1994). A combination of factors like peer monitoring, easy and flexible loaning procedures, lower interest rates, flexible repayment schedules, effective screening, etc., seem to have positively influenced in loan recovery. But the progress of Microfinance Sector is in the SEGMENT termed as small, short, unsecured. This implies that loans are really small amounts given for short duration without any security.

2.2.4 Role of NGOs in the Promotion of SHGs

NGOs have a role in bringing about the collaborative linkage between banks and groups. As facilitating institutions, NGOs organize the poor into groups, undertake training for them, help in arranging inputs, extension and marketing, introduce saving and internal lending, help in the maintenance of accounts, and link them with the banks for credit requirements. Here, banks directly provide credit to the SHGs with the NGOs' recommendations. In the second case, where the NGOs work as MFI they have to undertake some additional functions besides undertaking the function as a facilitator. Here, the loan is given to the NGOs, for on-lending to the SHGs. The NGOs will be legally responsible for repayment to the banks and will be bearing the risk in cases of non-payment.

The experiences of both NGOs and banks show that Microfinance groups have two distinct phases, viz., pre-formation and post-formation. Pre-formation phase include, identification of the village and target group, providing awareness to the members on the importance of groups and motivating them to come together. There are chances that the interests of the individuals may go against that of the group. In the post-formation phase, conflicts between individual interests and the group interests are resolved. The set of procedures to be followed by the group, rules to be adhered to by the members and the roles to be played by the leaders are arrived at by intense discussion among the members in these groups. Even though the basic steps in the pre-formation and post-formation stage are similar to both the NGOs and banks, NGOs seem to be better equipped to undertake SHG formation due to their nearness to the people and flexibility of operations (Emil Mathew, 2006).

The NGOs, which had better understanding of the situation of the area in which they were working, did well in the formation of microfinance groups. A comprehensive study by (Satish, 2001) into the problems and complexities faced by the NGOs and the banks in the pre-formation and post-formation stages of SHGs in three states of Karnataka, Maharastra and U.P has revealed that these groups enjoyed economics of scale in the procurement of raw material and marketing of the finished products by joining together as a group. Similarly, some of the NGOs could succeed in utilizing the collective efforts of the informal institutions of chit funds by converting them into

SHGs. But, the organizational skills in terms of maintaining discipline at meetings, interactions and participation in chit funds were less as compared to SHGs, which were considered essential for the success of SHGs. With a little effort, the spirit of cohesiveness could be inculcated among the former by the NGOs with the help of the animators appointed by them.

The NGO formed SHGs performed better in terms of targeting and recovery of loan as compared to DWCRA groups formed by the government. (Rajakutty's, 1997) study conducted in Tamil Nadu and Andaman Nicola Islands, has examined the implementation and status of the groups organized under DWCRA. The programme had succeeded in establishing groups and it had recorded 140 per cent growth in the number of groups by the end of the Eighth Plan. More than one third of the government groups formed under DWCRA had become defunct, where the revolving credit fund had not been used. Non posting of officials, inadequate supervision and follow up, utilization of loans for consumption purposes, lack of effort to revive defunct loans, lack of recovery of the loans were the main problems faced.

Cohesive groups and the collective action, which were central to microfinance groups, had largely been missing in these programmes. A comparison of the DWCRA programme to that of the NGO aided programme brought out that because of the NGOs support right from the group formation till the repayment and even after that enabled the groups to attain better results. The NGOs actively participated in the identification of the groups, initiation of training programmes, encouragement of training programmes and monitoring, whereby it succeeded in instilling group consciousness among the participants.

2.2.5 Challenges in the Growth of Microfinance in India:

Microfinance programme is not fully devoid of defects. It has certain problems and challenges in the course of its development. Often, the borrowers face problems of identifying those economic activities that yield a rate of profit necessary to cover the interest rate on loans. Even though the programme is meant for the promotion of income generating activities through the provision of loans, members are finding it difficult to find economically remunerative productive activities. A risk aversive character is quite observable among the members, where they restrict themselves to non-farm activities, which are traditional and less remunerative (Rajasekhar, 2005). Moreover, there are problems of getting loans on time, difficulty of getting raw materials, skilled labour and marketing opportunities. Thus, the members are finding it difficult to venture into those activities, which are diversified and remunerative (Nirmala et. al., 2004).

Usually, the programme is targeted at women as their contribution to the household income enables all the household members to receive the benefits of credit. This is because women contribute a larger proportion of their income to the welfare of the household as compared to men, and this throws light on the self-consumption nature of the men (Mencher, 1988). A study by (Rajasekhar, 2002) on the poverty alleviation programme of one south Indian NGO called SHARE has brought out the idea that participation of women in income generating activity contributed a higher proportion to household income. However, it had negative impact on the sharing of household responsibilities. It resulted in a situation where the male members withdrew from the labour market by transferring the household responsibilities entirely on to women. Rajasekhar suggests, therefore, that men too should be brought under the purview of development intervention, if women are to be empowered.

Studies on the performance of SHGs have brought out the idea that SHGs performed well in terms of recovery of loans (Rajakutty, 1997; Namboodiri and Shiyani, 2001; Satish, 2001; Madheswaran and Dharmadhikari, 2001). These studies are of the opinion that this was made possible because of the self-sustainable system of community organizations, constant and regular assistance from promoting agencies, social cohesion among group members and lower transaction costs. But, such a measurement only on the repayment capacity of the groups had not looked into the sources from where the members made repayments at the time of repayment. According to (Chavan and Ramakumar, 2002), group pressure sometimes forced the members to borrow from moneylenders at the time of repayment and hence, it created dependent. Another problem cited by the development scholars relate to the neglect of the poorest of the poor by the programme. According to (Madheswaran and Dharmadhikari, 2001), the exclusion of the poorest could be attributed to the less targeting on the poorest as compared to moderately poor. This was because the financial institutions presumed that the promotion of the poorest might hinder the sustainability of the programme. Their study has brought out that lack of awareness, social exclusion to join with other group members, improper identification techniques, difficulties faced at the time of appraisal and follow up and strict discipline in repayment requirements and penalties for delays acted as hindrances for the poorest to participate in the Programme.

SECTION – II
REVIEW OF EMPIRICAL STUDIES ON THE IMPACT OF MICROFINANCE

2.3 Review of Empirical Studies on the impact of Microfinance:

In this section an attempt has been made to critically review the literature of the past studies on the impact of Microfinance in India Roshan Singh et al. (1978) studied the pattern of flow of credit in Bichpuri development block of Agra district in Uttar Pradesh. They found that the pattern of financing agriculture was similar both at the national and district level. The proportion of bank finance to agricultural showed a steady but slow increase over a period of four years. The overall share of large farmers in total finance to agriculture was much higher as compared to the small and medium farmers in all the years (1972 to 1977). The share of small farmers showed an increasing trend mainly during the years 1976 and 1977 when deliberate efforts were made to direct the flow of bank credit in favour of small farmers. Ramlingam et al 1987 in their study entitled "socio economic impact of IRDP on weaker section: a comparative analysis" showed that the social status of the respondents had increased considerably from low status to higher status.

Desai (1988) assessed the institutional credit requirement for agriculture production in 2000 A.D. and observed the growth rate of total credit between 1972-73 and 1982-83 was 17 per cent in nominal terms. The commercial bank share has more than doubled from 16.31 per cent in 1972-73 to 35.85 per cent in 1982-83. He estimated short term credit requirement by taking the total value of crop output from the cost of cultivation scheme of government of India for the period from 1974-75 to 1984-85 and found that the growth rate in agriculture advance to be 16.28 per cent. Mahabub Hussain (1998) while assessing the performance of the Garmeena Bank in Bangladesh laid the hypothesis that " If the poor are supplied with the working capital, they can generate productive self-employment without additional external assistance", and the results showed that the Garmeena bank has reached 6 percent of villages and 4 percent target households (1987).

Ramdass (1989) measured the institutional credit flow in Pondicherry and observed that the short term credit advance by the institutions had grown enormously, while the long term credit lagged behind. He suggested the need for institution to come forward to provide long term credit and utilize the saving mobilized in rural areas exclusively for rural investment. Molly (1990) found that there is lion's share of NGOs programmes in the selected organizations related to the factory type employment such as readymade garments, Khadi and Village industry, candle making etc. The major productions schemes especially on house hold basis, which occupied 24 percent of total schemes, were animal husbandry, poultry, sericulture, fodder cultivation, kitchen garden and others.

Pathak (1992) reported that SHG being comprised of group of persons, gets empowered to solve most of their problems of non- financial nature like raw materials, inputs supply, marketing, better adoption of technology, education and training for realizing the human potential for development. Pathak (1992) SHG being comprised of group of persons, gets empowered to solve most of their problems of non-financial nature like raw materials, inputs supply, marketing, better adoption of technology education and training for realizing the human potential for development. The SHG's of Kerala have become centers for initiating social action against dowry system, alcoholism, illiteracy and divorce (NABARD 1997).

Pradeep Kumar (1993) used growth rate analysis to analyse the growth in physical and financial performance indicators of horticultural producer's cooperative marketing society limited, Bangalore. The indicators considered were membership share capital, owned funds, sales, inventories, fixed assets, current assets, total assets, current liabilities and total liabilities. Dinakar Rao (1994) reported that networking of

SHGs and Self-help promoting institution are elements of propagating self-help. And that SHGs linked with formal credit agencies had advantages of pooled enterprises, economic of scale and organisation to relish exploitation.

A World Bank study (1995) revealed that 67 per cent of the credit needs of poor people in India is for consumption needs and of the consumption credit required, 75 per cent was for short periods for emergent needs such as illness and household expenses during the lean monsoon seasons. They also estimate that 75 per cent of production credit (only 33% of total credit) was met by banks while 100 per cent of consumption credit requirement was met by informal resources at interest rate ranging from 30 per cent to 90 per cent per annum. Girija (1995) stated that the group provides the women a base for self-employment and empowerment through group dynamics. The peer pressure on group members has ensured proper utilization of credit and repayment of loans, savings provided self-insurance and self-assurance to the group members.

Harper (1996) in his study "Self-help groups – some issues from India" indicated that in India, as in other parts of the developing world, the banking community is extending its services to the poor by lending to self-help groups. By providing single larger loans, relying on the group, on NGOs, to monitor the on lending of micro-loans, the banks transaction charges are reduced, making the operation potential profitable. Kumaran (1997) examine self-help groups promoted by a voluntary agency in A.P and their role in promoting thrift and credit activities among the poor. Further he also examine in detail the process of development of self-help groups, structure and function, resource mobilization and socio-economic, activities. Various factors responsible for active functioning, passivity and disbandment of self-help groups are examined in detail.

Kumaran (1997) in his study on 21 SHGs found that 19 were active groups and one each was passive and dissolved group. According to him, the individual monthly contribution for savings varied from group to group (Rs.10-Rs.30) and the total savings for 18 groups in a year was Rs.33,013/- while the total credit generated during the same period was Rs.2,18,223/-, of which business took a large share of 29 per cent followed by others at 28 per cent, cumulative loan at 23 per cent, clearance of old debit at 12 per cent and health expense at 6 per cent. The interest rate on the loan varied from 5 percent to 3 percent between the groups on monthly basis.

McGuire and Conroy (1997) described two studies on "Bank NGO linkages and the transactions costs of lending to the poor through groups", one, in India and one in the Philippines. The India study compared the transaction costs incurred by banks while lending to the poor through various channels, and found that the transaction costs were much lower where banks used NGOs and self Help Groups as intermediaries. Transaction costs facing borrowers were also significantly lower. This suggests an important role for NGOs in the intermediation process. The Philippines study looked at the question from the prospective of NGOs. It found that NGOs could channel credit to the poor with lower transaction cost, as a proportion of loans granted, than most other institution. But the small loans and short maturities inherent in lending to the poor inevitably led to transaction costs being relatively high compared to the value of loans outstanding at any one point of time. The article also Highlights the need for NGOs to minimize the costs as for as possible.

Ramalakshmi (1998) pointed out that, inadequate working capital, is the most serious problem restricting the performance of many DWCRA groups and also the group members need training for skill enhancement especially for items such as soft made garments, foot wear, woolen blankets etc. Hartwig (1999) noted that SHG of Africa have increased the family income there by ensuring food security and children education. Nanda (1999) conducted impact studies of self-help and found that the most outstanding impact of the linkage programme could be the socio-economic empowerment of the poor more particularly the women. Puhazhendhi and Jayaram (1999) found that the in formal groups of rural poor with active intervention of NGOs adequately supported by training significantly improved women's participation both from economic and social aspects.

Puhazhendhi and Jayaraman (1999) reported that the SHG members taking up more than one activity increased from about 30% during pre group formation situation. They undertook supplementary activities such as animal husbandry, poultry etc, and non- farm activities like Petty shop, Kirana shop, Flower selling business etc. Pahazhendhi and Jayaraman (1999) concerned about the growth of agriculture advance during 1990-96, pointed out that despite the phenomenal growth in absolute terms, the proportion of amount outstanding advance to priority sector showed a declining trend from 16.9 per cent in June 1990 to 14.3 per cent in March 1996. The reversal trend was observed in 1996-97 March when the loans for agriculture constituted 16.3 per cent of net bank advances. The share of priority sector lending at all India level whose share had declined from the peak of 42.9 per cent in 1985 marginally improved to 41.7 per cent in March 1997. Sherin (1999) found that seventy six per cent of the respondents were highly self reliant in the functional SHGs whereas only 48.27 per cent of the respondents expressed high self-reliance in the non-functional SHGs. The male respondents were significantly greater in self-reliance in comparison with their female counterparts.

Abate (2000) studied the loan and advances to agriculture from all of the financial institutions shown significant compound growth rate over the study period. Compared to the growth in term loan (13.0 per cent), the growth in crop loan (17.2 per cent), which is a major index of agriculture production finance, has shown a higher growth rate in Karnataka state during the study period. Similarly, the growth in agricultural advances (12.5 per cent) has shown higher growth rate in direct agricultural advances (10.9 per cent). However the share of agriculture advance and weaker section had shown a declining trend during the study period. The recovery performance of agricultural advances in commercial banks, regional rural banks and co-operative banks has shown a positive trend. Only the recovery performance of primary cooperative agricultural and rural development bank had shown a declining trend. With respect to the problems encountered in Agriculture credit system misutilization of loan amount by borrower, willful and deliberate default by borrowers and diversion of income generated out of the investment have found prime importance in the order.

Gurumoorthy (2000) reported that the SHGs are linked with banks for the internal credit under the projects of rural development. The appraisal consists of bank managers, rural development officers, NGOs; project implementation units visit the groups for providing financial assistance to the respective entrepreneurial activities. Nair (2000) reviewing recent trends in rural financial intermediaries and commercial banks in India indicated that the commercial banks credit to rural areas during the late 1980's and early 1990's has shown a deceleration in growth. The relative proportion of bank credit flowing to priority sector, especially agriculture was fallen below the target of 18 per cent at a national level since the mid 1980's.

Prasad (2000) reported that in many villages, community issues like drinking water, roads, electricity and health services were addressed by the women's groups. The women involved themselves in various activities like desilting of tanks and working towards child development in addition to income generating activities. Suriakanthi (2000) reported that bank transactions are essential activities of SHG's. Credit and subsidy under the (SGSY) Swarna Jayanthi Gram Swarozgar Yojana Scheme can be availed only through banks.

Barik and Vannan (2001) reported that the project of linking SHGs with banks has gained momentum in India from 1992. And he reported that three broad models have emerged, model-I: Bank-SHG, member formed 14 per cent, model-II: bank (facilitating agency) SHG-members formed70 percent and model-III: Bank-NGO-MFI-SHG- members formed 16 per cent of SHGS linked during the 1999-2000. Dadhich (2001) stated that effective implementation of micro-finance can be a means not only to alleviate poverty and empower woman but also be a viable economic and financial proportion. Dwarakanath (2001) reported that the DWCRA programme helped the rural women to earn an additional monthly income ranging from Rs.250 - Rs.2000 depending on entrepreneurial activities taken up by them.

Namboodiri and Shiyani (2001) reported that the SHGs that are promoted by the NGOs had a better saving performance compared to that of SHIP. However, the repayment performance of the SHGs promoted by the SHIP was superior to that of NGOs. Pankaj (2001) reported that the SHG-bank linkage programme launched by NABARD in 1992 is activities land mark in the field of micro financing in India. This programme aims to organize SHGs 10 to 20 persons from the economically homogenous strata regularly same the amounts from their earnings. Satish (2001) reported that the NGOs due to the nearness to the people and flexibility of operations seem to be better equipped to undertake SHG formation. And linking SHGs to bank helps in overcoming the problem of high transaction costs to banks in providing credit to the poor.

Rangi et al. (2002) reported that about 59 per cent of the borrowings were for consumption purposes in the household. However, about 32 per cent of the respondents reported those consumption loans were exclusively for routine family expenditure because employment was not regularly available to the respondents" households. About

18 per cent of them took credit for repair of their houses and about five per cent each used it for the study of their children and installation of hand pumps.It was found that about 71 per cent of these bank loans were for productive purposes. Among the productive purpose, dairy farming was the most dominant (about 32%) followed by tailor shop (about 19%), cloth shop (about 10%), grocery shop (about 6%) and electrical shop (about 3%). The loans for consumption purposes accounted for about 29 per cent of the cases. The routine family expenditure was dominant reason for taking loans, for this purpose. The other purposes were social functions, medical treatment and house repairs (Rangi et al., 2002).

Vishvanath (2002) conducted a study in the management appraisal of district central co-operative bank in Uttar Kannada District of Karnataka and found that growth in number of branches, employees and membership was positive and significant. Except borrowing (8.17 per cent) all other financial variables showed a positive and significant growth. The recovery percentage for the selected Karnataka District Central Co- operative bank branches was found to be more than 90 per cent. Kothal et al (2003) stated that there could be four different models of linkage between SHGs and banks. Acceptance of a particular model depends on the perception of the bank and the strength of the SHGs and the NGO. The programme of SHGs organized by various NGOs and banks in different part of the country is reported to be highly satisfactory.

Raghavendra (2003) reported that the average participation level of SHG members has been quite good. Officials of Commercial Banks and RRB's together account for 50 percent of total participation followed by Co-operative banks at45 per cent and the balance 5 percent by NGO's. Southern region accounts for over 2/3rd of total participation. Raghavendra (2003) revealed that the total number of SHGs, which were credit linked in the country, reached a phenomenal figure of 4.61 lakh by March 2002. Almost 90 per cent of them were linked to banks were exclusive women groups and periodic studied have revealed that repayment of loans by SHGs to banks has been consistently over 95 per cent.

Vasudeva Rao (2003) in his study conducted at Andhra Pradesh pointed out that a majority of the people have taken loans for their own occupational development, whereas, only a few have taken for health, education and marriage purposes. The amounts taken are also varying with the purpose. About 75.60 per cent availed loan for dairy activities, while 4.00 and 3.60 per cent of the respondents" availed loan from the group for daughter's marriage and poultry, respectively (Ritu Jain et al, 2003). Arun Kumar (2004) reported that (53.33%) of the groups studied belong to medium level of performance category followed by high level of performance category (33.30%) of groups and remaining 13.33 per cent of groups belonged to low performance category.

Kala (2004) reported that the linkage of the Self Help Groups (SHG's) with formal rural banking started after the launching of the pilot scheme by NABARD in February

1992 and linkage of SHGs is possible only if the SHGs have successfully collected savings, made loans and recovered them for six months. Nataraj (2004) in his study on "Role and performance of SHGs in rural credit-an economic analysis" reported that the average savings per group and average savings per member in case of RRBs sponsored SHGs was better compared to NGO promoted SHGs Selvachandra (2004) stated that SHG and its linkage with banks is an important vehicle to promote micro finance in India. This programme helps to promote financial transactions between formal banking systems with the informal SHGs as clients.

Selvi and Rathna Krishnan (2004) observed that the majority of the SHG leaders (88.30%) performed the specified leadership roles to the medium level followed by 11.7 percent of them in lowland. Sentil and Sekar (2004) reported that income generation through SHG members gained additional income and employment through SHGs. Savitha (2004) reported that economic empowerment was high for agricultural laborers (53.33%) followed by small farmers (26.67%) and landless farmers (6.67%).

Asokan (2005) reported that National Institute of rural development (NIRD) conducted a study on micro enterprises, which are developed by SHGs in Kerala. The characteristics of micro entrepreneurs under SHGs revealed that a high proportion (90%) of them were unemployed prior to joining SHG and tailoring was found to be the most preferred activity (47%). The study also found that the average monthly turnover of micro project taken by members of SHGs members was around Rs. 1917 and net profit worked out to be Rs. 700 per month. This indicates a high level of profit i.e. 60 per cent of individual units have investments less than Rs. 5,000. A study conducted in Trchirapalli rural area found that before starting micro- enterprises their annual income was increased to the tune of Rs. 50,879.

Asokan (2005) reported that among the three models of linkages introduced, the second model i.e., SHG formed by NGOs and formal agencies but directly financed by bank is the best model. And he stated that the role of NGOs is very important to form SHGs Joseph. Asian productivity organization (2005) reiterated that on the way to improve the measurement of performance in productivity measurement, the total factor productivity should measure the synergy and efficiency of utilizing both labour and capital inputs. Further it stated that an appropriate productivity performance measurement system should cover financial, internal business process customers and learning and growing.

Ganesh (2005) reported that in Akola district of Maharashtra an SHG formed under SGSY in record time of one and half years, all the families belonging to BPL status have uplifted to "Owner of Brick Kiln" status. Their net profit per 1000 bricks amount to Rs.550/- to Rs.650/- approximately. And their turnover has increased to more than Rs.3.5 lakhs. Gosh (2005) studied that the share of allied activities in agricultural output, namely dairying, fisheries and poultry has been increasing significantly, the share of livestock in the gross value of agriculture (crop and livestock production) increased from under 16 per cent in 1970-71 to 26 per cent in 1995-96, that of fisheries went up over the same period from 1.7 per cent to 3.1 per cent. The share of non-food crop in the cropped area has increased from 25.7 per cent in the triennium ending 1971-72 to 35.1 per cent by 1999-2000.

Gosh (2005) studied that the short term credit remained nearly unchanged, significantly at about 14 per cent, the growth of long term credit slowed down from about 20 per cent in the 1970s to about 14 per cent in the 1990s which is too disturbing. Clearly, this trend is bound to have a crippling impact on the capacity of the agricultural sector to grow and prosper. NABARD (2005) studied the impact of SHGs on economic empowerment of its members in Ballir district, Uttar Pradesh. And reported there was an increase of the monthly income of each of the families by at least Rs.700/month and this increase was solely due to the business that they were able to do by virtue of taking loan after the activities of SHG started.

Rao (2005) reported that the highest average annual household income (Rs.45, 600) is from among respondents of papads and pickles and lowest (Rs.38, 600) from respondents of chalk making activity. And the micro enterprises roughly provided 117-mandays/respondent, which was a great contribution. Satya Sundaram (2005) stated that micro-finance in India is making steady and satisfactory progress. NABARD has set a goal of covering 10 million poor, i.e. one third of the country's poor population through one million SHG's by 2003.

Thorat (2005) stated that micro-financial services provided to the poor in sustainable manner is consistent with high repayment rates. Which meant that if the services to the poor were provided in a sustainable manner than the beneficiaries would go in for repayments that are quite high in consideration to a staggered manner of provision of services. Bhagwati (2006) stated that the micro- credit advanced through the mechanism of self-help groups linked to bank credit is associated with higher level of loan recoveries and that tree linkage project has facilitated socio-economic empowerment of weaker sections including women folk.

Dasaratharararamaiah et al. (2006) reported that 10.0 per cent of beneficiaries had income between Rs.7, 201 and above, 20.67 per cent have income between Rs.4, 801 to 7,200 and 31.33 per cent have income Rs.3, 601 to 4,800 and 38.00 per cent have income below Rs.3,600 per annum after implementation of DWCRA. And it was found that there are no persons without any income. And it was also found that 50 per cent of beneficiaries have less than 100 man-day of employment, 21.67 per cent of the beneficiaries have employment between 101 to 180 man-day, 20.00 per cent of the beneficiaries have employment between 181 to 240 man-day as against 8.33 per cent of the beneficiaries who have employment between 241 and above man-day of employment per annum.

Gangaiah et al (2006) conducted study on impact of SHGs on income and employment generation. They reported that on an average the loans received generated

184 person days of employment per household. Non-farm activities generated higher number of person days of employment. Idly shop, cloth business and tailoring generated 300 each and 240 person days of employment. They also found that SHGs had favorable impact in generation of income in the village selected. The averag3e income generated was Rs.19,578/-. Income generated in the selected activities shows that it b varies from Rs.5000 per annum in case of idly shop to Rs.26, 541 in the case of agriculture.

Joseph and Easwaran (2006) conducted a study to identify the constraints in functioning of SHGs and its impact on the members. And it was found that 51.28 per cent of respondents had income between Rs.25,000 to Rs.50,000. Majority of respondents had assets worth below Rs, 1 lakh and more than one-half of the respondents as whole (51.28%) had assets below Rs.1 lakh. They also studied the perceived impact of SHGs on tribal development. When studied the relationship between the composition and impact of SHGs. The perceived impact of SHGs was found to be significantly associated with three variables duration of membership, member's participation and perceived group cohesion. Joseph and Easwaran (2006) sated that in all parts of the country, self-help groups are organized by governmental and non-governmental organizations (NGOs). The government, banks and non-governmental organizations facilitate them by providing revolving fund, organizational and training, credit etc.

Reddy and Gupta (2006) studied the credit management in Self Help Groups(SHG's) under South Asia Poverty Alleviation Programme (SAPAP) revealed that the data on purpose wise allocation of credit showed that sample groups allocated 34 per cent, 22 per cent and 22 per cent of the total credit to small businesses, animal husbandry and agriculture respectively. Under animal husbandry, members take loan to purchase milch animals, sheep and goats, under agriculture members take crop loan to purchase, plough and bullock carts. The other major purposes include domestic consumption (13 per cent) and clearing of old debts (7 per cent) and share of health and education is only three per cent. Thus the members in the sample groups have taken credit mainly (78 per cent) for productive/ income generating activities during the study period.

Subbiah and Navaneetha (2006) reported that there are three models under the SHG's-bank linkage programme. About 72% of the SHGs are formed by NGOs/ government agencies and the like financed by banks. They stated the programme has been advantageous not only to members of SHG's but also to the banks. SavitaShankar (2006) conducted Studies on efficient credit models in micro finance, in Tamil Nadu; the most popular model for the dispensation of micro credit in India is the group-lending model. As per Sa-dhan (Industry Association of Community Development Finance Institutions in India) data, group loans account for 93% of the microfinance in India.

Thanarathnam (2006) while studying the working of primary agriculture co-operative banks analyzed the loan dispersed by the bank. He had used the annual average growth rate of different types of loans given by banks. It was found that the average annual growth rate for the period 1996-97 to 2001-02 with regard to short term loan was 2.07 per cent, for jewel loan it was 1.35 per cent deposit loan has 3.44 per cent of growth rate. It was really appreciable and it really showed the performance of the bank. According to the amount of loan dispersed by the bank, a large percentage share was taken by the jewel loan in all the six years and the amount was small with regard to deposit loan.

Ramappa and Sivasankaraiah (2007) studied that the share of agriculture loan in the total priority sector advances was considerably large and fluctuated from 73.02 per cent in 1993-94 to 76.79 per cent in 2004-05. It was also evident that of the total agriculture loan in 2004-05, crop loan alone accounted for 93.31 per cent. Among non- agriculture activities retail trade/business enterprise received large quantum of loan followed by Self Help Group's. The percentage share of non-priority sector in total outstanding advances showed increasing trend from 15.16 in 1993-94 to 34.2 in 2004-05. It signifies the change in the lending pattern of the Rayalseema Grameena bank in Andhra Pradesh.

Shylendra etal.,(2007) report the overall performance of the self-help group (SHG) intervention of the Sadguru Water and Development Foundation (SWDF) in India and identifies possible ways to take it forward for promoting savings and credit activities. The study was stated that Self-help groups have become an important instrument in the delivery of microfinance services like savings and credit for the poor.

2.4 Summary

The credit market scenario in India reveals that the formal financial system was not adequately developed to meet the increased credit demands of large number of small clients without adequate collateral. It had inherent problems of asymmetry of information pertaining to the identification of creditworthy borrowers, ensuring the utilization of the loans for those purposes for which they had borrowed and enforcing timely repayment. Since the transaction costs of credit market dealings of informal system was relatively cheaper, the needy relied on them, even though the interest rate was exorbitant. Although banking reforms were introduced, a large section of the poor remained inaccessible to credit. In this context, the microfinance programme assumed a significant place in the rural credit market of the country. The growth and the spread of microfinance activities achieved a considerable progress after the extensive implementation of bank linkage programme of the NABARD. Moreover, the NGOs also played significant roles in popularizing the microfinance through their development- oriented schemes. Though the group approach is well appreciated and accepted as a poverty alleviation strategy, it is not devoid of defects (Emil Mathew, 2006). At times, Microfinance groups faced problems of sustainability due to group and member specific characteristics. The empirical studies also revealed the same. Therefore, the issues pertaining to these aspects have been discussed in the ensuing chapters.

Reference:

Adams, D. W., Graham, D. H., & Pischke, J. V. (1984), *Undermining Rural Development with Cheap Credit,* Boulder and London: West view Press. Axelrod, R. (1981), *The Evolution of Cooperation*, Basic Books, New York.

Baland, J. M., & Platteau, J. P. (1996), "Halting Degradation of Natural Resources: Is there a Role for Rural Communities?", *Food and Agriculture Organisation of the United Nations*, Clarendon Press, Oxford.

Besley, T. & Coate S. (1995), "Group Lending, Repayment Incentives and Social Collateral", *Journal of Development Economics*, 46(1): 1-18.

Besley. T. (1994), "How Do Market Failures Justify Interventions in Rural Credit Markets?", *The World Bank Research Observer*, 9(1): 27-47.

Bhatt, N., & Tang, S. Y. (1998), "The Problem of Transaction Costs in Group Based Micro Lending: An Institutional Perspective" *World Development*, 26(4): 623-38.

Bhatt, V.V. (1987), "Financial Innovations and Credit Market Evolution", *Economic and Political Weekly*, 22(22): M45-M54.

Bouman, F. J. A. (1984), "Informal Saving and credit Arrangement in Developing countries: Observations from Sri Lanka", In Adams D.W et al. (eds.), *Undermining Rural Development with Cheap Credit*, West view Press, Boulder and London.

Bratton, M. (1986), "Financing Small Holder Production: A Comparison of Individual and Group Credit Schemes in Zimbabwe", *Public Administration and Development*, 6 (2): 115-32.

Braverman, A., & Guasch, J. L. (1993), Administrative Failures in Government Credit Programs, *The Economics of Rural Organization: Theory, Practice, and Policy*, 53-69.

Braverman, A., & Guasch, J. L. (1986), "Rural credit markets and institutions in developing countries: Lessons for policy analysis from practice and modern theory", *World Development*, 14(10): 1253-1267.

Buchanan, J.B. & Gorden, T. (1965), *The Calculus of Consent*, University of Michigan, Michigan.

Campbell, R., & Snowden, L. (Eds.). (1985), Paradoxes of Rationality and Cooperation: Prisoners Dilemma and Newcomb's Problem, University of British Columbia Press.

Coleman, J. S. (1988), "Social Capital in the Creation of Human Capital", *American Journal of Sociology*, S95-S120.

Cuevas, C. E., & Graham, D. H. (1984), "Agricultural Lending Costs in Honduras" In Adams, Dale W. Douglas H. Graham and J. D. Von Pischke (eds.), *Undermining Rural Development with Cheap Credit*. Westview Press, Boulder.

Desai, B.M. (1983), "Group Lending in Rural Areas", In Von J.D. Pischke, Dale W.

Adams and Gordon Donald (eds.), *Rural Financial Markets in Developing Countries*, Johns Hopkins University Press, Baltimore.

Devereux, J., & Fishe, R. P. (1993), "An Economic Analysis of Group Lending Programs in Developing Countries", *The Developing Economics*, 31 (1): 102-121.

Floro, S. L., & Yotopoulos, P. A. (1991), *Informal Credit Markets and the New Institutional Economics: The Case of Philippine Agriculture,* Westview Press, Boulder.

Gaiha, R., Imai, K., & Kaushik, P. D. (2001), "On Targeting and Cost Effectiveness of Anti-Poverty Programmes in Rural India", *Development and Change,* 32 (2): 309-342.

Ghatak, M. (1999), "Group lending, local information and peer selection", *Journal of development economics*, 60 (1): 27-50.

Ghatak, M., & Guinnane, T. W. (1999), "The Economics of Lending with Joint Liability: Theory and Practice", *Journal of Development Economics*, 60 (1): 195-228.

Godquin, M. (2004), "Micro-Finance and Repayment Performance in Bangladesh: How to Improve the Allocation of Loans by MFIs", *World Development*, 32 (11): 1909- 1926.

Goetz, A. M., & Gupta, R. S. (1996), "Who Takes the Credit? Gender, Power and Control over Loan Use in Rural Credit Programs in Bangladesh", *World Development*, 24 (1): 45-63.

Hashemi, S. M., Schuler, S. R., & Riley, A. P. (1996), "Rural Credit Programs and Women's Empowerment in Bangladesh", *World Development*, 24 (4): 635-653.

Hoff, K., & Stiglitz, J. E. (1990), "Introduction: Imperfect information and rural credit markets- puzzles, policy perspectives." *The World Bank Economic Review*, 4(3): 235-250.

Hulme, D., & Mosley, P. (1996), *Finance against poverty, Vol. 1*, Routledge Publication, New York.

Huppi, M., & Feder, G. (1990), "The Role of Groups and Credit Cooperatives in Rural Lending", *The World Bank Research Observer*, 5 (2): 187-204.

Jain, S., & Mansuri, G. (2003), "A Little at a Time: The Use of Regularly Scheduled Repayments in Micro-Finance Programs", *Journal of Development Economics*, 72 (1): 253-79.

Khandker, S. R. (1998), "Micro-Credit Programme Evaluation: A Critical Review1", *IDS bulletin*, 29(4): 11-20.

Yifu Lin, J., & Nugent, J. B. (1995), "Institutions and Economic Development", *Handbook of Development Economics*, 3: 2301-2370.

Llanto G. M. (1990), "Asymmetric Information in Rural Financial Markets and nterlinking of Transactions through Self-help Groups", *Saving and Development*, 14(2): 137-52.

Mayoux, L. (1998), "Participatory Learning for Women's Empowerment in Micro- Finance Programmes: Negotiating Complexity, Conflict and Change", *IDS Bulletin*, 29 (4): 39-50.

Mayoux, L. (2001), "Tackling the Down Side: Social Capital, Women's Empowerment and Micro-Finance in Cameroon", *Development and Change*, 32 (3): 435-64.

Morduch, J. (1999), "The Roles of Subsidies in Micro-Finance: Evidence from the Grameen Bank", *Journal of Development Economics*, 60 (1): 229-48.

Morduch, J. (1999), "The Micro-Finance Promise", *Journal of Economic Literature*, 37(4): 1569-1614.

Mosley, P., & Dahal, R. P. (1985), "Lending to the Poorest: Early Lessons from the Small Farmers' Development Programme, Nepal", *Development Policy Review*, 3(2): 193-207.

Oakerson, R. J. (1986), "A Model for the Analysis of Common Property Problems", *In proceedings of the Conference on Common Property Resource Management,* Washington: National Academic Press.

Olson, M. (1965), *The Logic of Collective Action,* Oxford: Oxford University Press. Chavan, P., & Ramakumar, R. (2002), "Micro-Credit and Rural Poverty", *Economic and Political Weekly*, 37(10): 955-965.

Poteete, A. R., & Ostrom, E. (2004), "Heterogeneity, Group Size and Collective Action: The Role of Institutions in Forest Management", *Development and Change*, 35(3): 435-461.

Putnam, R. D., Leonardi, R., & Nanetti, R. Y. (1994), *Making democracy work: Civic traditions in modern Italy*, Princeton university press.

Rahman, A. (1999), "Micro-Credit Initiatives for Equitable and Sustainable Development: Who Pays?", *World Development*, 27(1): 67-82.

Rajasekhar, D. (1996), "Problems and Prospects of Group Lending in NGO Credit Programmes in India", *Savings and Development*, 20 (1): 79-104.

Reinke, J. (1998), "Does Solidarity Pay? The Case of the Small Enterprise Foundation, South Africa", *Development and Change*, 29(3): 553-576.

Rutherford, S. (2001), *The Poor and Their Money*, New Delhi, Oxford University Press (Oxford India Paperbacks).

Sahu, G. B., & Rajasekhar, D. (2005), "Banking Sector Reforms and Credit Flow to Indian Agriculture", *Economic and Political Weekly*, 40(53): 5550-5559.

Schaefer-Kehnert, W. (1980), "Success with group lending in Malawi", *Quarterly Journal of International Agriculture*, *19*(4): 331-337.

Schneider, H. (Ed.) (1997), *Microfinance for the Poor?,* OECD Publishing.

Sharma, M., & Zeller, M. (1997), "Repayment Performance in Group Based Credit Programs in Bangladesh: An Empirical Analysis", *World Development*, 25 (10): 1731-1742.

Stiglitz, J. E. (1990), "Peer Monitoring and Credit Markets", *The World Bank Economic Review*, 4 (3): 351-366.

Varian, H. (1990), "Monitoring Agents with Other Agents", *Journal of Institutional and Theoretical Economics*, 146(1): 153-174.

Gonzalez-Vega, C. (1982), "Credit Rationing Behaviour of Agricultural Lenders: The Iron Law of Interest rate Restrictions", In Adams D.W et al. (eds.), *Undermining Rural Development with Cheap Credit,* Boulder and London: Westview Press.

Vogel, R. C. (1984), "The effect of subsidised Agricultural Credit on Income Distribution in Costa Rica", In Adams D.W et al. (eds.), *Undermining Rural Development with Cheap Credit*, Boulder and London: Westview Press.

Woolcock, M. J. (1999), "Learning from failures in microfinance", *American Journal of Economics and Sociology*, 58(1): 17-42.

Wydick, B. (1999), "Can Social Cohesion be Harnessed to Repair Market Failures?

Evidence from Group Lending in Guatemala", *The Economic Journal*, 109 (457): 463-475.

Young, H. P. (2001), *Individual strategy and social structure: An evolutionary theory of institutions,* Princeton University Press.

3

Methodology

3.1 Introduction

One of the most essential features of development is the transformation of society, which embraces the movement form traditional relations, social norms, and traditional ways of health care, education and methods of production to more modern ones. Development enriches the lives of individuals by widening horizons of the choices and freedoms and at the same time by reducing their sense of isolation. Hence, the development strategy must be aimed at facilitating the transformation of society in identifying the potential catalysts and barriers to change. In this chapter, an attempt is made to present the methodology and socio-economic profile of the study area and sample respondents. This chapter has been divided into three sections. Section-I presents the survey methodology. Section-II presents the socio-economic profile of the study area. Section-III presents the socio-economic profile of the sample households.

SECTION-I
SURVEY METHODOLOGY

3.2 Survey Methodology

The methodology used in this study, has been presented under three heads viz., sampling design, data base, and techniques of analysis.

Sampling Design

In this study, multi stage sampling technique is used in the selection of units. Accordingly, at the first stage, Visakhapatnam district is selected purposively. The second stage of sampling is the selection of Mandal*. Chodavaram mandal is selected keeping in view that it should satisfy the two criteria viz., (i) cover the maximum number of rural poor households and (ii) cover the maximum number of Self-Help Group (SHG) households. The Third stage of sampling is the selection of villages.

* Mandal is at the middle rung of the local Self –Government the two being Village Panchayat and Zilla (District) Praja (People) Parishad.

As Chodavaram village is a big village it is selected for the study, in order to cover the required number of sample households (See Appendix 3.1 A, B, C). The Fourth stage of sampling involved the selection of households. In all, 400 SHG households were selected for the study. While 200 are members of old Self Help Groups (OSHG) and 200 are member of New Self Help Groups (NSHG). For selecting OSHG, the SHGs who have completed more than 5 years membership and for selecting NSHG, the SHGs having a membership of less than 5 years is considered. These two groups of households have been chosen keeping in view the probability proportion to their actual number in the total SHG households in the study area i.e., 10 per cent of the households.

Data Base

Both primary and secondary data were collected for the present study. The primary data were collected through well-designed and pre-tested schedules. The tools employed for the collection of the primary data was direct personal interview schedules. In addition, discussions were held with officials concerned. The Survey was conducted during the period from 1st April 2012 to 30th November 2012. In addition to primary data, the secondary data were collected from different sources for the present study. They are All-India Debt and Investment Survey (AIDIS); Reserve Bank of India (RBI); National Sample Survey Organisation (NSSO); NABARD and Microfinance 2012-13; District Rural Development Agency (DRDA), Hand Book of Statistics, Visakhapatnam.

Techniques of Analysis

In analyzing the data, different statistical techniques are used. To study the employment among the sample households Worker Population Ratio (WPR), Labour Force Participation Rate (LFPR) and Unemployment Rate (UR) are used. To judge the income variation among the households, Co-efficient of Quartile Deviation, Co-efficient of Variation is calculated. The significance of difference between average incomes of OSHG and NSHG households is tested with the help of Z-test and F – distribution measures the ratio of the variance between groups to the variance within groups. To examine the poverty levels, the Head Count Ratio (HCR) is used. Since all the sample households are poor, to measure shortfall and severity of poverty, Poverty Gap Ratio (PGR) and Sen's Index and Modified Sen's Index of poverty are used. To find out whether the microfinance programme participation has led to empower the members, Chai-square test is used and the empowerment is measured with indices (See Appendix 3.2).

Regression Analysis: Determinants of Income

Multiple regression analysis is used to identify the factors that determine the level of income of poor households.

Where:

$$PCIH\ (Y) = b_1 + b_2SH, + b_3PWH + b_4WRag + b_5WRnag + b_6SLHH + b_7PCIOS + b_8PCILS + b_9LH + b_{10}AH + b_{11}SAH + \ldots\ldots + \mu$$

PCIH	=	Annual per capita income of the household (Dependent Variable)
SH	=	Size of the household
PWH	=	percentage of workers in the household
WR_{ag}	=	wage rate of agricultural labour
WR_{nag}	=	wage rate of non-agricultural labour
SLHH	=	size of the landholding of the household
PCIOS	=	per capita income from other source (self-employment)
PCILS	=	per capita income from livestock
LH	=	literacy level of the head of the household
AH	=	Age of the head of the household
SAH	=	Age squared of the head of the household.

Regression Analysis:

Determinants of Borrowings and Repayments

Multiple regression analysis is used to identify the factors that determine the borrowings and repayment of loans of poor households.

Borrowings (Y) = $Y = a + b_1x_1 + b_2x_2 + b_3x_3 + b_4x_4 + b_5x_5 + \ldots\ldots + b_nx_n + \mu$ ---*Model-I*

Repayments (Y) = $Y = a + b_1x_1 + b_2x_2 + b_3x_3 + b_4x_4 + b_5x_5 + \ldots\ldots + b_nx_n + \mu$ ---*Model-II*

Where Borrowings = Different types of borrowings from different sources by the rural respondents of the selected area

Where Repayments = The repayment of loans borrowed by the rural respondents of the selected area.

Age (x_1)	=	Age of the respondent
Head (x_2)	=	Dummy variable, whether the respondent is head of Household
Literacy Level (x_3)	=	Number of Years of Education of the respondent
Earner (x_4)	=	Dummy variable, whether the respondent is working or not
Occupational Pattern (x_5)	=	Dummy variable, whether the respondent is employee
Size of the family (x_6)	=	Family size of the household
Asset holdings (x_7)	=	Value of the Assets owned by the household
Income (x_8)	=	Annual income of the household
Dependency ratio (x_9)	=	Dependency ratio of the household
Recurring Expenditure (x_{10})	=	Food and non-food Expenditure of Household
Non- Recurring Expenditure (x_{11})	=	Sickness of family members, ceremonies, etc.

Regression Analysis

Determinants of Empowerment:

A multiple linear regression is used to statistically measure the impact of all these determinants on the level of Empowerment. In this model we have estimated 2 regression models taking Economic Empowerment Index (EEI) and Social Empowerment Index (SEI) of the sample households where EEI and SEI of the respondents has taken as dependent variable and other relative variables are taken as independent variables. Those independent variables are like Age, Literacy level, Employment Days, Income, Loan Amount, Asset Holding and Mobility.

$$EEI\ (Y) = b_0 + b_1AGE + b_2EDU + b_3EMPL + b_4HHINC + b_5PROLOAN + b_6ASSETS + b_7MOBLITY + \ldots. + u\text{---}Model\text{-}I$$

$$SEI\ (Y) = b_0 + b_1AGE + b_2EDU + b_3EMPL + b_4HHINC + b_5PROLOAN + b_6ASSETS + b_7MOBLITY + \ldots. + u\text{---}Model\text{-}II$$

Where:

EEI	= Economic Empowerment Index (Dependent variable)
SEI	= Social Empowerment Index (Dependent variable)
AGE	= Age of the members in years
EDU	= Education level of the members
EMPL	= Employment in person days in Post SHG
HHINC	= Household income of the members in rupees
PROLOAN	= Amount of loan used for productive purposes in rupees
ASSETS	= Assets (house + land +jewellery)
MOBLITY	= Level of mobility of the members

SECTION - II
SOCIO-ECONOMIC PROFILE OF THE STUDY AREA

3.3 Socio Economic Profile of the Visakhapatnam District:

It is one of the backward districts in North Coastal Andhra Pradesh and it lies between 170-15" and 180-32" northern latitude and 810-54"and 830-30" of eastern longitude. It is bounded on the north partly by Orissa state and partly by Vizianagaram district, on the south by East Godavari district, on the west by Orissa State and on the east by the Bay of Bengal.

Historical Aspect and Etymology

Inscriptions indicate that the district was originally a part of Kaling kingdom, subsequently conquered by the Eastern Chalukyas in the 7th Century, A.D. who ruled over it with their Head Quarters at Vengi. The district was also under the occupation of various rulers, such as the Reddy Rajahs of Kondaveedu, the Gajapathis of Orissa, the Nawabs of Golkonda and the Moghal emperor, Aurangazeb through a Subedar. This territory was passed on to the French occupation, in view of the succession dispute among Andhra kings and finally it came under the British reign. There were non geographical Graftings till 1936. Consequent on the formation of Orissa state, the talukas namely Bissim Cuttack, Jaypore, Koraput, Malkanagir, Naurangapur, Pottangi and Rayagada entirely and parts of Gunupur, Paduva and Parvathipur were transferred to Orissa state.

The district was reconstituted with the remaining area and residuary portions of Ganjam district, namely Sompeta, Tekkali and Srikakulam Taluks entirely and portion of Parlakimidi. Ichchapuram, Berhampur were retained in Madras Presidency. With the passage of time, the reconstituted district was found administratively unwieldy and therefore, it was bifurcated into Srikakulam and Visakhapatnam districts in the year 1950. The residuary district of Visakhapatnam was further bifurcated and the taluks of Vizianagaram, Gajapathinagaram, Srungavarapukota and portion of Bheemunipatnam taluk were transferred to the newly created Vizianagaram district in the year 1979. Coming to etymology of the name Visakhapatnam, tradition has it that some centuries ago a king of Andhra dynasty, encamped on the site of the present head quarter town of Visakhapatnam, on his pilgrimage to Banaras and being pleased with the place, has built a shrine in Honour of his family Deity called Visakeswara to the south of the Lawsons Bay from which the district had derived its name as Visakheswarapuram which is subsequently changed to Visakhapatnam. The encroachment of waves and currents of the sea were supposed to have swept away the shrine into off shore area.

Physical Features

The District presents two distinct geographic divisions. The strip of the land along coast which covers 56.4% of total area of the district, the interior called the plains division and the hilly area of the Eastern Ghats with an altitude of about 900 to 1200 meters, Sankaram forest with an altitude of 1615 meters, Machkhand River which on reflow becomes Sileru, drains and waters in the area in their flow and reflow which are tapped for power generation, formed the first geographic division. The other division forms the plains division with an altitude not exceeding 75 meters, watered and drained by the rivers Sarada, Varaha and Thandava and rivulets Meghadrigedda and Gambheeramgedda. Since no major irrigation system exists, significant sub regions for agronomic variations exist in this division. Along the shore lies series of salt and sand swamps. The coast line is broken by a number of bald-head mounts, the important being the Dolphin's Nose which has afforded the establishment of Natural Harbour at

Visakhapatnam, Rushikonda (v), Polavaram rock and the big Narasimha Hill and Bheemunipatnam. Administratively, the District is divided into three Revenue Divisions and 43 Mandals.

Andhra Pradesh

Visakhapatnam

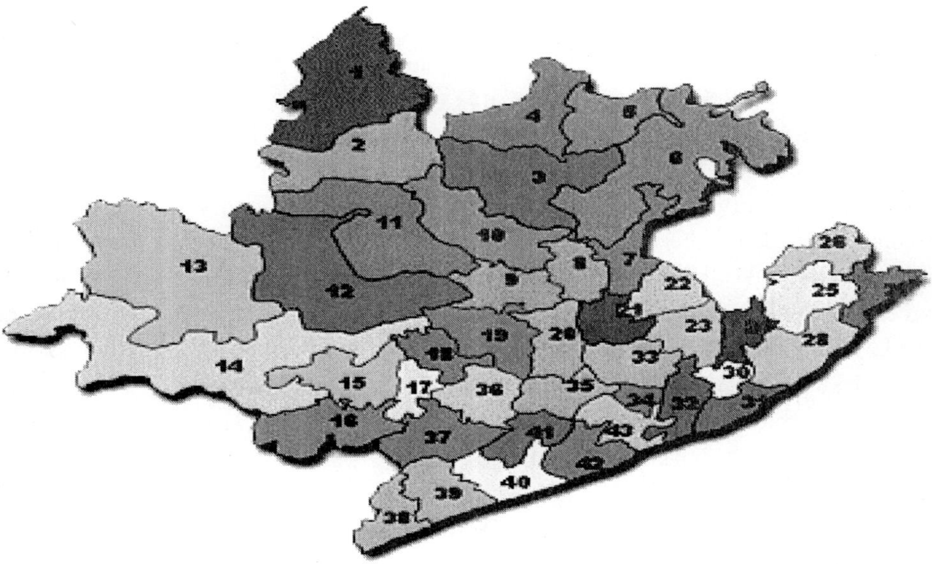

Mandal Code	Mandal Name	Mandal Code	Mandal Name	Mandal Code	Mandal Name
1	Munchingiputtu	16	Nathavaram	31	Pedagantyada
2	Pedabayalu	17	Narsipatnam	32	Paravada
3	Hukumpeta	18	Rolugunta	33	Anakapalli
4	Dumbriguda	19	Ravikamatham	34	Munagapaka
5	Arakuvalley	20	Butchayyapeta	35	Kasimkota
6	Ananthagiri	21	Chodavaram	36	Makavarapalem
7	Devarapalle	22	K Kotapadu	37	Kotauratla
8	Cheedikada	23	Sabbavaram	38	Payakaraopeta
9	Madugula	24	Pendurthi	39	Nakkapalli
10	Paderu	25	Anandapuram	40	S. Rayavaram
11	G. Madugula	26	Padmanabham	41	Yelamanchili
12	Chintapalle	27	Bheemunipatnam	42	Rambilli
13	Gudemkothaveedhi	28	Visakhapatnam	43	Atchutapuram
14	Koyyuru	29	Visakhapatnam (U)		
15	Golugonda	30	Gajuwaka		

Demographic Characteristics

The population of the District is 42.88 lakhs as per Directorate of Economics and Statistics, Andhra Pradesh as per 2011 Census, and this constituted 5.06 per cent of the population of the state while the geographical area of the District is 11161 Sq. Km., which is only 4.1 percent of the area of the State. Out of the total population, 21.41 lakhs are males and 21.47 lakhs are females. The Sex Ratio is 1003 females to 1000 males. The District has a density of population of 384 per Sq. Km. Agency area shows lesser density and plain area shows a higher density. About 47.50 percent of the population resides in the 10 hierarchic urban settlements, while rest of the population is distributed in 3100 villages. As per 2011 census Scheduled Castes constitute 7.60 percent of the population, while scheduled tribes account for 14.55 percent of the population of the district. The district has a work force of 16.03 lakhs constituting about 41.83 percent of the population besides the "marginal workers" to a tune of 2.97 lakhs. Among the main workers, the cultivators constitute 36.31 percent; agricultural labourers 23.60 percent and the balance of 40.09 percent are engaged in primary, secondary and territory sectors. As per 2011 census there are 26.13 lakhs literates forming 60.94 percent of the total population of the district. Male literates constitute 55.53 percent while female literates forming 44.47 percent excluding 0-6 age group of the total population.

Climate and Rainfall

The district has different climatic conditions in different parts of it. Near the coast, the air is moist and relaxing, but gets warmer towards the interior and cools down in the hilly areas on account of elevation and thick vegetation. April to June are the warmest months. The temperature (at Visakhapatnam Airport) gets down with the onset of south west monsoon and tumbles to a mean minimum of 21.00 C by January, after which there is reversal trend till the temperature reaches mean maximum of 32.70 C by the end of June during 2010-11. The district annual normal rainfall is 1202 mm of which south-west monsoon accounts for 50 percent of the normal, while north-east monsoon contributes 17.6 percent of the normal rainfall during 2010-11. The rest is shared by summer showers and winter rains. Total rainfall received is 1762.8 mm during the year 2010-11 and it excess 46.6 percent to normal rainfall. Agency and inland Mandals receive larger rainfall from the South West monsoon, while Coastal Mandals get similarly larger rainfall from North-East monsoon.

Soils

Red loamy soils predominate with coverage of 69.9 percent of the villages of the district. The soils are poor textured and are easily drained. Sandy loamy soils come next with 19.2 percent coverage, largely confined to the coastal areas. As much as 45 percent of the soils in the district are low inorganic content and 55 percent are in phosphorous content.

Land-Use

The total geographical area of the District is 11.16 lakh hectares, of this 35.9 percent alone is cultivable area while 39.52 percent is forest area. The rest is distributed among "Barren and uncultivable land" about 11.7 percent and "Land put to non-agricultural uses" about 9.6 percent. Out of the cultivable area, the net area sown form 23.1 percent while cultivable waste and fallow (current and old) lands constitute about 12.8 percent during 2010-11.

Agriculture and Animal Husbandry

Agriculture is the main stray of nearly 70 percent of the households. Though Visakhapatnam city is industrially developing, the rural areas continued to be backward. Rice is a staple food of the people and paddy is therefore the principal food crop of the district followed by Ragi, Bajra and Jowar and cash crops such as sugarcane, groundnut, sesamum, niger and chillies are important. Since there is no major irrigation system, only about 36 percent of the cropped area is irrigated under the ayacut of the medium irrigation system and minor irrigation tanks. The rest of the cultivated area is covered under dry crops depending upon the vagaries of the monsoon. The productivity of the crops is low.

Animal husbandry is an important allied economic activity to agriculture. Next to draught animal which are main source of energy for agriculture, milch animals, sheep and goat are important for income generation of the rural households. A sizable number of households earn subsidiary income by selling milk to visakha dairy and in local markets. The total livestock of the district is 17.87 lakhs of which working animals account for 2.24 lakhs while milch animals account for 4.33 lakhs. Goats and sheep's totaling upto 6.03 lakhs are important for the livelihood of the considerable population.

Irrigation

As a percentage to the Net area sown, the Net area irrigated is 25.8 during 2002- 03. The irrigation intensity is 1.4 percent. The total area irrigated under canals is 19,698 hectares, under tanks 11,404 hectares, under tube wells 10,322 hectares, under dug wells 7,576 hectares and under other wells 22,644 hectares. The irrigation sources as per Minor Irrigation Census 2001 are 26358 Dug wells, 7486 Tube wells, 6234 Surface flow sources and 54 lift irrigation sources.

Minerals

The district has mineral deposits of Bauxite Apatite (Rock Phosphate) Calcite, Crystalline limestone in rural tracts. Bauxite deposits at Sapparla, Jerrila and Gudem of G.K.Veedhi Mandal are considered to be the largest in the country. Bauxite deposits are also identified at Galikonda, Katuki, Chittemgondi of Araku group deposits and Katamrajukonda of Gurthedy sub-group of deposits. Phosphate apatite is available in Kasipatnam village of Ananthagiri Mandal. Rich deposits of crystalline limestone and calcite are mapped in Borra caves and along the valley from Borra to Araku and around Valasi village of Ananthagiri Mandal. Ruby mica is another mineral available in the district, which is essential for electrical and electronic industries. This mineral is available in the form of Philogopite and it is confined to Borra tract.

Industries

Industrial development is conspicuous in Visakhapatnam Urban agglomeration, with the establishment of large scale Industries like Hindustan Shipyard, Hindustan Petroleum Corporation, Coromandal fertilizers, Bharath Heavy Plates and Vessels, L.G. Polymers ltd., Hindustan Zinc, the recent giant Visakhapatnam Steel Plant and a host of other ancillary industries. In the countryside, the agro based industries like Sugar Factories, Jute Mills and Rice Mills are there, besides brick and tile units. The district has 385 registered factories under factories act, functioning with a work force of about 36,828 persons and the working capital of Rs. 10246 lakhs. The total inputs are 12522.50 lakhs; the value of output and Net value added being 14302.71 and 1120.82 lakhs respectively. As per Economic Census 1977, the total no. of enterprises and persons working in these enterprises is 90356 and 200283 respectively.

Infrastructure

The distribution of households with sanitary facilities available shows that out of the total households, only 30.9 percent of households are having bathroom facility within the house and 28.23 percent of households with latrine facility within the house. By the type of water outlet 12.4 percent is in closed drainage, 39.5 percent is with open drainage and remaining 57.5 percent is without drainage. The distribution of households with type of fuel used for cooking indicates that 59.8 percent households are using firewood and 4.2 percent of households are using crop residue, cow dung and coal combined as fuel and 8.5 percent of households are using Kerosene and 26.5 percent of households are using LPG as fuel for cooking. The distribution of households with source of drinking water indicated that 22.5 percent are with wells, 32.4 percent are with tap water and 35.7 percent are having hand pumps and tube wells, 2.3 percent are using rivers, canals as sources of drinking and 7.1 percent depend on springs and other sources. The distribution of households availing banking services and households having specific assets shows that 32.3 percent of total households are using banking services, 75.7 percent of households are having radio, 33.4 percent are having TV, 9.0 percent are having Telephone, 26.9 percent are having bicycle, 13.6 percent are having Scooter/Motor cycle, 1.9 percent are having car and 45.8 percent of the total households are not having any of the specified assets.

SECTION-III
SOCIO-ECONOMIC PROFILE OF THE SAMPLE HOUSEHOLDS

3.4 Socio-Economic Profile of the Sample Households

In this section an attempt is made to study the social aspects like age, literacy, family size, caste and economic aspects like number of earning members and assets of the sample households. The survey was conducted during the period from 1st April 2012 to 30th November 2012. In all, 400 SHG households were selected for the study. While 200 are members of Old Self Help Groups (OSHG) and 200 are members of New Self Help Groups (NSHG). The rationale for selecting the mandal is that the mandal have maximum coverage of SHG programme and also have maximum number of rural poor households. The major objective behind this classification is to assess whether access to microcredit has reduced the dependence of rural poor on informal credit agencies in rural areas.

Age Composition

The age of the head of the household may influence his decision making capacity. If he is too young, he lacks experience in decision making and if he is old, he cannot take decision in time and this may influence the productive capacity of the household. Similarly, the age of family members help to assess the available workforce in the family and its impact on productivity of the household. The age of the heads of the households and the age of the family members for OSHG and NSHG categories are presented in Tables-3.1A and 3.1B. It could be seen from the Table that almost half of the heads of households are in the age group of 18-39 for both the categories. The age composition of the family members (Table 3.1B) shows that around 30 per cent are in the age group of below 18 and 40 per cent are in the age group of 18-39 in both the categories. The majority of the members are young persons because they want to do some income generating activities to increase the income. It has also been found that old people are not generally intended to become members of SHGs. Since, they cannot undertake any income generating activities.

Table 3.1A Distribution of the Head of Households by Age Composition

Age in Years	OSHG	NSHG	All
Below 18	0	0	0
18-39	42.0	49.0	45.5
40-49	24.5	25.5	25.0
50-59	21.0	16.0	18.5
Above 60	12.5	9.5	11.0
Total	100.0 (200)	100.0 (200)	100.0 (400)

Source: Field survey

Note: Figures in brackets are Heads of Households.

Table 3.1B Distribution of Total Family Members by Age Composition

Age in Years	OSHG	NSHG	All
Below 18	31.9	31.6	31.7
18-39	40.3	44.1	42.2
40-49	11.9	12.7	12.3
50-59	9.9	6.9	8.4
Above 60	6.0	4.7	5.4
Total	100.0 (697)	100.0 (699)	100.0 (1396)

Source: Field survey

Note: Figures in brackets are Heads of Households.

Family Size

The size of the family of sample households is presented in Table-3.2A. It could be seen from the table that majority of households in OSHG (85.5) and NSHG (88.5) are having a family size of 4 and below. This implies that in rural areas also people have awareness of the two child norm and family planning techniques. Further, the distribution of households by average family size is calculated and presented in Table-3.2B. In both the households the average family size is low i.e., 3.49.

Table 3.2A Distribution of the Households by Size of the Family

Family Size	OSHG	NSHG	All
1 - 2 Members	21.5	18.5	20.0
3 - 4 Members	64.0	70.0	67.0
5 & Above	14.5	11.5	13.0
Total	100.0 (200)	100.0 (200)	100.0 (400)

Source: Field survey

Note: Figures in brackets are Heads of Households.

Table 3.2B Distribution of the Households by Average Family Size

	OSHG	NSHG	All
No. of Households	200	200	400
No of Family Members	697	699	1396
Average Family Size	3.48	3.49	3.49

Source: Field survey

Literacy Level

Education is recognized as one of the important components of human resource development. In view of this, the Government has taken a number of measures to promote literacy level, especially among rural masses. Apart from increasing enrolment, measures are also taken to check the dropouts. The literacy levels of the heads are presented in Table-3.3A. The proportion of illiterate heads are high in both OSHG (33.0) and NSHG (39.5) households. To have a complete understanding, one has to examine the literacy levels among all the members of the family. The details of the literacy levels of all family members are presented in Table-3.3B. The proportion of illiterate members are high in both OSHG (19.1) and NSHG (24.7) households. It implies that micro finance doesn"t help much in increasing the educational status of the heads of households as well as other family members in the family.

Table 3.3A Distribution of Head of Households by Literacy Level

Literacy Level	OSHG	NSHG	All
Illiterate	33.0	39.5	36.2
Primary	34.0	22.0	28.0
Secondary	25.5	28.5	27.0
Post-Secondary	7.0	9.0	8.0
Technical	0.5	1.0	0.8
Total	100.0 (200)	100.0 (200)	100.0 (400)

Source: Field survey

Note: Figures in brackets are Heads of Households.

Table-3.3B Distribution of Total Family Members by Literacy Level

Level of Education	OSHG			NSHG			All		
	Male	Female	Total	Male	Female	Total	Male	Female	Total
Illiterate	17.0	21.5	19.1	19.5	29.7	24.7	18.2	25.6	21.8
Primary	42.8	48.3	45.4	36.4	37.6	37.0	39.8	42.9	41.3
Secondary	29.3	24.9	27.2	32.6	20.5	26.4	30.9	22.7	26.8
Post-secondary	8.9	4.1	6.6	9.3	10.7	10.0	9.1	7.5	8.3
Technical	2.0	1.3	1.7	2.2	1.5	1.9	2.1	1.4	1.8
A. Total Adults	(348) 100.0	(317) 100.0	(665) 100.0	(313) 100.0	(327) 100.0	(640) 100.0	(661) 100.0	(644) 100.0	(1305) 100.0
B. Child below 5	13	19	32	30	29	59	43	48	91
Total (A+B)	361	336	697	343	356	699	704	692	1396

Source: Field survey

Note: Figures in brackets are total Members.

Caste

Caste is one of the characteristic features of the households that specify the social status of the household in the society. The details of the distribution of sample households by caste are given in Table-3.4. It could be seen from the Table that backward caste households are figured high in both the groups.

Table 3.4 Distribution of Head of Households by Caste

Caste	OSHG	NSHG	All
OC	34.5	40.0	37.2
BC	58.0	58.5	58.3
SC	7.5	0.5	4.0
ST	0.0	1.0	0.5
Total	100.0 (200)	100.0 (200)	100.0 (400)

Source: Field survey

Note: Figures in brackets are Heads of Households.

Assets:

The value of assets will explain the economic status of the household. The assets represent all assets that were owned by the household and that have money value.

These include all physical assets like land, house, furniture, ornaments, utensils etc. The distribution of sample households according to the total value of assets is presented in Table-3.5. It may be observed from the table that the percentage of households having assets worth above Rs.2,00,000/- is around 50 per cent in both the groups. This may be due to the impact of urban culture in chodavaram and it is nearer to the Visakhapatnam.

Table 3.5 Distribution of Households by Value of Assets

Value in Rs.	OSHG	NSHG	All
Less than100000	25.0	29.0	27.0
100000 - 200000	28.5	23.0	25.7
200000 - 300000	27.0	19.0	23.1
More than 300000	19.5	29.0	24.2
Total	100.0 (200)	100.0 (200)	100.0 (400)

Source: Field survey

Note: Figures in brackets are Heads of Households.

Earning Status and Dependency Ratio

Earning status of the family members is an important concept that will determine the family income of the household. In recent years, non-farm activities are also gaining importance in rural sector which will provide livelihood for the poor. Data regarding the distribution of the earners, non-earners and dependency ratio are presented in Table 3.9. It could be observed from the Table 3.9 that the non-earners are lower in all households.

From the Table, it could also be observed that in all households, there is a lower dependency ratio.

Table – 3.6 Distribution of Family Members by Earning Status

Category of SHGs	Earners			Non- Earners				Total members	Dependency Ratio
	Male	Female	Total	Male	Female	Children	Total		
OSHG	30.5 (213)	27.7 (193)	58.2 (406)	8.6 (60)	8.2 (57)	24.10 (174)	41.8 (291)	100.0 (697)	0.72
NSHG	30.8 (215)	28.5 (199)	59.2 (414)	5.0 (35)	10.6 (74)	25.2 (176)	40.8 (285)	100.0 (699)	0.69
All	30.5 (426)	28.0 (391)	58.5 (820)	6.8 (95)	9.4 (131)	25.3 (353)	41.5 (579)	100.0 (1396)	0.71

Source: Field survey

Note: Figures in brackets are total Members

3.5 Summary

The socio-economic profile of the sample households shows that almost half of the heads are in the age group of 18-39 for both the OSHG and NSHG. The family size is less than four members in majority of the households. Regarding literacy levels of the heads of households, the proportion of illiterate heads are high in both the households. Around 50 per cent of households are in the assets range of above Rs. 2,00,000/- in both the groups. More than half of the total members in both the households are earners. The dependency ratio is lower in both the households. To sum up, but for literacy the performance is satisfactory.

4

Employment, Income and Poverty among Sample Households

4.1 Introduction

It has been observed that indebtedness among the rural poor is acute and the credit policy for the rural is not effective to meet the credit needs of the rural poor and that as an alternative, micro credit strategy has emerged to provide credit for rural poor. Even though the main objective in the promotion of SHGs is to provide the rural poor an access to formal credit, and to improve employment opportunities, raising incomes and reducing poverty are the other achievements gained through the SHGs. The poor participate in micro credit programmes with the expectation that borrowing will increase their income and sustain self-employment. The pertinent question now is whether participation does in fact reduce poverty in terms of consumption and help increase and employment on a sustained basis? This Chapter tries to answer the above question by making a comparative analysis between the Old SHG (OSHG) and the New SHG (NSHG) households. The major objective behind this classification is to assess whether participation of a household member in the OSHG leads to improvement in the household's endowment.

This chapter has been divided into four sections. The first section deals with the differences in the employment and occupational patterns between the OSHG and NSHG households. The second section deals with the differences in the level and determinants of income between the households. The third section deals with the differences in the levels of expenditure between the households and the forth section deals with the differences in the incidence, magnitude and dimensions of poverty between the households.

SECTION - I
EMPLOYMENT

4.2 Employment

Indian Agriculture sector provide employment usually for a period of 240 days in a year. The period from May to August and that from November to February are considered peak seasons for farm employment, while March, April, September and October (120 days) are considered as slack seasons. It is observed that some workers also engage themselves as wage labourers in non-farm sector during the slack season. The total employment therefore includes both employment in the farm sector and employment in non-farm sector, in addition to self-employment. Some of the poor, apart from wage employment cultivate tiny bits of land. Agriculture is a household enterprise involving all the workers in the family including children. In view of this, the estimation of effective and gainful employment per worker in the household is complex. In fact, this is true in the case of many self-employed activities, carried out by all the workers in the family. The workers in agricultural sector participate in different processes and sometimes work virtually only for three to four hours a day and still contribute to the output. Not all the family members work throughout the day. On an average a male worker toils for six hours, while female and children for four hours. This clearly suggests that none of them works for eight hours a day, which is the usual norm.

The National Sample Survey Organization (NSSO) has developed and standardized the concepts and definition of labour force, employment and unemployment suiTable to Indian socio-economic conditions and adopted them in its quinquennial surveys on employment and unemployment since 1972-73 (27th Round). The various estimates are based on three concepts, viz., usual status, weekly status and daily status. These are explained below:

(a) **Usual Principal Status Concept & Usual Principal Subsidiary Status:** In this approach, the status of activity on which a person spent relatively longer time of the preceding 365 days from the date of survey, is considered the Usual Principal Status (UPS) activity of the person. In addition to UPS, if a person spends some time in another activity, it is called subsidiary activity and the two put together are called Usual Principal and Subsidiary activity Status (UPSS).

Accordingly, a person is considered "working" or "employed", if the person was engaged for a relatively longer period during the previous year, in any one or more work- related activities (economic activities). The person is considered "seeking" or "available" for work or "unemployed", if the person was not working but was either seeking or available for work for a relatively longer period during the preceding year.

(b) **Weekly status Concept:** The activity status is determined with reference to a period of preceding seven days. A person who worked at least for one hour a day, during the reference period of one week, while pursuing a gainful occupation, was deemed to be employed. A person, who did not work during the reference period but was seeking or available for work, was deemed to be unemployed.

(c) Daily Status Concept: The activity status of a person, for each day of the preceding 7 days, is recorded. A person who worked for one hour but less than four hours was considered as having worked for half day. It he worked for four hours or more during a day, he was considered as employed for the whole day.

Taking into consideration, the number of persons usually employed (i.e., those who had worked for a relatively longer period during a reference period of 365 days preceding the date of survey), and the number of persons usually unemployed for a relatively longer period during the reference period of the year preceding the date of survey, Worker Population Ratio (WPR), proportion of usually unemployed and Labour Force Participation Rate (LFPR) are estimated for OSHG and NSHG households in the study area. The details are presented in Tables 4.1, 4.2, 4.3 and 4.4.

It may be seen from the Table 4.1, that the proportion of persons employed in the principal status according to usual status approach was higher among the OSHG than the NSHG households. This may be due to the empowerment by the Programme. In case of UPSS the proportion was higher among NSHG households.

Table 4.1 Worker- Population Ratio (Usual Status)

Category of Households	No. of Persons	No. of persons employed for greater part of the year	No. of persons employed per 1000 persons
OSHG	697	134	192
NSHG	699	126	180
All	1396	260	186

Source: Filed Survey.

Table 4.2 Workers – Population Ratio (Usual Principal Status)

Category of Households	No. of Persons	No. of persons employed for the year	No. of persons employed per 1000 persons
OSHG	697	406	582
NSHG	699	414	592
All	1396	820	585

Source: Filed Survey.

The estimates of proportion of usually unemployed as per UPSS approach for OSHG and NSHG are presented in Table 4.3. It may be seen that proportion of unemployed during the study year was higher among NSHG than OSHG group.

Table 4.3 No. of Persons Unemployed per 1000 persons (UPSS)

Category of Households	No. of Persons	No. of persons unemployed for greater part of the year	No. of persons employed per 1000 persons
OSHG	697	87	125
NSHG	699	90	129
All	1396	177	127

Source: Filed Survey

Labour force, or in other words, the "economically active" population refers to the population which supplies or seeks to supply labour for production and therefore, includes both "employed" and "unemployed". For measuring the labour force participation, UPSS approach. The labour force measured in terms of UPSS includes persons who had for a relatively longer part of the year either worked or were looking for work and also those who had worked at least for some time from among the rest.

Accordingly, the estimates of labour force participation rates for the OSHG and the NSHG groups as per the UPSS approach are presented in Table 4.4.

Table 4.4 Labour Force Participation Rate (LFPR)

Category of Households	No. of Persons	Labour Force Participation Rate
OSHG	697	707
NSHG	699	721
All	1396	714

Source: Filed Survey

It may be noted that no insignificant differences in the proportion of economically active persons were observed between the groups.

Various studies conducted on micro credit indicated that the number of days of family employment increased slightly for micro credit beneficiaries after receiving the loans. Hossain (1988) conducted a study on beneficiaries of Grameen Bank in Bangladesh in 1988 and found that 20 per cent of the borrowers of the Bank were earlier unemployed. There was a small movement away from agricultural labour towards vocations like poultry farming, livestock rearing, processing and manufacturing, trading and shop-keeping. On an average, the number of days of family employment per month went up by 11 to 15 days. Mosley (1996) conducted a study on beneficiaries of Banco Sol in Bolivia in 1996 and found that only 38 per cent of the borrowers experienced an increase in employment days after taking the loans. The remaining 62 per cent of the borrowers either experienced a decrease or no change in employment days. Phazhendhi and Satyasai (2000) conducted a study in India on SHGs members in 2000 and found that the employment per household during pre SHGs situation was 318 man days which increased to 375 during post-SHG situation. While 52 per cent of the employment generated was from farm activities during pre-group situation, it was only 47 per cent during post-group situation. On the other hand, the proportion of employment generated through non-farm and off farm activities increased to 28 per cent and 37 per cent respectively.

Apart from the magnitude of employment, the data on the occupational pattern of the workers are studied and presented in Table 4.5. Based on the occupational distribution of the workers, the majority of the workers under the OSHG households are depending on household industry (33.5 per cent) followed by construction labour (29.4 per cent) etc. But in the case of NSHG households majority of the workers are depending on construction labour (27.4 per cent) followed by salaried people (22.8 per cent) etc. (See Figures 4.1 & 4.2).

Table 4.5 Occupational Distribution of Workers among Groups (as % of Total Workers)

Sl. No	Occupation	OSHG		NSHG		All	
		Main	Secondary	Main	Secondary	Main	Secondary
1	Cultivation	1.0	2.5	8.7	1.5	4.9	2.0
2	Agricultural labour	0.5	0.0	0.7	2.9	0.6	1.5
3	Construction labour	29.4	0.0	27.4	1.2	28.4	0.6
4	Rearing milch cattle	3.7	3.2	1.7	5.1	2.7	4.2
5	Household industry	33.5	-	18.7	-	26.0	-
6	Trade	9.9	-	16.7	-	13.3	-
7	Salaried people	21.0	-	22.8	-	21.9	-
8	Profession	1.0	-	3.2	-	2.1	-
	Total	100.0	100.0	100.0	100.0	100.0	100.0

Source: Filed Survey

Note: In OSHG the total workers are 406 & in NSHG the total workers are 414.

Figure 4.1 Occupational distribution of workers of OSHG group

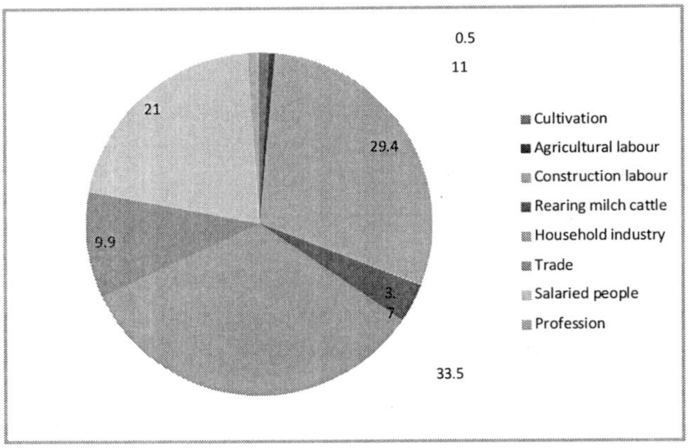

Figure 4.2 Occupational distribution of workers of NSHG group

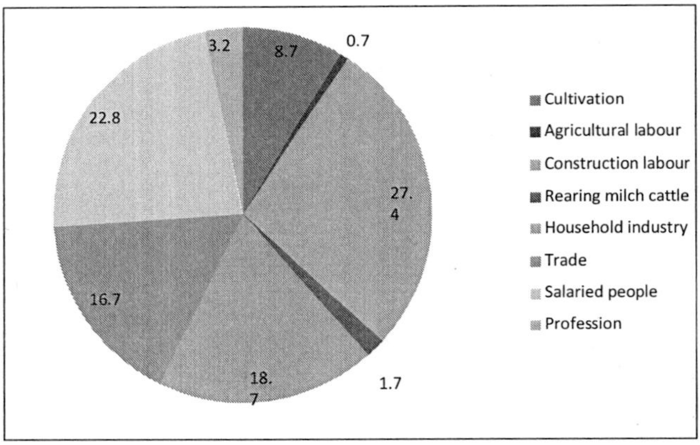

Papola and Partha Pratim Sahu (2012) in their paper based on the NSS data noted that the agriculture accounts for an overwhelmingly major share in rural economy and growth in employment in agriculture has been small, overall employment growth turns out to be low in rural areas. Aggregate employment in rural areas grew at a rate of 2.1 per cent during 1972-73/1983, but saw a decline to 1.7 and 1.4 per cent in the two subsequent periods. It has declined in absolute terms during 2004-05 to 2009-10 at a rate of 1.65 per cent per annum. Construction registered the fastest growth and the growth rate has increased over the years. During 1993-94/2004-05, employment growth in construction - 8.3 per cent has been recorded. Financial services had an employment growth of 6.30 per cent and other services 0.64 per cent in rural. Despite a decline in aggregate employment, construction employment grew at 13.6 per cent per annum. Non- farm employment has registered a fast growth in employment in rural areas. (Table-4.6)

The focus of the analysis is now shifted to the examination of determinants of income of the poor households in next section.

Table - 4.6 Growth of Rural Employment 1972-73 to 2009-10 (UPSS)

Sector	1972-73 to 77-78	1977-78 to 83	1983 to 87-88	1987-88 to 93-94	1993-94 to 99-2000	1999-00 to 2004- 05	2004-05 to 2009-10	1972-73 to 83	1983 To 93-94	1993-94 to 2004- 05	1999-00 to 2009-10
1	2	3	4	5	6	7	8	9	10	11	12
Primary Sector	1.66	1.49	0.28	2.17	0.20	1.29	-1.65	1.60	1.35	0.69	-0.19
Mining & Quarrying	5.82	6.11	5.58	1.09	-1.25	2.11	5.21	6.09	2.99	0.26	3.65
Manufacturing	5.36	3.50	4.33	0.35	1.62	4.09	-2.74	4.47	2.04	2.74	0.62
Utilities	17.17	1.66	11.12	5.15	-8.29	1.83	1.19	8.95	7.66	-3.82	1.51
Construction	0.92	6.32	18.45	-3.50	6.44	10.50	13.61	3.79	5.36	8.27	12.04
Secondary Sector	4.71	4.08	7.57	-0.53	2.55	6.03	4.65	4.47	2.87	4.11	5.34
Trade, Hoteling etc.	7.62	3.19	4.06	3.37	3.76	6.23	0.66	5.38	3.67	4.88	3.41
Transport & Communication etc.	6.77	8.07	5.13	3.79	6.75	6.33	2.58	7.60	4.36	6.56	4.44
Financing, Insurance, Real estate & business services	10.62	15.32	-7.21	4.45	4.27	8.41	2.07	13.33	-0.72	6.13	5.20
Community, social and personal services	4.08	2.26	0.40	5.99	-0.99	1.38	0.16	3.19	3.56	0.08	0.77
Tertiary Sector	5.72	3.58	2.13	4.64	2.12	4.52	0.90	4.69	3.56	3.20	2.70
All Non- Agricultural	5.23	3.82	4.91	1.98	2.32	5.25	2.83	4.58	3.22	3.64	4.03
Total	2.21	1.89	1.19	2.12	0.67	2.29	-0.34	2.08	1.72	1.40	0.96

Source: Own estimates based on various rounds of NSS data on employment and unemployment

SECTION – II
LEVELS AND DETERMINANTS OF INCOME

4.3.1 Levels and Determinants of Income

The increased employment opportunities or improvement in the already pursuing employment will lead to increase in the earnings. Puhazhendhi and Satyasai (2000) in their Study found that average net income/household income increased from Rs. 20,177/- or to Rs. 26,889/- or by about 33 per cent in pre and post group formation situation. Another study conducted by Puhazhendhi (2000) in Tamil Nadu covering 70 SHGs and 1041 members found that net incremental income due to the programme implementation was Rs. 2,424/- for all groups and it was relatively more in good performance groups (Rs. 2,967/-) than average and poor performance groups (Rs. 1,650/- and Rs. 1,299/- respectively). Sebastian Titus (2001) conducted a survey of 340 SHG members drawn from SHGs functioning under NGOs in Central Tamil Nadu and found that the overall average incremental income for all households who took loans for productive purposes was Rs. 376.75 per month. More than 60 per cent of the respondents reported a monthly increase in income above Rs. 300/- arising out of income generating activities.

Studies on Grameen Bank have, in general shown a positive change in the income of the beneficiaries. However, all these studies use recall method and therefore suffer from memory bias. Further, these studies have not attempted to isolate the income flows from assets acquired through loans. Therefore comparing the beneficiary income with a control groups income, rather than its own income will be a reliable method. In their analysis Pallavi Chavan and Ramakumar (2002) concluded that both NGO-led micro-credit and state-led credit institutions have led to positive but only marginal increases in the earnings of their beneficiaries. However, given the methodological problems associated with studies on income changes, more empirical evidence is required in order to substantiate such a conclusion.

The income of the household generally indicates the economic status of the household. In rural areas, households are engaged in diversified occupations for their livelihood. Therefore, in arriving at the total annual income, income from wage, income from livestock, income from household enterprises-like horticulture, basket making, fruit vending and finally income from agriculture are considered. To overcome the problem of recall, the wage-income from casual labour and income obtained from household enterprises for seven days preceding the date of survey has been taken up as the basis and similarly 30 days income from the livestock. The annual income from agriculture as declared by the sample households has been taken up, as there are no problems of credit in this regard. The details of the distribution of the households by income groups and average annual income and average per capita income of the sample households by source are presented in Tables 4.7, 4.8 and Figure 4.3.

Table 4.7 Distribution of Households by Annual Household Income Groups

Total Income Group	OSHG	NSHG	All
Below 25,000	8.0	12.0	10.0
25,000 - 50000	29.25	30.25	29.75
50,000 – 75,000	27.75	27.25	27.5
75,000 – 1,00,000	26.0	22.0	24.0
Above 1,00,000	9.0	8.5	8.7
Total	100.0 (200)	100.0 (200)	100.0 (400)

Source: Filed Survey

Note: Figures in brackets are Households

Figure 4.3 Annual Household income group among OSHG & NSHG Households

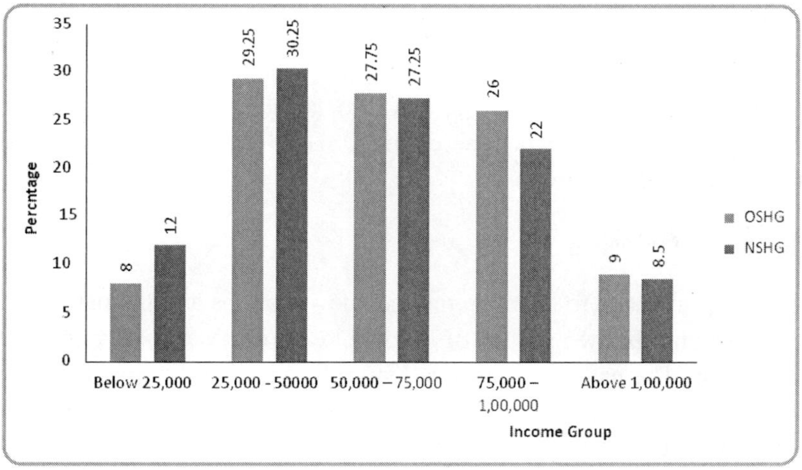

Table 4.8 Average Annual Household Income of the Sample Households by Source

Source	OSHG	NSHG	All
Crop income	1.7	5.6	3.6
Wage income	30.2	30.0	30.1
Livestock/rearing of cattle	1.4	2.5	1.9
Household industry	24.8	11.2	18.2
Trade	12.5	19.1	15.7
Salaried income	22.7	25.4	24.0
Profession	3.2	3.1	3.2
Others	3.5	3.1	3.3
Total Average income	100.0 (99123)	100.0 (93929)	100.0 (96526)
Per Capita Income (annual)	28443	26875	27658
Per Capita Income (per month)	2370	2240	2305

Source: Filed Survey

Note: Figures in brackets are Household Income.

It could be observed from the Table 4.7 that 65 per cent of the OSHG households and 69.5 per cent of the NSHG households are in the income range of below Rs 75,000/- per year indicating that the microfinance has marginal impact on their income levels. The distribution of income by source as indicated in Table 4.8 shows that income from household industry (24.8 per cent) and income from wage (30.2 per cent) are the major sources in OSHG households and income from wage (30 per cent) and salaried income (25.4 per cent) in NSHG households. The per capita income of the OSHG and NSHG households is estimated separately and is presented in Table 4.8. It may be observed from the Table that the average per capita income of the OSHG households is relatively higher than that of the NSHG.

The distribution income by source (Table 4.8) show that incase of the OSHG households, household industry and trade are the major one accounting from around 40 per cent followed by income from other sources but in case of the NSHG households wage income in the major one accounting for 30 per cent followed by household industry and trade (around 30 per cent). The per capita income of the households is estimated separately for the OSHG and NSHG households. It can be seen from the Table 4.8 that the per capita income of the OSHG household's is relatively higher than that of the NSHG households.

4.3.2 Income Variation

An attempt is made to examine the income variations and the pattern of income distribution among the two groups of households in order to assess the significance of the variations. The pattern of income distribution among the sample households is studied by using the quartile deviation method. Co-efficient of variation is calculated to examine the degree of variation around the mean in the incomes and is also used to compare variations between two groups of households. Co-efficient of Quartile Deviation is calculated by using the formula and the results of the analysis are presented in Table 4.9.

1) Co-efficient of Quartile deviation (Q.D.) = (Q3 - Q1) / (Q3 + Q1) Where

   Q1 = lower quartile value

   Q3= upper quartile value

2) Co-efficient of variation (C.V.) is calculated by using the formula

   C.V. = σ / mean × 100

Table - 4.9 Income Distributions by Category of Households

Sl. No	Item	Household Income			Per capita Income		
		OSHG	NSHG	All	OSHG	NSHG	All
1	Mean Income (Rs. In 000's)	99.12	93.93	96.53	30.74	28.02	29.38

2	Value of upper quartile (Q3) (Rs. In 000's)	108.00	108.00	108.00	36.75	26.25	26.59
3	Value of lower quartile (Q1) (Rs. In 000's)	78.00	70.19	72.00	21.60	20.00	21.00
4	Difference between upper and lower quartiles (Q3- Q1) (Rs. In 000's)	30.00	37.81	36.00	15.15	12.56	15.00
5	Co-efficient of Quartile deviation in % form	16.13	21.22	20.00	25.96	23.90	26.32
6	Standard Deviation	47.46	41.14	44.43	14.07	10.61	12.52
7	Co-efficient of variation (in %)	47.88	43.80	46.03	45.76	37.85	42.60

Source: Filed Survey

It can be observed from the Table that the household income of the first and third quartiles ranged from Rs. 78000/- to Rs. 108000/- for OSHG households. Whereas in case of NSHG households the range is from Rs. 70190/- to Rs. 108000/-. To know the extent of income variation between the OSHG and NSHG households, the Co-efficient of Quartile Deviation and the Co-efficient of Variation are calculated. The Co-efficient of Quartile Deviation of OSHG households (16.13) is lower than that of NSHG households (21.22). The value of Co-efficient of Variation for OSHG households is 47.88 as against 43.80 for NSHG households. It implies that the NSHG households are homogeneously distributed than OSHG households. The same analysis is carried out for per capita income of these two categories of households. The differences in the values of Co-efficient of Quartile Deviation (25.96 and 23.90 for OSHG and NSHG respectively) and Co-efficient of Variation (45.76 and 37.85 for OSHG and NSHG households respectively) contrast more in terms of per capita income.

The significance of the differences between the mean household income and mean per capita income of two groups was tested with the help of Z - test. The statistic used for testing the significance of difference between two population means is

$$Z = \frac{x_1 - x_1}{\sqrt{\frac{\sigma_1^2}{n_1} + \frac{\sigma_2^2}{n_2}}}$$

Where

x1 = Mean of the first population

x2 = Mean of the second population

σ1 = variance of the first population

σ2 = variance of the second population

n1 = size of the first population

n2 = of the second population

- The test procedure is summarized below:

1. Null hypothesis: there is no difference between the means of the population i.e., 1 = 2
2. Alternative hypothesis 1< 2
3. Level of significance: $\alpha = 0.05$
4. Criterion: Reject the null hypothesis if Z < - 1.96 or Z > 1.96

It is hypothesized that there are no differences in household income and per capita income between the OSHG and NSHG households.

Before testing the significance of the differences in between means the differences between standard deviations were also tested.

The statistics used for testing the equality of two population, is

$$F = \frac{S_1^2}{S_2^2} \text{ or } \frac{S_2^2}{S_1^2}$$

Whichever is larger (John E. Freund (1984))

- The test procedure is as follows:

1. Null hypothesis: $\sigma 1 = \sigma 2$

   Alternative hypothesis: $\sigma 1 \neq \sigma 2$
2. Level of significance: $\alpha = 0.05$
3. Criterion: Reject the null hypothesis it calculated value is greater than Table value of F, the value of F for n1 – 1 and n2 – 1 degrees of freedom.

The values of F-statistic are presented in Table 4.10. Since, the value of F- statistic is less than the Table value, we accept from the null hypothesis that there are no differences between the standard deviations of the two household groups with respect to household income as well as per capita income and the Z values are significant at 5% level. It implies that the differences in household income and per capita income between OSHG and NSHG households are statistically significant. Therefore, we reject the null hypothesis. It shows that the mean household income as well as per capita income of OSHG are higher than those of NSHG households. It can be inferred from the above analysis that households who participated in the groups for longer time are able to make significant improvements in their incomes compared to the households who do not have group help.

Table - 4.10 Significance of Difference between Mean Income of OSHG and NSHG

Statistic	Household Income			Per capita Income		
	Critical value	Calculated value	p-value	Critical value	Calculated value	p-value
F- Statistic	3.865	1.368	0.243	3.865	4.773**	0.029
Z-Statistic	1.645	1.170	0.121	1.645	2.185**	0.014

Source: Filed Survey

** Significant at 5% level.

4.3.3 Determinants of Income and Results of Regression Analysis:

With the help of regression analysis, an attempt is made to identify the determinants of income of the households. The crucial variables that influence the income generally are: (i) size of the household, (ii) percentage of workers in the household, (iii) wage rate of agricultural labour (annual wage income/number of man- days employed), (iv) wage rate of non-agricultural labour (v) per capita income from live stock (vi) size of the landholding of the household, (vii) per capita other income (self- employed), (viii) literacy level of the head of the household, (ix) age of the head of the household and (x) age squared of the head of the household. Specification of the model is the first step in a systematic study of the relationship. This involves the determination of (i) the dependent and the explanatory variables, (ii) the number of equations of the Model and their precise mathematical form and (iii) a prior theoretical expectation about the size and magnitude of the parameters.

Accordingly, per capita income is taken as the dependent variable for the present study. We can easily identify the variables that influence per capita income based on discussion presented in this Study and may write the following function.

Where

PCIH = f (SH, PWH, WRag, WRnag, SLHH, PCIOS, PCILS, LH, AH, SAH)

PCIH = Annual per capita income of the household (Dependent variable)

SH = Size of the household

PWH = per centage of workers in the household

WRag = wage rate of agricultural labour

WRnag = wage rate of non-agricultural labour

SLHH = size of the landholding of the household

PCIOS = per capita income from other source (self-employment)

PCILS = per capita income from livestock

LH = literacy level of the head of the household

AH = Age of the head of the household

SAH = Age squared of the head of the household.

As mentioned above, the dependent variable (PCIH) is the per capita income of the household. Income includes all the earnings of the household from wage employment, cultivation, livestock and other self-employment activities. The size of the household (SH) is expected to have a negative correlation with the annual per capita income. The percentage of workers in the household (PWH) is expected to have a positive correlation with the per capita income. As the percentage of workers increases, the levels of per capita income also will increase. An increase in wage rate of agricultural labour and non-agricultural labour (either WRag, or WRnag) is expected to have a positive correlation with the per capita income.

As the size of the landholding of the household (SLHH) increases, the size of return/produce from the land will increase. Due to this reason, the level of the per capita income will increase and a positive correlation is always expected. An increase in the level of the income from livestock and other self-employment activities will raise the income level of the household. Hence, the level of per capita income from livestock and other self-employment activities PCILS, PCIOH, are expected to have positive correlation with the annual per capita income. Literacy level of the head of the household (LH) is expected to have a positive correlation with the per capita income of the household, as the literacy level helps improve the income level. Number of years of schooling is taken to assess the literacy level of the head of the household.

The age of the head of the household (AH) is expected to have a positive correlation with the annual per capita income. The variable age squared of the head of the household (SAH) is expected to have a negative relationship with income. As the age of the head (up to the age of 60 years) of the household increases, the level of income will also increase with an increasing rate, but later as the age increases, the level of income will increase with a decreasing rate i.e., there exists an inverse relationship between age squared and per capita income of the household.

Based on the above assumptions, multiple regression analysis is used to specify the function and relationship between the dependent and independent variables. Accordingly, in this Study, the following multiple regression model is used.

$$PCIH = b_0+b_1SH+ b_2PWH+ b_3WR_{agl}+ b_4WR_{nagl}+ b_5SLHH+ b_6PCIOH+ b_7PCILS+b_8LH+ b_9AH+ b_{10}SAH$$

Since there exists an inverse relationship between the size of the household and per capita income, the parameter b_1 is expected to have a negative sign. The parameters b_2, b_3, b_4, b_5, b_6, b_7, b_8, and b_9 are expected to have positive signs and finally, parameter b_{10} is expected to have a negative sign since there exists an inverse relationship between the age squared of the head of the household and per capita income.

Table 4.11 Regression Coefficients of the independent variables of OSHG and NSHG Households

Independent variables	OSHG		NSHG		All	
	B	Sig.	B	Sig.	B	Sig.
(Constant)	2606.287 (.545)	.587	8518.696 (1.498)	.136	8303.011** (2.056)	.040
SH	-2823.582* (-7.736)	.000	-2740.535* (-5.771)	.000	-2973.029* (-9.304)	.000
PWH	20.517 (0.945)	.346	79.012* (3.035)	.003	39.835** (2.188)	.029
WR agl	13.186 (1.564)	.120	22.078* (3.572)	.000	25.735* (5.200)	.000
WR nagl	72.067* (26.564)	.000	47.856* (13.583)	.000	58.355* (24.930)	.000
SLHH	6828.482* (3.767)	.000	-2414.107** (-2.341)	.020	-1849.468** (-2.113)	.035
PCIOS	.881* (38.220)	.000	.695* (16.185)	.000	.794* (34.085)	.000
PCILS	-.010 (-.047)	.963	.457 (1.833)	.068	.178 (1.056)	.291
LH	23.967 (.316)	.752	165.107 (1.695)	.092	72.863 (1.107)	.269
AH	450.960** (2.120)	.035	276.518 (1.018)	.310	298.830 (1.597)	.111
SAH	-5.099** (-2.239)	.026	-3.844 (-1.315)	.190	-3.561 (-1.776)	.077
R^2	0.932		0.738		0.828	
Adjusted R^2	0.919		0.724		0.824	
F-value	227.548*		53.216*		187.243*	

Source: Filed Survey

Note: Figures in brackets indicate" values.

* Significant at 1% level. & ** Significant at 5% level.

Results of the Regression Analysis

The regression coefficients of independent variable estimated through regression analysis together with their coefficient of multiple determinations (R^2) are presented in Table 4.11. The correlation matrix for all the variables is presented in Appendix 4.1.

It can be seen from the Table that the estimated regression coefficient of variable SH has the expected negative sign and it is significant at 1 per cent level in both the OSHG and the NSHG households. The estimated coefficient of variable PWH has the expected positive sign in both the OSHG and NSHG cases and it is significant at 1 per cent level in the NSHG households. The variable WR_{ag} has a positive sign as expected in both OSHG and NSHG cases and it is significant at 1 per cent level in the case of the NSHG. The variable WR_{nag} has a positive sign as expected in both OSHG and NSHG cases and it is significant at 1 per cent level in both the cases. The variable SLHH has a positive sign as expected in both OSHG and NSHG cases and it is significant at 1 per cent level in the case of the OSHG and 5 per cent level in NSHG. The variable PCIOS has a positive sign as expected in both OSHG and NSHG cases and it is significant at 1 per cent level in the case of both the OSHG and NSHG The variable PCILS has negative sign in OSHG and positive sign in NSHG and it is insignificant in both the cases. The variable LH has a positive sign in case of the OSHG and the NSHG households but not significant. This may be due to the reason that the increased employment opportunities may not be sensitive at significant level to the literacy level of the head of the household. However, the variable is not significant in both the cases.

The variable AH, as expected, has a positive sign only in both groups of households, but has significant in case of the OSHG households. Finally, variable SAH has the expected negative sign in case of the OSHG and the NSHG households. The reason in case of households is that the increased employment of the other members of the family reduces the need of the head of the household's participation in economic activities at an older age. The explanatory variables have explained 93 per cent of variation in the OSHG group of households and around 73 per cent in case of the NSHG households indicating the overall goodness of fit. Thus, in analyzing the factors influencing the per capita income of the rural poor households, it is found that the size of the household, per centage of workers in the household, wage rates of agricultural laboures, wage rates of non -agricultural labourers, size of landholding of household, per capita income from other sources like self-employment, age of the head of the households and age squared of the head of the households are the significant factors.

Having presented the income levels and the determinants the focus of the analysis is shifted to the examination of income-expenditure relationship of the poor households.

SECTION- III
EXPENDITURE

4.4 Expenditure

In this Section it is proposed to examine the Expenditure levels of the OSHG and the NSHG Households. The household's expenditure is divided into two categories viz., recurring expenditure and non-recurring expenditure. Amount spent on food items and non-food items like clothing housing, fuel, education is considered as recurring expenditure. Non-recurring expenditure is the amount spent on events like birth, sickness, marriage, death etc. Data for recurring expenditure was collected on daily, weekly, monthly and annual basis for different items. To assess the non-recurring expenditure of the households, the amount spent on non-recurring expenditure items during the past three years of the reference period was considered. By making an average for the three-year period the annual non-recurring expenditure was arrived at. Total annual expenditure was arrived at accordingly. The details of the distribution of the households according to the annual recurring expenditure is presented in Table 4.12 and Figure 4.4.

Table 4.12 Distribution of the Households by Annual Recurring Expenditure

Category of Households	Recurring Expenditure (in Rupees)					
	Below 25,000	25,000-50,000	50,000-75,000	75,000-1,00,000	Above 1,00,000	Total
OSHG	22 (11.0)	70 (35.0)	63 (31.5)	40 (20.0)	5 (2.5)	200 (100.0)
NSHG	22 (15.0)	74 (33.0)	70 (35.0)	29 (14.5)	5 (2.5)	200 (100.0)
All	44 (11.0)	144 (36.0)	133 (33.2)	69 (17.2)	10 (2.6)	400 (100.0)

Source: Filed Survey

Figure 4.4 Per centage Distribution of Households by Recurring Expenditure Groups

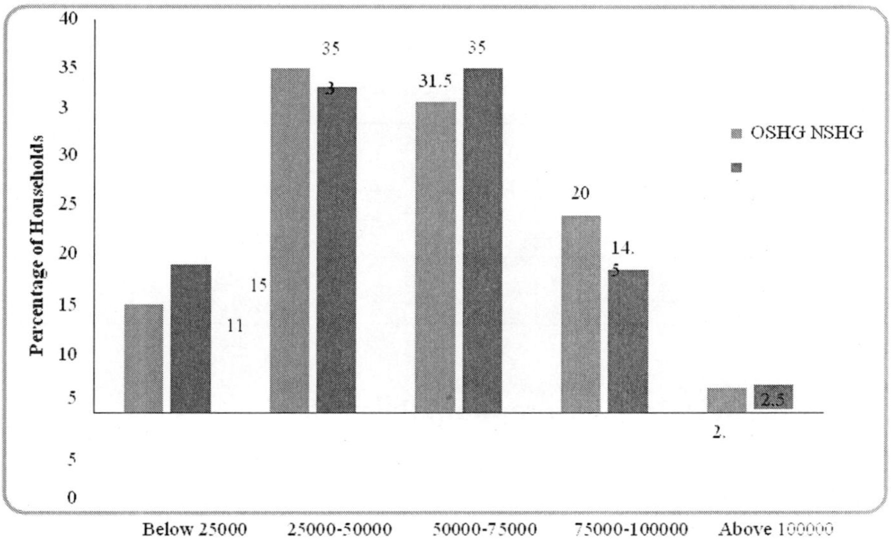

Expenditure Group

It could be observed from the Table 4.12 that the percentage of households reporting an annual recurring expenditure of Rs. 75,000/- and below is 77.5 percentage in the OSHG households and 83 percentage in the NSHG households. The details on recurring expenditure on food items and non-food items are examined later. Distribution of the households according to the annual non-recurring expenditure is presented in Table 4.13. This Table reveals that majority of the households are reporting low non-recurring expenditure.

Table 4.13 Distribution of the Households by Annual Non-Recurring Expenditure

Category of households	Non-Recurring Expenditure (in Rupees)				
	Below 25,000	25,001-50,000	50,001 – 1,00,000	Above 1,00,000	Total
OSHG	170 (85.0)	17 (8.5)	6 (3.0)	7 (3.5)	200 (100.0)
NSHG	173 (86.5)	18 (9.0)	4 (2.0)	5 (2.5)	200 (100.0)
All	343 (85.8)	35 (8.8)	10 (2.5)	12 (3.0)	400 (100.0)

Source: Filed Survey

The average annual amount of recurring and non-recurring expenditure is presented in Table 4.14. It could be observed from the Table that the per capita expenditure (recurring and non-recurring) for the OSHG households is greater compared to the NSHG households. This may be due to the OSHG households are having more access to formal institutions. These aspects can be analyzed in detail with the help of level of borrowing in the next chapter.

Table 4.14 Average Annual Recurring and Non-Recurring Expenditure (in Rupees)

Category of households	Recurring	Non-Recurring	Total	Per capita expenditure (Per month)
OSHG	82658 (85.69)	13885 (14.31)	96543 (100.00)	2308
NSHG	80606 (87.52)	11764 (12.48)	92371 (100.00)	2202
All	81632 (86.31)	12824 (13.69)	94457 (100.00)	2255

Source: Filed Survey

Income-Expenditure (Consumption) Relationship

Duesenberry and Engle widely discussed the relationship between income and expenditure of the households in the economic literature. In fact, the relationship between income and expenditure on food and non-food items has assumed much more importance in the thinking of many economists. Engle's hypothesis regarding income- consumption relationship (popularly know as Engle's law) is "as income of a family increases, the proportion of its income spent on food falls and that spent on non-food items increases". Against this backdrop of Engle's hypothesis, the income consumption relationship of the sample households is analyzed. As the present study refers to a single point of time, cross section analysis is attempted.

The national scenario on income and expenditure on food and non-food items is presented for the purpose of general understanding. The data presented in Table 4.15 provide a broad picture on the changes in the pattern of income-consumption relationship at the national level. The consumption pattern over the period indicates that with an increase in the per capita income, there is a decline in the share of food expenditure and vice versa.

Table 4.15 Percentage Distribution of Family Monthly Per Capita Consumer Expenditure by NSS in Rural India (in Rupees)

Years (NSS Round)	Per Capita Income (at current prices)	Per Capita Income (at 2004-05 prices)	Per Capita Expenditure	
			Food items	Non-food items
1972-73	792	9855	72.80	27.20
1977-78	1421	10748	64.30	35.70
1983	2634	11742	65.60	34.40
1987-88	3670	12417	63.80	36.20
1993-94	8166	15181	63.20	36.80
1999-2000	16437	19993	59.40	40.60
2004-05	24143	24143	55.00	45.00
2009-10	46243	33961	53.60	46.40

Source: 1) NSS KI (66/1.0): Key Indicators of Household Consumer Expenditure in India, 2009-10.
2) Statistical Appendix, Economic Survey 2012-13.

Details of the pattern of the relationship between expenditure (recurring) and income of the sample households are given in the Table 4.16 and Figures 4.5 & 4.6.

Table 4.16 Percentage Distribution of Annual Per Capita (Recurring) Expenditure on Food and Non-Food Items

Per Capita Income Groups	OSHG		NSHG		All	
	Food	Non food	Food	Non food	Food	Non food
Below 10000	58.69	41.31	39.91	60.09	47.28	52.72
10001 - 15000	46.68	53.32	46.04	53.96	46.32	53.68
15001 - 20000	43.76	56.24	45.92	54.08	44.85	55.15
20001 - 25000	43.76	56.24	45.81	54.19	44.69	55.31
Above 25000	42.89	57.11	46.69	53.31	44.48	55.52
All	44.27	55.73	45.61	54.39	44.93	55.07

Source: Filed Survey
Note: Figures are in per centages

Figure 4.5 Percentage of Expenditure on Food items among OSHG & NSHG Households

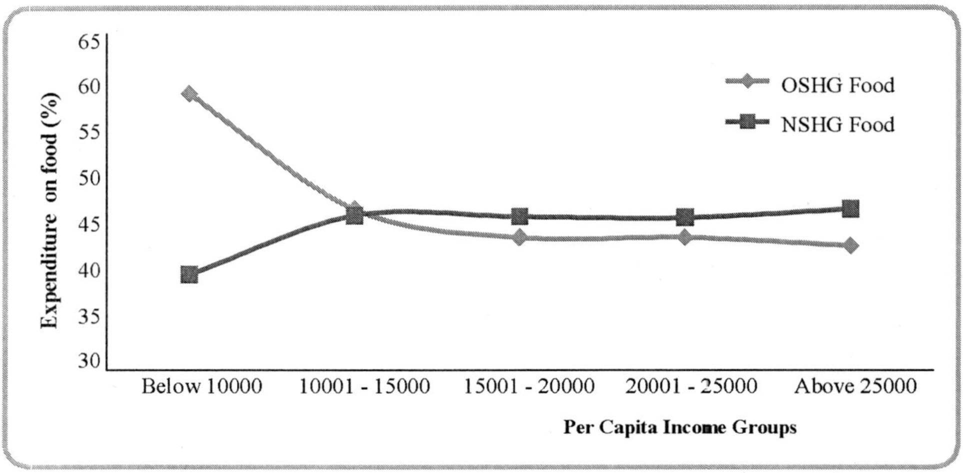

Figure 4.6 Percentage of Expenditure on Non-Food items among OSHG & NSHG Households

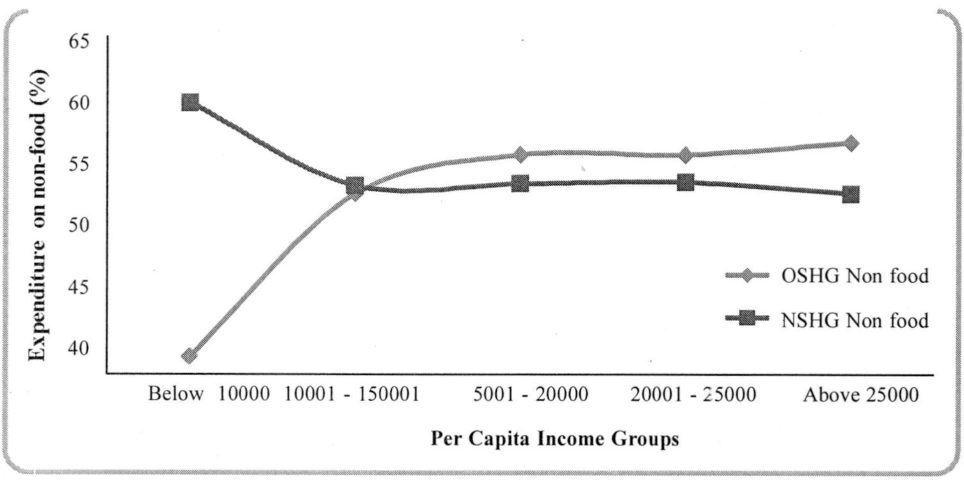

All the sample households, category wise, are classified into different income groups and the average per capita expenditure on food and non-food items is estimated. There is a decline in the share of food expenditure as income size increases indicating an inverse relationship between the per capita income and the share of food expenditure. This phenomenon is similar in the OSHG households. This may be due to the fact that OSHG households are having access to formal institutions since several years.

SECTION – IV
INCIDENCE AND DIMENSIONS OF POVERTY

4.5.1 Incidence and Dimensions of Poverty

Poverty reduction has been one of the major objectives of India's planned development. In spite of massive financial assistance of credit and subsidy provided by the government in implementing various poverty alleviation programmes, the achievement made in terms of households crossing the poverty levels has not been up to the expectations. The main reason for this is due to lack of effective participation and involvement of the poor in the progrmmes meant for their own development. Considering the importance of grass root level organizations in promoting socio-economic development of the poor, the recent efforts have been to provide a conductive atmosphere among the poor to develop their own organizations. Although several types of people's organizations are formed, the most prominent among them are the SHGs (Kumaran, 2001). Micro level studies such as the role of the SHGs in reducing poverty are limited in number. Therefore, an attempt is made in this section, to examine and analyze: (a) The concept and measurement of poverty; (b) Review of major studies on poverty (c) The methodology adopted in the study regarding poverty line. The above aspects are analyzed and presented in this section.

Concept and Measurement of Poverty

The concept of poverty has been defined mainly as a concept of nutritional deficiency and lack of minimum subsistence. At the conceptual level, a distinction is frequently drawn between the "absolute" and "relative" poverty. A household is considered poor, in the absolute sense when it is unable to provide itself with the minimum subsistence, which is the nutritional standard. Relative poverty is defined as deprivation of income and wealth of a household in relation to that of community. On this basis, a household is said to be poor when its income falls short of a certain proportion of the average income of the community. The concept of "relative poverty" has limited applicability to low income countries like India since the problem here is low level of subsistence. If this concept is used for estimating the levels of poverty, many households whose income does not provide minimum subsistence are likely to be considered as non-poor. Therefore, the concept of "absolute poverty" is more relevant to the measurement of poverty for low-income countries like India.

To distinguish the poor from non-poor, a particular level of income/expenditure that satisfies the minimum level of living is considered in determining the poverty line. While fixing the poverty line, different methods have been employed by various poverty studies. Some of the important methods ate noted below. According to the first method, poverty line is fixed by taking the norm fixed by several working groups set up by the Planning Commission in 1962 and adjusting it for temporal and spatial price variations. According to the second method, the poverty line estimates the expenditure-calories intake relationship and decides expenditure required to meet the requirement of given calories. Poverty line is based on the optimum food basket arrived at by minimizing the food cost, subject to the fulfillment of the nutritional norm, according to the third method.

Therefore, on the basis of the minimum nutritional requirements of some conventionally determined consumption basket, which constitutes the minimum level of living, a particular level of consumption expenditure is, considered as poverty line i.e., people whose consumption expenditure falls below such a norm are considered "poor".

4.5.2 Studies Relating to Poverty in India:

A number of studies have been conducted to measure the extent of poverty in India. It is important to study some of the estimates as suggested by famous economists.

Dandekar and Rath (1971) in their study estimated the cost of minimum living at 1960-61 prices to be Rs. 180/- per capita per annum for rural households, and Rs. 270/- per capita per annum for urban households. When they applied this criterion, they found that 40 per cent of the rural population and about 50 per cent of the urban population fell below the poverty line in 1960-61. In his study, (Minhas, 1991) used two norms, Rs. 240/- and Rs. 200/- per capita consumer expenditure per annum at 1960-61 prices as poverty line and estimated the proportion of the poor in the rural areas. On the basis of Rs. 240/- norm, he arrived at the conclusion that the number of people below the poverty line has changed much but the proportion below the poverty line declined from 65.00 to 50.60 per cent during the period, from 1956-57 to 1967-68. When the second norm (Rs. 200/-) was considered, not only the proportion below the poverty line fell from 52.40 in 1965-67 to 37.10 per cent in 1967-68, but the number of people below the poverty line also declined from 173 million to 154 millions. This decline was attributed to the growth of average per capita income at an annual rate of 1.25 per cent over this period rather than to the fall in the concentration ratio.

Contesting Minhas, Bardhan (1974) showed a sharp rise in the incidence of poverty from 38 per cent in 1960-61 to 54 per cent in 1968-69. He used expenditure norm of Rs. 15/- per cent per month at 1960-61 prices as the poverty line for the rural India and showed that this amount satisfied the cost of the minimum diet. In the absence of consumer price index numbers, he adopted the series pertaining to agricultural labourers on the basis of the NSS rural retail prices and the weighting diagrams provided by the Second Agricultural Labour Enquiry. The use of price index number of agricultural labourers might have been responsible for this high incidence of poverty in 1968-69. However, this is more appropriate than the use of national income deflator implicitly used by Mukherji, Bhattacharya and Chatterji in 1972.

Ahluwalia (1978) provided state-wise rural poverty estimates for 14 years, from 1956-57 to 1973-74. The poverty line used was the consumer expenditure level of

Rs. 15/- at all India 1960-61 prices. (Ahluwalia 1978) applied the consumer price index for agricultural labour to the poverty line at current prices for each of the years for which the NSS Consumer Expenditure distributors are available. Using the above procedure, rural poverty lines were obtained for 14 years and the percentage of rural population below poverty line for the respective years was calculated. It can be inferred from Ahluwalia's estimates that the trend in the incidence of poverty fluctuated overtime. Rural poverty in India declined initially from 53.4 per cent in 1957-58 to 42.0 per cent in 1960-61. However, it started rising from 42.3 per cent to 57.9 per cent during 1961-62 to 1967-68 and then declined to 47.6 per cent in 1973-74. Therefore, he opined that in general, the time series have shown a pattern of fluctuation with the incidence of poverty falling in periods of good agricultural performance and rising in the periods of poor performance.

Mahendra Dev (1988) estimated the poverty line for the reference years by making use of the estimates derived by Bardhan in 1974 for the year 1960-61. He adjusted the poverty lines by the consumer price index for agricultural labourer for the reference years. He found that the percentage of rural Indian population living below the poverty line was continuously declining from 46.4 percentage in 1964-65 to 44.78 per cent in 1972-73 and from 40.45 per cent in 1977-78 to 33.20 per cent in 1983. Kakwani and Subha Rao (1992) attempted a study on rural poverty for the period 1973-86. They used relative price levels in the middle group of the rural population. Using these price relatives and consumer price indices for agricultural labourers available, they worked out the state specific poverty lines at the current prices for the years 1973-74, 1977-78, 1983 and 1986-87. According to their estimates, the incidence of rural poverty in India showed a continuous decline over the period. In 1973-74 as much as 60.5 per cent of the rural population was living below the poverty line, which declined to 56.2 per cent in 1977-78 and to 47.7 per cent in 1983 and registered a further decline to 41.5 per cent by 1986-87.

Minhas, Jain and Tendulkar (1991) measured the incidence of poverty by using exact procedure for the three years: 1970-71, 1983 and 1987-88. They converted the poverty norms to prices prevailing in the year for which the NSS consumer expenditure data are available. They worked out state specific cost of living indices. Then, applying these indices, they calculated state specific poverty norms for 1970-71, 1983 and 1987- 88. The poverty norms for rural India were Rs. 33.01, Rs. 93.16 and Rs. 122.63 respectively for the years considered. Corresponding to these poverty lines, the percentage of population below the poverty lines was 57.33 in 1970-71, 49.02 in 1983 and 44.88 in 1987-88. The estimates indicated that the incidence of rural poverty during 17 years period declined by 12.55 percentage points.

Rohini Nayyar (1991) measured the poverty lines for 13 years from 1960-61 to 1983-84 and estimated the incidence of rural poverty. Her conclusions of poverty lines are based on actual consumption data by broad categories. She made use of the calorie norm of 2200 to arrive at the poverty lines. According to her estimates, the incidence of rural poverty in India fluctuated between 51.69 per cent and 30.23 per cent. The rural poverty declined from 40.65 per cent in 1960-61 to 33.98 per cent in 1961-62. However, it moved upwards from 33.98 per cent in 1961-62 to 51.59 per cent in 1966-67. Then, it started declining continuously from 51.59 per cent in 1966-67 to a low of 30.23 per cent in 1983-84.

Gaurav Datt and Martin Ravallion (1989) have developed the concept of poverty gap along with the poverty line. The authors have used Rs. 89/- as the poverty line. Since all NSS data on consumption expenditure are in current local prices, the study has used rural inter-state prices relative (ratio of rural price in a state to all-India prices) for 1973-74 constructed by Bhattacharya updated to 1983 using Consumer Price Index for agricultural labourers as the rural price deflator. According to this Study, 45 per cent of the rural population was below the poverty line in 1983.

Gupta (1995) has studied the changes in poverty ratios during the post-liberalization phase (after 1991) based on the NSS data (49th Round). According to his study, the poverty ratios in the rural fell down from 57 per cent in 1970-71 to 35 per cent in 1990-91 but moved up to 41.7 per cent in 1992. From 1988-89, these findings are based on NSS thin samples. Therefore, one should carefully compare these estimates with earlier ones, which were based on full sample. However, even when we compare all the estimates available since 1988-89, we observe the same declining trend with an upward turning in 1992. Gaurav Datt (1996) of the World Bank has made a study of poverty in India for the period 1951-1992 using NSS data. The poverty line is based on a nutritional norm per capita daily intake of 2400 calories in rural area. This implies a per capita monthly expenditure of Rs. 49/- as the rural poverty line at 1973-74 prices. Using all India consumer price index for agricultural labourers for the survey period, the study revealed that between 1951-52 and 1991-92, the national head count index of rural poverty declined from about 55 per cent to 39 per cent.

Ravallion and Datt (1996) using time series of consistent consumption for 40 years (1950-90) and on the basis of poverty measures made an attempt to assess the extent to which India's poor shared the country's economic growth. Three poverty measures used by the authors for this study are: the headcount index; the poverty gap index; and the squared poverty; urban growth benefitted only urban poor; and growth in the primary and tertiary sectors reduced poverty both in rural and urban areas; and finally it is concluded that secondary sector growth did not reduce poverty in either of the rural or urban areas.

Malik (2000) using data based on NSSO from 1952 onwards showed that there was no long-term trend in poverty reduction from 1952-1973. But, thereafter up to 1986-87, a sharp decline in poverty has been observed. The decline however at a lower rate has been reported to continue till 1989-90. The study also showed that there took place a sharp increase in poverty in 1992 which declined after 1993-94. Trends in rural poverty have been found to observe a close proximity with trends in agricultural wages. The author pointed out the fact that the period of decline in poverty is one when rural poverty declines faster than urban poverty. He found that the initial impact of economic reforms undertaken by the government in 1990s was adverse. But subsequently a reversal of adverse trend has been observed.

Sundaram (2001) examined the incidence of poverty on the basis of the monthly per capita consumption expenditure. The author developed empirical relationship between employment and poverty in 1990s. He compared data for 1993-94 with that of 1999-2000. He computed the proportion of population below poverty line by gender, age and rural/urban location. The study estimated 7.5 per cent decline in incidence of poverty among agricultural labour households, 6 per cent fall among other labour households, and 2.3 per cent fall among self-employees. Overall, the study emphasized that the results based on NSSO data 55th round confirmed the direction of change i.e. decline in poverty over 1990s. The same conclusion was found valid for major states. The study found that, rural poverty and urban poverty declined in eight out of the fifteen major states.

Rajan (2002) studied the impact of international trade on 100 developed and developing countries during 1960-90. The author provided the empirical evidence that the countries that managed to reduce poverty were those that have adopted trade liberalization policies. Trade leads to rapid growth and it reduced poverty at the same time. But only growth cannot be taken as a sufficient condition for poverty reduction, so the author further suggested the need of social safety nets to protect the poor from the bad impacts of liberalization. He emphasized that trade liberalization should be backed by sound macro policies, strong institutions and good investment environment.

Mishra and Rao (2003) made an attempt to show that trade liberalization accelerates growth and thereby reduces poverty. The study, is based on cross country regression analysis from 1978-79 to 1999-2000 period. They discussed macro-economic policies such as growth performance, investment, agricultural export and recent policy developments in their paper. The authors on the basis of their study prepared analytical framework and model estimation. They examined relationship through auto regressive integrated moving average method (ARIMA), in which the dependent variables are explained by their own past i.e. lagged trends. The study shows that the lower tariff during the process of economic reforms in 1991 reduced the relative prices of manufacturing. It influenced the terms of trade in favour of agriculture and lifted private investment in agriculture. These have facilitated in increasing the aggregate crop output over the period. The increase in agricultural output has reduced rural poverty.

Sundaram and Tendulkar (2003) found that poverty declined during 1994-2000. They examined rural and urban poverty separately for 15 states. For comparison they resolved the problem of comparability of monthly per capita expenditure in 50th round (1993-94) based on URP (uniform reference period) and 55th round (1999-2000) based on MRP (mixed reference period) by re-computing the data of 50th round on the basis of MRP (mixed reference period). While measuring changes in poverty over 1990s at the state-level, the authors calculated the headcount ratio (HCR), i.e. size of the poor population; the poverty gap index (PGI) i.e. the depth of poverty; and squared poverty gap (FGT) i.e. the severity of poverty. The study found that poverty increased over the six years from 1993-94 to 1999-2000 in Assam, Madhya Pradesh and Orissa. Assam recorded rise in poverty in terms of HCR, PGI and FGT. Madhya Pradesh showed a rise in HCR, and a decline in PGI and FGT. Orissa registered a decline in HCR, and rise in PGI and FGT. In the remaining 12 states, a decline in poverty ratio has been observed.

The weighted average of PGI on MRP (mixed reference period) of 15 states declined from 0.0933 to 0.00653 and FGT declined from 0.0308 to 0.0202. The crux is that despite diversity across the states, poverty declined in 1990s.

Sundaram and Tendulakar (2004) examined the change in magnitude of poor in India labour force between 1993-94 and 1999-2000. The authors estimated size of poor in labour force in four segments: rural males, rural females, urban males and urban females. They presented the gender, activity status, and rural urban composition of these groups based on employment and unemployment for the 50th and 55th rounds of NSSO. The study found that poverty prevalence is more among rural and urban women workers than those for men. The aggregate magnitude of working poor was estimated to be 93.9 million in rural India and 20.9 million in urban India in 1994. Total number of working poor was 114.8 million, which was 30 per cent of the working force. As per the estimates, from a level of 115 million, the number of working poor declined by a little over 12 million, almost entirely in rural area. The overall picture that emerged from the study is that there is a correlation between reduction in poverty and education. Education endowment increases the productivity of workforce and reduces poverty. Thus, the overall picture presented is that poverty declined in 1990s.

Mehta and Bhandari (2005) explored trends in poverty in Asian developing countries. The authors examined trends in poverty in Asian countries using international poverty line at less than $1 and $1.08 per day (a standardized global poverty line at 1993 purchasing power parity) and using national poverty line. The whole frame work shows that poverty incidence has remained same between 1987 and 1993. After 1993, incidence of poverty appears to have declined rapidly again (World Bank, 1997). The authors pointed out that there are two causes of the low rate of poverty reduction in South Asia: first, low economic growth in the poorest countries; and secondly, persistent inequalities (in income and non-income dimensions) that prevented the participation of poor in growth. They concluded that pro-poor, sustainable economic growth, social development, good governance and micro finance can reduce poverty. Micro finance provides financial services to low income clients, like landless marginal farmers or poor urban dwellers etc. Micro financing has potential to increase the physical capital of poor and it builds human and social capital.

Himanshu (2007) found that poverty did decline during 1993-2005, but the annual rate of reduction during this period had been lower than that of in 1970s and 1980s. The author confirms the earlier findings that the 1990s has indeed been the lost decade for poverty reduction. In this study, a little reduction in poverty has been observed in 1993-2000; the bulk of decline having occurred in 1999-2005. Poverty declined faster during 1999-2005 but the annual rate of decline was lower than that of in the previous decade of 1983-1994. The picture emerging from the poverty reduction during 1999-2005 shows that poverty reduction at national level was due to poverty reduction in the states with above national average poverty till 1999. Further, his research paper shows evidence of improvements in non-income indicators during 1993-2005.

Thakur (2010) examined the impact of growth on poverty and income distribution. It found that, at all India level, headcount ratio was 53.07 per cent in 1977-78 and declined the 39 per cent in 1991. Inverse relation between growth and poverty has been observed in this study. Quoting the IGIDR (Indira Gandhi institute of Development and Research) estimates, the author noticed that the Gini co-efficient was 27.71 per cent in rural areas in 1991. During 1997-98, it increased to 30.11 per cent in rural areas. Thus, with development, magnitude of inequality has widened during post reform period, as per the study of the IGIDR, the World Bank (1955), the Planning Commission (1977) and the Tendulkar estimates.

Some empirical studies in India have observed reduction in poverty during the post reform period. Poverty reduction is observed to be associated with economic growth. However, rate of reduction and factors affecting poverty differ from study to study.

The estimates of state-wise poverty lines for rural and urban areas for 2011-12 are given in Table 4.17. The percentage and number of persons below poverty line for all

States/UTs for rural areas, urban areas and combined are given in Table 4.18. The all India poverty ratio is obtained as state-population weighted average poverty ratio, and the all India poverty line is the per capita per month expenditure that corresponds to the all India poverty ratio.

The NSSO tabulates expenditure of about 1.20 lakh households. Since these households have different number of members, the NSSO for the purpose of comparison divides the household expenditure by the number of members to arrive at per capita consumption expenditure per month. This is called Monthly Per Capita Consumption Expenditure (MPCE) and is computed on the basis of three different concepts: Uniform Reference Period (URP), Mixed Reference Period (MRP), and Modified Mixed Reference Period (MMRP). As per Tendulkar Methodology, the poverty line has been expressed in terms of MPCE based on Mixed Reference Period. State-wise estimates of Average Monthly Per Capita Expenditure for rural and urban areas separately for the year 2011-12 are given in Table 4.19.

For 2011-12, for rural areas the national poverty line using the Tendulkar methodology is estimated at Rs. 816 per capita per month and Rs. 1,000 per capita per month in urban areas. Thus, for a family of five, the all India poverty line in terms of consumption expenditure would amount to about Rs. 4,080 per month in rural areas and Rs. 5,000 per month in urban areas. These poverty lines would vary from State to State because of inter-state price differentials.

The national level poverty ratio based on comparable methodology (Tendulkar Method) for 1993-94, 2004-05 and 2011-12 estimated from Large Sample Survey of Household Consumer Expenditure data of 50th, 61st and 68th round respectively are given in Table 4.20.

Table 4.17 Percentage and Number of Poor Estimated by Tendulkar method, using Mixed Reference Period (MRP)

	Poverty Ratio (%)			Number of Poor (million)		
	Rural	Urban	Total	Rural	Urban	Total
1. 1993-94	50.1	31.8	45.3	328.6	74.5	403.7
2. 2004-05	41.8	25.7	37.2	326.3	80.8	407.1
3. 2011-12	25.7	13.7	21.9	216.5	52.8	269.3
Annual Average Decline: 1993-94 to 2004-05 (percentage points per annum)	0.75	0.55	0.74	-	-	-
Annual Average Decline: 2004-05 to 2011-12 (percentage points per annum)	2.32	1.69	2.18	-	-	-

Source: Government of India, Planning Commission July 2013, Press Note on Poverty Estimates, 2011-12.

The percentage of persons below the Poverty Line in 2011-12 has been estimated as 25.7 per cent in rural areas, 13.7 per cent in urban areas and 21.9% for the country as a whole. During the 11-year period 1993-94 to 2004-05, the average decline in the poverty ratio was 0.74 percentage points per year. It accelerated to 2.18 percentage points per year during the 7-year period 2004-05 to 2011-12. Therefore, it can be concluded that the rate of decline in the poverty ratio during the most recent 7-year period 2004-05 to 2011-12 was about three times of that experienced in the 11-year period 1993-94 to 2004-05.

Since several representations were made suggesting that the Tendulkar Poverty Line was too low, the Planning Commission, in June 2012, constituted an Expert Group under the Chairmanship of Dr. C. Rangarajan to once again review the methodology for the measurement of poverty. The Rangarajan Committee is deliberating on this issue and is expected to submit its report by the middle of 2014. Since the data from the NSS 68th round (2011-12) of Household Consumer Expenditure Survey is now available, and the Rangarajan Committee recommendation will only be available a year later, the Planning Commission has updated the poverty estimates for the year 2011-12 as per the methodology recommended by Tendulkar Committee.

Table 4.18 State specific Poverty Lines for 2011-12

S.No.	States	Monthly per capita (Rs.)	
		Rural	Urban
1	Andhra Pradesh	860	1,009
2	Arunachal Pradesh	930	1,060
3	Assam	828	1,008
4	Bihar	778	923
5	Chhattisgarh	738	849
6	Delhi	1,145	1,134
7	Goa	1,090	1,134
8	Gujarat	932	1,152
9	Haryana	1,015	1,169
10	Himachal Pradesh	913	1,064
11	Jammu & Kashmir	891	988
12	Jharkhand	748	974
13	Karnataka	902	1,089
14	Kerala	1,018	987
15	Madhya Pradesh	771	897
16	Maharashtra	967	1,126
17	Manipur	1,118	1,170
18	Meghalaya	888	1,154
19	Mizoram	1,066	1,155
20	Nagaland	1,270	1,302
21	Odisha	695	861
22	Punjab	1,054	1,155
23	Rajasthan	905	1,002
24	Sikkim	930	1,226
25	Tamil Nadu	880	937
26	Tripura	798	920
27	Uttarakhand	880	1,082
28	Uttar Pradesh	768	941
29	West Bengal	783	981
30	Puducherry	1,301	1,309
	All India	816	1,000

Note: computed as per Tendulkar method on Mixed Reference Period (MRP)

Source: Government of India, Planning Commission July 2013, Press Note on Poverty Estimates, 2011-12.

Table 4.19 : Number and Percentage of Population below poverty line by states 2011-12 (Tendulkar Methodology)

S.No	States	Rural		Urban		Total	
		% age of Persons	No. of persons (lakhs)	% age of Persons	No. of persons (lakhs)	% age of Persons	No. of persons (lakhs)
1	Andhra Pradesh	10.96	61.80	5.81	16.98	9.20	78.78
2	Arunachal Pradesh	38.93	4.25	20.33	0.66	34.67	4.91
3	Assam	33.89	92.06	20.49	9.21	31.98	101.27
4	Bihar	34.06	320.40	31.23	37.75	33.74	358.15
5	Chhattisgarh	44.61	88.90	24.75	15.22	39.93	104.11
6	Delhi	12.92	0.50	9.84	16.46	9.91	16.96
7	Goa	6.81	0.37	4.09	0.38	5.09	0.75
8	Gujarat	21.54	75.35	10.14	26.88	16.63	102.23
9	Haryana	11.64	19.42	10.28	9.41	11.16	28.83
10	Himachal Pradesh	8.48	5.29	4.33	0.30	8.06	5.59
11	Jammu & Kashmir	11.54	10.73	7.20	2.53	10.35	13.27
12	Jharkhand	40.84	104.09	24.83	20.24	36.96	124.33
13	Karnataka	24.53	92.80	15.25	36.96	20.91	129.76
14	Kerala	9.14	15.48	4.97	8.46	7.05	23.95
15	Madhya Pradesh	35.74	190.95	21.00	43.10	31.65	234.06
16	Maharashtra	24.22	150.56	9.12	47.36	17.35	197.92
17	Manipur	38.80	7.45	32.59	2.78	36.89	10.22
18	Meghalaya	12.53	3.04	9.26	0.57	11.87	3.61
19	Mizoram	35.43	1.91	6.36	0.37	20.40	2.27
20	Nagaland	19.93	2.76	16.48	1.00	18.88	3.76
21	Odisha	35.69	126.14	17.29	12.39	32.59	138.53
22	Punjab	7.66	13.35	9.24	9.82	8.26	23.18
23	Rajasthan	16.05	84.16	10.69	18.73	14.71	102.92
24	Sikkim	9.85	0.45	3.66	0.06	8.19	0.51
25	Tamil Nadu	15.83	59.23	6.54	23.40	11.28	82.63
26	Tripura	16.53	4.49	7.42	0.75	14.05	5.24
27	Uttarakhand	11.62	8.25	10.48	3.35	11.26	11.60
28	Uttar Pradesh	30.40	479.35	26.06	118.84	29.43	598.19
29	West Bengal	22.52	141.14	14.66	43.83	19.98	184.98
30	Puducherry	17.06	0.69	6.30	0.55	9.69	1.24
31	Andaman & Nicoba	1.57	0.04	0.00	0.00	1.00	0.04
32	Chandigarh	1.64	0.004	22.31	2.34	21.81	2.35
33	Dadra & Nagar	62.59	1.15	15.38	0.28	39.31	1.43
34	Daman & Diu	0.00	0.00	12.62	0.26	9.86	0.26
35	Lakshadweep	0.00	0.00	3.44	0.02	2.77	0.02
	All India	**25.70**	**2166.58**	**13.70**	**531.25**	**21.92**	**2697.83**

Notes: 1. Population as on 1st March 2012 has been used for estimating number of persons below poverty line. (2011 Censes population extrapolated)

2. Poverty Line of Tamil Nadu has been used for Andaman and Nicobar Island

3. Urban Poverty Line of Punjab has been used for both rural and urban areas of Chandigarh.

4. Poverty Line of Maharashtra has been used for Dadra & Nagar Haveli.

5. Poverty Line of Goa has been used for Daman & Diu.

6. Poverty Line of Kerala has been used for Lakshadweep

Table 4.20 State-wise estimates of Average Monthly Per Capita Expenditure (MPCE) as per Mixed Reference Period (MRP) for 2011-12

S.No	States/UTs	Rural	Urban
1	Andhra Pradesh	1563.21	2559.30
2	Arunachal Pradesh	1455.87	2241.63
3	Assam	1056.98	2090.18
4	Bihar	970.41	1396.65
5	Chhattisgarh	904.04	1776.21
6	Delhi	2690.24	3160.76
7	Goa	2460.77	2934.87
8	Gujarat	1430.12	2472.49
9	Haryana	1925.96	3346.32
10	Himachal Pradesh	1800.62	3173.30
11	Jammu & Kashmir	1601.51	2320.28
12	Jharkhand	919.59	1894.41
13	Karnataka	1395.10	2898.94
14	Kerala	2355.53	3044.22
15	Madhya Pradesh	1024.14	1842.35
16	Maharashtra	1445.89	2937.06
17	Manipur	1334.55	1448.91
18	Meghalaya	1315.11	2293.82
19	Mizoram	1384.44	2426.53
20	Nagaland	1756.70	2279.42
21	Odisha	904.78	1830.33
22	Punjab	2136.39	2743.07
23	Rajasthan	1445.74	2206.93
24	Sikkim	1445.06	2528.11
25	Tamil Nadu	1570.61	2534.32
26	Tripura	1194.14	1996.66
27	Uttarakhand	1551.42	2452.02
28	Uttar Pradesh	1072.93	1942.25
29	West Bengal	1170.11	2489.89
30	Andaman & Nicoba Islands	2508.19	4439.03
31	Chandigarh	2543.57	3000.27
32	Dadra & Nagar Haveli	1094.20	2346.15
33	Daman & Diu	2239.45	2163.94
34	Lakshadweep	2533.07	2666.49
35	Pondicherry	2309.92	2959.82
	ALL INDIA	1287.17	2477.02

Source: NSSO Report No. KI. (68/1.0) on Key Indicators of Household Consumer Expenditure in india 2011-12, NSS 68th round, National Sample Survey Office

It is very clear from the preceding review that there are wide differences in the methodology used for fixing the norm to identify the poverty line. Nevertheless, all these studies showed that the incidence of poverty is on a decline in India. The above estimates are given by way of illustration. Majority of the studies referred to above are macro-level studies using aggregate data and the results indicate only a broad picture of economic phenomenon of poverty. The present study focuses, as mentioned earlier at the micro level. The fixing of poverty line and income/expenditure, depend on the ultimate objective of the study. Firstly, some of the studies on poverty mainly wanted to work out the minimum level of living to determine the poverty line in terms of a particular level of consumption expenditure as poverty threshold. Secondly, some studies have adopted the poverty line estimated already and adjusted it to price variations. In case, one's objective is restricted to having an estimate of number of households living below the poverty line, the exercise of the second one mentioned above may serve the purpose. In this Study, the second method is adopted. The methodology used in this Study is discussed below.

4.5.3 Methodology and Poverty Measures

A number of researchers and organizations have used many alternative ways of measuring poverty. Many of these studies have considered the income dimension of poverty. These are also differences among researchers as to how to adjust a given poverty line to the changes in relative prices over different periods and across different regions.

In this study, to know the level of living of the poorest of the poor households, the estimates of poverty are computed. These estimates are based on the primary household expenditure data, which are collected by the Researcher. In other words, using per capita household consumer expenditure as a measure of standard of living the poverty analysis is carried out. (Accordingly, by using weighted average of family size, per capita monthly total expenditure of each household, is computed). Therefore, for identifying the poor, one looks at the level of personal expenditure that enables the individual to satisfy a certain minimum consumption level. Proportion of population not able to attain the specified level of expenditure is segregated as poor. Defining this level of expenditure, the poverty line is the first step in estimating poverty. However, in this Study, instead of estimating poverty line for the purpose of our Study, we updated the poverty line, which is adopted by the Expert Group of the Planning Commission.

The Expert Group of Planning Commission has estimated the poverty line for each state for the year 1973-74 and in the subsequent years. Since the present Study area is located in Andhra Pradesh, the poverty line estimated by Expert Group for this state for the year 2011-12 is taken and adjusted to the reference year 2012-13 i.e., Rs. 860 per capita monthly total expenditure in rural Andhra Pradesh corresponded to an intake of 2400 Kael and it served as the cut-off line for dividing the poor from the non-poor.

The above given poverty line is adjusted to the reference year with the help of Consumer Price Index for Rural Labourers (CPIRL). Accordingly, to calculate the poverty line (Z-value for the year 2012-13) we adopted the following procedures as indicated below.

$$\text{Z-value (2012-13)} = \text{Coefficient of inflation} \times \text{Z-value (Rs. 860) (2011-12)}$$

First of all the coefficient of inflation is obtained by dividing the consumer price index for rural labourers for the year 2012-13 by the consumer price index for agricultural rural labourers for the year 2011-12. This is done only after different base years are converted into the same base. Coefficient of inflation can be written as:

$$\text{Coefficient of Inflation} = \frac{\text{CPIRL(2012-13)}}{\text{CPIRL(2011-12)}}$$

$$\text{Coefficient of Inflation} = \frac{777^{**}}{665^{*}} = 1.16$$

Source: *Annual Report 2011-12, Consumer Price Index Numbers for Agricultural and Rural Labourers, Government of India. BASE: 1986-87=100, Table no: 2.02.

** All-India Consumer Price Index Numbers for Agricultural and Rural Labourers on Base 1986-87=100, November, 2013, HYPERLINK http://labourbureau.nic.in/ http://labourbureau.nic.in/.

Finally, to obtain the poverty line (z-value for the year 2012-13), the computed coefficient of inflation is multiplied by the poverty line (z-value for the year 2011-12). Accordingly, Rs. 997.6 per capita monthly total expenditure is estimated for the rural areas. This poverty line is adopted in all the poverty measures of study.

Poverty Measures

To measure the three different aspects of poverty i.e., incidence, shortfall and severity of poverty among the sample households in the study area, we have used all the three poverty measures. These measures are Head Count Ratio, Poverty Gap Ratio and Modified Sen's Index of Poverty. Each of these measures is separately discussed below:

Head Count Ratio (HCR)

Head Count Ratio at the individual level is calculated by comparing household per capita monthly expenditure with updated poverty line for rural areas. It can be written as:

$$HCR = \frac{q}{n}$$

Where

"q" is the number of poor,

"n" is the total population.

This measure ignores how poor the poor are and, therefore, remains unchanged when poor become poorer or move upward on the income ladder.

Poverty Gap Ratio (PGR):

The total income needed to bring all the poor up to the poverty line is given by an average poverty gap (GAP) as:

Where

$$GAP = (z\text{-}m) \times q$$

"m" is mean per capita monthly expenditure of the poor,

"z" is the poverty line expressed in the monetary terms.

From the above expression, we have derived the second measure known as the Poverty Gap Ratio Index as derived by Sen (1976). If the degree of misery suffered by an individual is proportional to the expenditure shortfall of that individual from the poverty line, then the sum total of these shortfalls may be considered as an adequate measure of poverty. Such a measure is called poverty gap ratio index (PGR) and can be written as:

$$PGR = \frac{(z\text{-}m)}{Z} HCR$$

The measure PGR will provide adequate information about the intensity of poverty if and only if all the poor households are assumed to have exactly the same expenditure, which is less than the poverty line. In practice, the expenditure of the poor is unequally distributed and, therefore, PGR cannot be an adequate measure of poverty. It is an improvement on Head Count Ratio, nonetheless. Besides, it has an interpretation which makes it extremely attractive from a policy point of view. It indicates the poverty gap as a fraction of total expenditure needed to support every one in the population at the poverty line. Thus, the transfer of resources required to eradicate poverty completely could be assessed with this index. Although, perfect targeting of resources is not possible, this index provides at least a lower limit on the amount of transfers.

Sen Index (Sp)

Amartya Sen (1976, 1981) applied following measure for poverty index. In this way HCR measures incidence (proportion of poor), PGR measures intensity (depth of poverty or how poor the poor are?) and GP measures severity (income concentration inequality). GP is Gini coefficient of income distribution among poor (Bhowmik, 2007). Sen Index combines the three ratios:

a) Headcount ratio (HCR)

b) Income poverty gap ratio (PGR)

c) Gini coefficient (GP) (measurement of income inequality developed by Prof. Gini in1912)

$$SP = HCR[PGR+(1-PGR)G_p]$$

Modified Sen's Index of Poverty (P):

The Sen-Shorrocks-Thon (SST) index is an index of poverty intensity. It is also called the modified Sen Index of poverty intensity. This index is proposed by Shorrocks (1995) as an extension of the Sen (1976) index. The SST index measures poverty incidence, depth, and inequality jointly and hence is a comprehensive poverty measure. In addition, this index can be decomposed into its constituting parts transparently.

Xu and Osberg (2002) also show that based on the Sen index and two of its constituting components (poverty rate and average poverty gap), one can always compute the SST index from the Sen index as follows:

SST index = (poverty rate) × (Sen index) + 2 × (poverty rate) × (1 –poverty rate) × (average poverty gap)

As the poverty gap ratio's is insensitive to the redistribution of income among the poor is corrected by modified Sen's index (P) that assigns a specific rank order to individuals according to the extent of poverty.

Empirical Results: Head Count Ratio

For the OSHG as whole, about 43 per cent of total households are found to be below the poverty line, while this picture is accounted for by 40 per cent in case of the NSHG. Based on the above facts, it can be concluded that the incidence of poverty among OSHG and NSHG households is high (Table 4.21).

The Poverty Gap Ratio

From Table 4.21 the estimates of Sen's poverty gap ratio clearly indicate the poverty, as a fraction of total expenditure needed to support everyone in the population at the poverty line. Thus, the larger the estimate, the larger is the requirement of resources to guarantee the entire population an expenditure equivalent to the poverty line. Moreover, its smaller estimated value denotes lesser resources requirement to do needful. The empirical results, when analyzed, helped us in deriving the following inferences. The results of this poverty measure show that, the poverty gap ratio was found to be higher in the OSHG households.

Sen's Index (Sp)

Sen's Index (Sp) is a composite index that measures simultaneously the incidence and intensity of poverty as well as inequalities in income distribution of below poverty line households. The incidence, intensity and inequality as measured by (Sp) values are in both the OSHG (0.1199) and NSHG (0.1060). This indicates that the incidence and intensity of the poverty is high in OSHG comparably with NSHG.

Modified Sen's Index of Poverty

As said earlier, Sen's modified poverty measure overcomes the limitation of his earlier measure, viz., poverty gap ratio. The latter measure suffers from the limitation of being insensitive redistribution of income among poor. The Modified Sen's Index of Poverty overcomes this drawback by the use of a specific rank order weighing scale. Empirical values of modified measure of poverty lie between zero and unity. It assumes zero value when every one's income is above the poverty line and becomes unity when everyone has zero income. There by we may infer that the lower the value of this measure, the closer is the distribution of the poor to the poverty line and vice versa. The measure of Sen's Index of poverty assumed values in both the OSHG and NSHG groups (for OSHG (0.0853) and for NSHG (0.0669)) (Table 4.21). This indicates that the distribution of the poor is closer to the poverty gap.

Table 4.21 Group-wise Estimates of three poverty measures

Measures	Old SHG	New SHG	Total
Head Count Ratio(HCR)	0.43	0.40	0.42
Poverty Gap Ratio(PGR)	0.069	0.051	0.061
Gini Coefficient	0.2255	0.2256	0.2282
Sen's Index (Sp)	0.1199	0.1060	0.1156
Sen's Modified Index(P)	0.0853	0.0669	0.0783

Source: Field Survey

4.6 Summary

The proportion of persons employed in the UPS and UPSS is higher among the OSHG and NSHG households indicating the positive effect on employment pattern of the micro credit. Apart from the magnitude of employment, the analysis on the occupational pattern of the works showed that, the majority of the workers under the OSHG households are depending on household industry (29.6 per cent) followed by construction labour (29.4 per cent) etc. But in the case of NSHG households majority of the workers are depending on construction labour (27.4 per cent) followed by salaried people (22.8 per cent) etc., this implies that there is an occupational shift towards non- farm or off-farm activities through micro credit.

The distribution of the households according to income range showed that 65 per cent of the OSHG households and 69.5 per cent of the NSHG households are in the income range of below Rs 75,000/- per year indicating that the microfinance has marginal impact on their income levels. The distribution of income by source shows that income from household industry (24.8 per cent) and income from wage (30.2 per cent) are the major sources in OSHG households and income from wage

(30 per cent) and salaried income (25.4 per cent) in NSHG households. It may be observed from the Table that the average per capita income of the OSHG households is relatively higher than that of the NSHG. With the help of multiple regression model, the determinants of income of poor were analysed. The analysis found that size of the household, percentage of workers in the household, wage rates of agricultural and non-agricultural labourers, size of landholding, per capita income from other sources like self-employment, age of the head of the household and age squared of the head of the household are the significant factors.

It could be observed from the Table that the per capita expenditure (recurring and non-recurring) for the OSHG households is greater compared to the NSHG households. This may be due to the fact that the OSHG households are having more access to formal institutions. In order to observe the income-expenditure relationship, the Eagle's law was tested. It was observed that there is a decline in the share of expenditure on food items as the income size increases. This decline is so sharp in the OSHG compared to the NSHG households.

The Planning Commission takes into consideration the monthly per capita expenditure norm to estimate the poverty. Having wide methodological differences in the methodology used for fixing the norm to identify the poverty line, all the estimates showed that the incidence of poverty is on a decline in India. In this study also monthly per capita expenditure as a measure of standard as a measure of standard of living is used for the analysis of poverty. The official poverty line is adjusted to the year 2012-13 by using the consumer price Index for Rural Labourers. Accordingly the estimated poverty line of Ra. 997/- is taken for the rural areas in this Study. The empirical result shows that the incidence of poverty is high in both the households. A lower Poverty Gap Ratio was found in the NSHG households compared to the OSHG. The Sen's Index reveals that the incidence and intensity of the poverty is high in OSHG comparably with NSHG and Modified Sen's Index of Poverty indicated that the distribution of poor is closer to the poverty line in both the households.

References

Ahluwalia, M. S. (1978), "Rural poverty and agricultural performance in India", The Journal of Development Studies, 14(3): 298-323.

Bardhan, P. K. (1974), "On life and death questions", Economic and Political Weekly, 9(32/34):1293-1304.

Bhowmick. (2007), Economics of poverty, New Delhi: Deep and Deep Publications. Chavan, P., & Ramakumar, R. (2002), "Micro-credit and rural poverty: An analysis of empirical evidence", Economic and Political weekly, 37(10): 955-965.

Dandekar, V. M., & Rath, N. (1971), "Poverty in India-I: Dimensions and Trends", Economic and Political Weekly, 6(1): 25-48.

Datt, G., Ravallion, M., & Mundial, B. (1990), Regional disparities targeting, and poverty in India, Agriculture and Rural Development Department, World Bank, W.P.S. 375.p.37.

Dev, S. M. (1988), "Regional disparities in agricultural labour productivity and rural poverty in India", Indian Economic Review, 23(2): 167-205.

Gaurav, D. (1996): "Poverty in India (1951-52): Trends and Decompositions', Mimeo, World Bank.

GOI, (2012), Annual Report 2011-12, Consumer Price Index Numbers for Agricultural and Rural Labourers, Government of India. BASE: 1986-87=100, Table no: 2.02.

GOI, (2013), All-India Consumer Price Index Numbers for Agricultural and Rural

Labourers on Base 1986-87=100, November, 2013, HYPERLINK http://labourbureau.nic.in/ http://labourbureau.nic.in/.

Gupta S.P. (1995), "Recent Economic Reform and its Impact on Poor", Paper presented at the National Conference on poverty and Employment, New Delhi, pp. 8-9, March 27-29.

Gupta, S. P. (1995), "Economic reform and its impact on poor", Economic and Political Weekly, 30(22):1295-1313.

Himanshu (2007), "Recent Trends in Poverty and Inequality: Some Preliminary

Results", Economic and Political Weekly, 42(6): 497-508.

Hossain Mahabub (1988): "Credit for Alleviation of Rural Poverty: the Grameen Bank in Bangladesh", IFPRL Research report 65, International Food Policy Research Institute, Washington D.C.

Kakwani, N., & Subbarao, K. (1990), Rural poverty in India, 1973-86, Population and Human Resources Department, World Bank.

Kumaran, K. P. (2001), "Changing Role of Grass Root Level Organisations in the Context of Participatory Rural Development", Social Action-New Delhi, 51(1): 74-82.

Malik M.S. (2000), "Economic Reforms and Effect on Poverty", Yojana, 44 (7): 10-18. Mehta, R. & Bhandari, S. (2005), "Poverty in Asia: Trends Issues and Polices in Poverty in India", in Nageswar Rao (ed.), Global and Regional Dimensions, Deep and Deep Publications, New Delhi, pp. 50-66.

Minhas, B. S., Jain, L. R., & Tendulkar, S. D. (1991), "Declining incidence of poverty in the 1980s: Evidence versus artefacts", Economic and Political Weekly, 26 (27/28): 1673-1682.

Mishra, V.N. and M. Rao (2003), "Trade Policy, Agricultural Growth and Rural Poor", Economic and Political Weekly, 38 (43): 4588-4603.

Mosley, P. (1996), "Metamorphosis from NGO to Commercial Bank: The Case of BancoSol in Bolivia", in Hulme, D. & Mosley, P. (ed.), Finance against Poverty, Vol. 2, Routledge Publications, London.

Mukherjee, M. N. Bhattacharya and GS Chatterjee, (1972), "Poverty in India: Measurement and Amelioration", Commerce, 125(3198): 19.

Nayyar, R. (1991), Rural poverty in India: an analysis of inter-state differences, Oxford University Press, Mumbai, pp.27-61.

Papola, T.S. & Sahu, P.P. (2012), "Growth and Structure of Employment in India Long- Term and Post-Reform Performance and the Emerging Challenge", Institute for Studies in Industrial Development, ICSSR, New Delhi. Available at HYPERLINK http://isidev.nic.in/pdf/ICSSR_TSP_PPS.pdf http://isidev.nic.in/pdf/ICSSR_TSP_PPS.pdf

Puhazhendhi V. & Satyasai K. J. S. (2000), "Micro Credit for the Rural People: An Impact Evaluation", National Bank for Agriculture and Rural Development, Mumbai. Also see HYPERLINK http://www.nabard.org/mcid/impactstudy.htm http://www.nabard.org/mcid/impactstudy.htm.

Rajan, R.S. (2002), "Trade Liberalisation and Poverty; Revisiting the Age Old Debate", Economic and Political Weekly, 37 (49): 4941-4946.

Ravallion, M., & Datt, G. (1996), "How important to India's poor is the sectoral composition of economic growth?", The World Bank Economic Review, 10(1): 1-25.

Shorrocks, A. F. (1995), "Revisiting the Sen Poverty index", Econometrica: Journal of the Econometric Society, 63(5): 1225-1230.

Sundaram, K. (2001), "Employment and Poverty in 1990s", Economic and Political Weekly, 36 (32): 3039-3049.

Sundaram, K., & Tendulkar, S. D. (2004), "The Poor in India Labour Force", Economic and Political Weekly, 39(48): 5121-32.

Sundaram, K., & Tendulkar, S. D. (2003), "Poverty in India in the 1990s: An analysis of changes in 15 major states", Economic and Political Weekly, 38 (14): 1385-1393.

Thakur, R. (2010), "Poverty-Progeny of Progress", in N.S Iyengar (ed.), Poverty and Sustainable Development, Deep and Deep Publications, New Delhi, pp. 90-112.

Xu, K., & Osberg, L. (2002), "The social welfare implications, decomposability and geometry of the Sen family of poverty indices", Canadian Journal of Economics, 35(1): 138-152.

5

Indebtedness of Rural Households

5.1 Introduction

Generally, the poor need credit for various requirements and raise credit from different sources. In order to enhance their participation in microcredit programmes and to make appropriate changes in the policies, one has to analyze the structure of their borrowings and their participation in different sources of credit. This chapter has been organized into four sections. Section-I deals with Overview of Indebtedness, Borrowing and Repayment. Section-II presents the theory of Asymmetric Information. In Section- III, the structure of borrowings of sample households in relation to purpose of borrowing, source of borrowing, rate of interest and nature of security offered is analyzed. In Section–IV, the repayment performance of loans are examined. A comparative analysis between OSHG and NSHG households is carried out for the above said aspects so as to identify the factors influencing borrowing and repayments.

SECTION – I
OVERVIEW OF INDEBTEDNESS, BORROWINGS AND REPAYMENTS

5.2 Overview of Indebtedness, Borrowings and Repayments

Since independence and mainly after the introduction of Green Revolution the developments in agricultural sector have resulted in changes, which had both beneficial and adverse effects on the conditions of rural households. For instance, developments in bio-chemical technology resulting in a spectacular rise in agricultural output, institutional reforms such as land reforms and policy measures like minimum wage legislation have had a positive impact on the economic welfare of rural poor. On the other side, which may off-set the advantages of bio-technology, namely increasing adoption of labour- displacing machinery in high growth regions and demographic factors like increase in proportions of rural labour in the total work-force, may even-out the marginal benefits that emanated from the spectacular growth in the agricultural sector. The effect of these variables on the conditions of the rural poor has been widely discussed with reference to employment, real wages and other related issues by the academics. It is inferred that though the incomes of this class have been on the increase, the real income is on the decline and they are forced to borrow for both production and consumption.

Indebtedness has long been treated as a distress phenomenon. It is indeed so if the debt taken is not used for productive purposes and instead is used for consumption purpose and ceremonies. Debt can also become a distress phenomenon if the borrower's crop fails due to natural calamities, or if production becomes uneconomic because of high input costs, stagnant technology and lack of remunerative prices which make it impossible for the farmer to repay his capital and interest. Finally, interest becomes a heavy liability if the loan is taken from non-institutional sources at high rates of interest.

The accumulated liability of principal and compound interest can sometimes become crippling, and the borrower is forced to mortgage or sell his land losing thereby his only means of livelihood Radhakrishnna R. (2007). Therefore, the growing indebtedness of the rural poor households is a matter of concern and deserves one's attention.

In this Section, an attempt is made to examine the trends in indebtedness of rural households at the All -India level to ascertain the contributing factors. Since what is intended is to get an over view of the magnitude of the problem and its relationship to aspects having a bearing on indebtedness, the conceptual differences widely noted on various issues in All-India Debt and Investment Surveys (AIDIS) are not considered as insurmountable impediments, though the need for caution in interpreting the trends should not be lost sight off.

Methodology:

The incidence of indebtedness of households has been estimated based on AIDIS and the Situation Assessment Survey of Farmers (SAS) Jan-Dec 2003, both conducted by the National Sample Survey Organization (NSSO). SAS covered outstanding debt during Jan-Dec 2003 of farmer households defined as those operating some land and engaged in agricultural activities on that land in the past year whereas AIDIS covered outstanding debt at the end of June 2002 for cultivator households operating at least 0.002 hectares of land in the past year. Though the two surveys have some differences in definitions and coverage, their broad conclusions appear comparable. This chapter is devoted to an analysis of their key results.

The first decennial country-wide enquiry on household indebtedness, viz., All- India Rural Credit Survey (AIRCS), 1951-52 was conducted by the Reserve Bank of India for the purpose of formulating credit policies in the area of agriculture. The second decennial survey viz., All-India Rural Debt and Investment Survey (AIRDIS), 1961-62, was conducted again by the Reserve Bank of India (RBI) and attempted to arrive at statistically valid and reliable estimates of debt, investment and other related characteristics of rural households for the country as a whole, and for major individual states, which served as bench mark data. The Third (1971-72) and the Fourth (1981-82) decennial surveys covered the urban households as well and were carried out by the NSSO in the 26th and 27th Rounds of the NSS, respectively, at the instance of the Reserve Bank of India.

The AIDIS, 1991-92, fifth in the series of the decennial surveys formed the main subject of the programme for the 48th Round of the NSSO and was conducted during the year 1992. The latest decennial AIDIS and the SAS, both conducted by the NSSO during Jan-Dec 2003 in its 59th Round, provide insights into varied dimensions of farmers" indebtedness in India for the year 2003. The rural households are broadly categorized as cultivators and non-cultivators. The latter covers agricultural laborers, artisans and other non-cultivator households. The published data of these surveys are used in this chapter to assess the levels and changing trends in the indebtedness of the rural households.

Incidence of Indebtedness

The first two surveys (i.e., 1951-52 and 1961-62) were conducted by the RBI while the next two surveys i.e., (1971-72 and 1981-82) were conducted jointly by NSSO and RBI, with the responsibility of field work vested with the former and the processing of data and publication of the results with the latter. As against this, the NSSO was vested with the complete responsibility of conducting the survey, processing and publication of the results of the fifth decennial survey relating to 1991-92. The SAS conducted by NSSO during Jan-Dec 2003 in its 59th Round, provide insights into varied dimensions of farmers" indebtedness in India for the year 2003 (Table-5.1 and Figure 5.1).

Table 5.1 Proportion of Households Reporting Debt (As on June 30)

	1951	1962	1971	1981	1991	2003
Rural households	63.3	62.8	41.3	19.4	32.0	48.6

Source: All- India Debt and Investment Survey

Figure 5.1 Proportions of Households Reporting Debt (As on June 30)

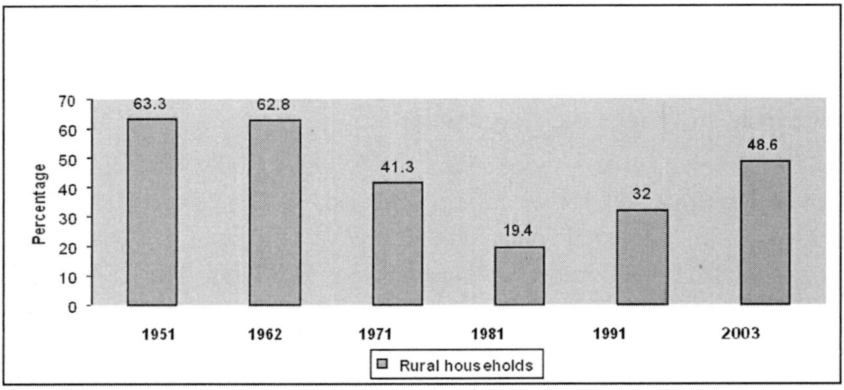

Source: All- India Debt and Investment Survey

It may be seen that the indebtedness of rural households was marginally lower at 62.8 percent in 1962 over that of 1951 (63.3 percent) which decreased significantly to 41.3 per cent in 1971 and further to 19.4 per cent in 1981 (Table 5.1). The incidence had increased to 32 per cent in 1991 and 48.6 per cent in 2003. The steep decline in the proportion of rural households reporting debt during 1971 and 1981 gave rise to much debate all though the decline in the proportion between 1961 and 1971 did not raise any debate as the shift in pattern of households debt from non-institutional debt to institutionalized debt was a welcome sign during this period. In view of the expansion of branch network of scheduled commercial banks into the rural and unbaked areas during 1971 and 1981, the decline in the incidence of indebtedness of rural households was contrary to general expectations. The debate pointed towards the limitations of sampling design adopted for the survey and to certain other non-sampling issues. A brief review of the debate is presented below before reviewing the trends revealed by 1991-92 survey.

Seetha Prabhu et.al., (1988), examined the substantial decrease in the proportion as well as absolute number of households reporting debt between 1971 and 1981, at all- India and state level, from the viewpoints of (i) under estimation arising out of method of sampling used for the survey; (ii) steep rise in incomes of the household resulting in their reduced dependence on external sources of credit; (iii) expansion in network of institutional credit agencies in rural areas; and (iv) excess demand for credit which was not met by the institutional credit agencies. Although they have pointed towards the smaller sample size in 1981 compared to that in 1971, they have agreed that the sample size per se need not be a contributory factor for decline in the proportion. They added that the incomes of rural households could not have grown so high as to reduce their dependence on credit agencies.

Gothoskar (1988), compared the estimates of outstanding debt of rural households derived from the 1971-72 and 1981-82 surveys with similar estimates available from the viewpoint of suppliers of credit, such as commercial and cooperative banks. He observed that the estimates derived from 1981-82 survey (as also 1971-72 survey) were underestimated and added that the state sample estimates are generally lower than the central sample estimates for 1981. He referred to both sampling and non-sampling errors in the derivation of estimates from such large-scale surveys. From the sampling point of view, he suggested that (i) enquiry into financial characteristics of households should not be clubbed with other socio-economic enquiries for the purpose of sample selection; (ii) villages may be grouped into two strata, viz., villages having institutional credit facilities; and (iii) households in selected villages should further be stratified as those availing of loans from institutional agencies and others. He also suggested that information may also be collected from agencies supplying credit in selected villages; and informal loans in the nature of trade credit and bills payable may be treated separately as formal loans.

In 2003, of the 89.33 million farmer households estimated, the SAS shows that 43.42 million (48.6 per cent) were indebted (Table 5.2). In other words, more than half i.e., 45.91 million or 51.4 per cent – were not indebted either from institutional or non- institutional sources. A large proportion of them might have been financially excluded. The average outstanding debt per farmer household was at Rs.12, 585 and per indebted farmer household was at Rs.25, 902. A state-wise analysis showed that in 2003 incidence of indebtedness was higher in states which had input-intensive or diversified agriculture. The incidence of indebtedness was the highest in Andhra Pradesh followed by Tamil Nadu, Punjab, Kerala, Karnataka, Maharashtra and Haryana (Table 5.2 Figure 5.2). Average debt per farmer was higher in states with higher incidence of outstanding debt. For instance, average outstanding debt per farmer household was higher in the state of Punjab followed by Kerala, Haryana, AP and Tamil Nadu all relatively developed and better banked states. Clearly, neither indebtedness nor outstanding debt per farmer was an indicator of backwardness.

In five states viz., Andhra Pradesh, Karnataka, Kerala, Maharashtra and Punjab where suicides were reported, both indebtedness and outstanding debt per farmer household were higher than the all-India level. As will be seen, in these states except for Kerala, large proportion of the debt was incurred for productive purposes. Strikingly, sources of debt were different. For instance, in Maharashtra the institutional sources accounted for a major portion of the debt whereas in Andhra Pradesh it was from moneylenders.

Table 5.2 Incidence of Indebtedness in Major States: 2003

State	Estimated Number of Indebted Farmer Households	Per cent of Indebted Farmer Households	Average loan Per Household, Rupees
Andhra Pradesh	49493	82.0	23965
Tamil Nadu	28954	74.5	23963
Punjab	12069	65.4	41576
Kerala	14126	64.4	33907
Karnataka	24897	61.6	18135
Maharashtra	36098	54.8	16973
Haryana	10330	53.1	26007
Rajasthan	27828	52.4	18372
Gujarat	19644	51.9	15526
Madhya Pradesh	32110	50.8	14218
West Bengal	34696	50.1	10931
Orissa	20250	47.8	5871
Uttar Pradesh	69199	40.3	7425
Himachal Pradesh	3030	33.4	9618
Bihar	23383	33.0	4476
Jammu & Kashmir	3003	31.8	1903
Assam	4536	18.1	813
All -India	434242	48.6	12585

Source: NSSO: Situation Assessment Survey of Farmers, 2003

Figure 5.2 Incidence of Indebtedness in Major States: 2003

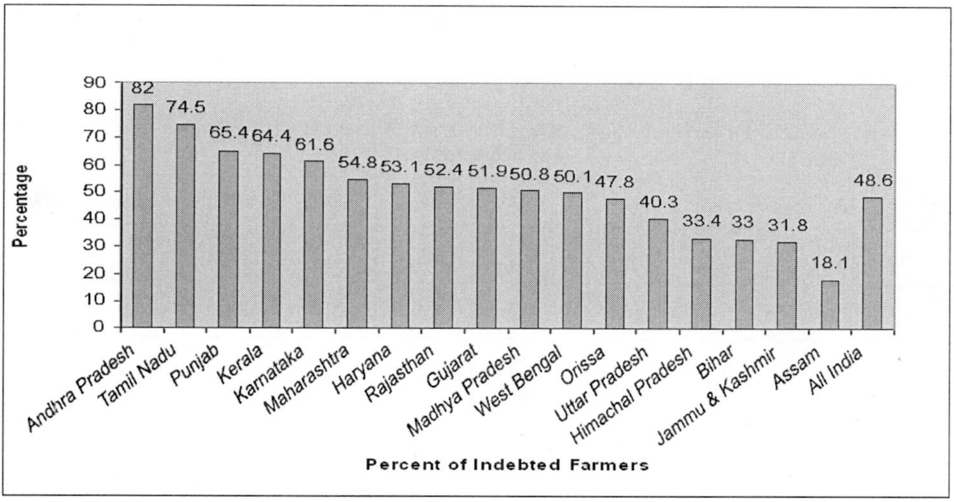

Source: NSSO: Situation Assessment Survey of Farmers, 2003

The inter-state variations in the incidence and amount of debt per farmer household could be on account of the difference in their level of development and commercialization of agriculture. The southern states have a relatively more diversified agriculture as the proportion of their area devoted to food grain was relatively less than that of all-India. On the other hand, Punjab and Haryana are primarily food grain producing states using high doses of inputs purchased from the market. In both the categories of agriculturally developed states, farmers need to borrow for financing investment, production and marketing. There were differences in the incidence of indebtedness among different social groups (SAS, 2003). The incidence of indebtedness was 36.3 percent for STs, 50.2 percent for SCs, 51.4 percent for other backward classes and 49.4 percent for others. The average amount of outstanding debt was Rs 5,506 for STs, Rs 7,167 for SCs, Rs 13,489 for other backward classes and Rs.18, 118 for others. The incidence of indebtedness as well as average amount of debt was lowest for the most deprived group viz., STs. In the case of other groups, the incidence of indebtedness was closer to that of all-India (48.6 percent). Average outstanding debt was also lower for SCs.

Debt by Source

In 2003, the total debt of farmer households was estimated at Rs. 1.12 lakh crore. Of which Rs.65,000 cr was from institutional agencies and Rs. 48,000 cr from non-institutional agencies. Private moneylenders accounted for Rs.29,000 cr and traders Rs.6,000 cr. About Rs 18,000 cr of debt from non-institutional sources, a major portion of which was from moneylenders, carried an interest rate greater than 30 percent. There is an urgent need to relieve the farmers from private debt carrying high interest rate by transferring it to institutional agencies. The share of institutional sources in cultivators" debt improved in the years following bank nationalization, from about 32 percent in 1971 to 66 percent in 1991, but in 1990s, there was a loss of momentum and the share declined to 61 percent in 2002 (Table 5.3).

Table 5.3 Share of Debt* of Cultivator Households from Different Sources: 1951-2002 (in percentages)

Sources of credit	1951	1961	1971	1981	1991	2002
Institutional	7.3	18.1	31.7	63.2	66.3	61.1
Cooperative Societies/ Banks, etc.	3.3	2.6	22.0	29.8	30.0	30.2
Commercial Banks	0.9	0.6	2.4	28.8	35.2	26.3
Non-institutional	92.7	81.3	66.3	36.8	30.6	38.9
Moneylenders	69.7	49.2	36.1	16.1	17.5	26.8
Unspecified	-	-	-	-	3.1	-
Total	100.0	100.0	100.0	100.0	100.0	100.0

*Debt refers to outstanding cash dues.

Source: RBI All-India Rural Credit Survey 1951-52; RBI, All - India Rural Debt and Investment Survey, 1961-62 and NSSO. All -India Debt and Investment Surveys. 1971-72, 1981-82, 991-92 and 2003

In the post-nationalization period, the increase in the share of commercial banks was rapid and sizeable. The cooperative sector's share increased from 22 percent in 1971 to about 30 percent by 1981 and stagnated since then. In the1990s, while cooperatives sustained their, albeit low, share at 30 percent, the share of commercial banks slipped from 35 percent in 1991 to 26 percent in 2002. The decline in the share of institutional agencies in 1990s could be attributed to the decline in the share of commercial banks. In the share of institutional and non- institutional sources of farmers" debt there are wide variations across states (SAS, 2003). In majority of states, the outstanding debt of the farmer was financed more by the institutional agencies than by non-institutional agencies (Figure 5.3). However, in few states such as AP, Rajasthan, Assam, Bihar and Punjab the financing of the debt was more by the non-institutional sources. Credit cooperative societies were an important source of finance only in five states: Maharashtra, Gujarat, Kerala, Haryana and Tamil Nadu. At all-India level, the share of cooperatives in the total outstanding debt of farmers was 19.6 percent, whereas these states had shares in the range 23-49 percent (Table 5.4).

Table 5.4 Distribution of Debt by Sources across Major States: 2003 (in percentages)

State	Institutional				Non- Institutional				Total
	Gover-nment	Coope-ratives	Bank	All	Money lenders	Traders	Others	All	
Maharashtra	1.2	48.5	34.1	83.8	6.8	0.8	8.6	16.2	100.0
Kerala	4.9	28.3	49.1	82.3	7.4	1.7	8.5	17.6	100.0
Uttaranchal	31.5	4.8	39.8	76.1	5.9	1.7	16.3	23.9	100.0
Orissa	13.0	18.1	43.7	74.8	14.8	0.8	9.5	25.1	100.0
Chhattisgarh	1.3	20.6	50.5	72.4	13.0	4.2	10.5	27.7	100.0
Gujarat	0.5	41.8	27.2	69.5	6.5	4.4	19.6	30.5	100.0
Karnataka	1.9	16.9	50.1	68.9	20.0	1.9	9.3	31.2	100.0
Haryana	1.1	23.9	42.6	67.6	24.1	3.1	5.3	32.5	100.0
J & K	13.1	0.2	54.3	67.6	1.1	15.5	15.7	32.3	100.0
H.P	6.1	11.6	47.6	65.3	7.2	5.5	22.0	34.7	100.0
Jharkand	3.9	4.5	55.7	64.1	19.0	1.7	15.2	35.9	100.0
Uttar Pradesh	2.4	6.7	51.2	60.3	19.1	2.9	17.7	39.7	100.0
West Bengal	10.3	19.2	28.5	58.0	13.0	10.7	18.4	42.1	100.0
Madhya Pradesh	1.9	16.9	38.1	56.9	22.6	9.0	11.4	43.0	100.0
Tamil Nadu	2.0	23.3	28.1	53.4	39.7	0.4	6.4	46.5	100.0
Punjab	1.9	17.6	28.4	47.9	36.3	8.2	7.6	52.1	100.0
Bihar	2.2	2.5	37.0	41.7	32.8	1.1	24.6	58.5	100.0
Assam	7.0	2.7	27.8	37.5	15.5	12.0	35.1	62.6	100.0
Rajasthan	1.3	5.9	27.0	34.5	36.5	19.2	10.1	65.8	100.0
Andhra Pradesh	1.0	10.4	20.0	31.4	53.4	4.8	10.4	68.6	100.0
All -India	2.5	19.6	35.6	57.7	25.7	5.2	11.5	42.4	100.0

Source: NSSO: Situation Assessment Survey of Farmers, 2003.

Another set of six states viz., Chhattisgarh, West Bengal, Madhya Pradesh, Orissa, Punjab, and Karnataka had shares in the range of 17-21 per cent. In Maharashtra and Gujarat, the share of cooperative societies was higher than that of commercial banks. In Jammu and Kashmir, Bihar, Assam, Jharkand and Uttaranchal the share of cooperatives in farmers' outstanding debt was negligible at less than 5 per cent. The share of moneylenders in the farmers" outstanding debt was higher in Andhra Pradesh (53 percent), Tamil Nadu (40 per cent), Rajasthan (37 per cent), Punjab (36 per cent), and Bihar (33 per cent). In all these states, except Bihar, the share of moneylenders in farmers" outstanding debt was higher than that of commercial banks. Traders were a significant source of financing debt in Rajasthan, Jammu & Kashmir, Assam and West Bengal.

Figure 5.3 Distribution of Debt by Sources across Major States-2003

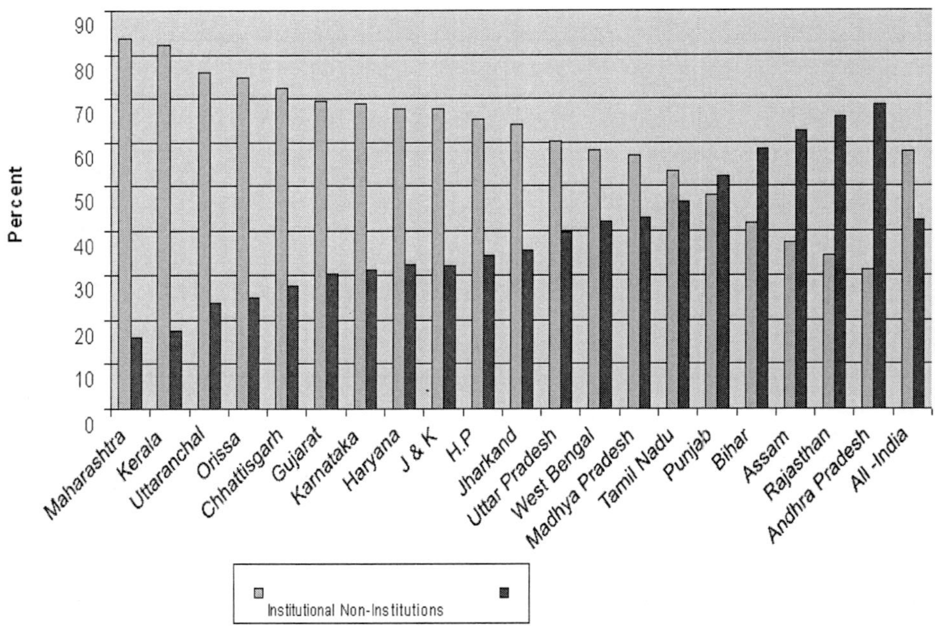

Source: NSSO: Situation Assessment Survey of Farmers, 2003.

It is indeed a matter of concern that in spite of all the efforts made for the spread of institutional finance, it accounted for only two-fifths of farmers" total outstanding debt. Further, in some states like Andhra Pradesh, Rajasthan and Assam it was less than two-fifths. Since the interest rates charged by the non-institutional sources are high, this might have imposed heavy burden on the farmers.

Debt by Land Size:

The incidence of indebtedness and the share of institutional finance in outstanding debt for all India increased with the size of land holding (Table 5.5). The incidence of indebtedness increased from 46 percent for marginal and small farmer households to 66 percent for large farmers and the share of institutional agencies in the debt increased from 51 to 68 percent. The average size of loan per farmer also increased with the landholding size. Small and marginal farmer households, which accounted for 80 percent of indebted farmer households, absorbed 51 percent of the total outstanding credit from institutional agencies. The dependent of marginal and small farmers was more on non-institutional agencies than of large farmers. As against large farmers, one- third of whose debt was from non-institutional sources, one-half of the debt of small and marginal farmers was from non-institutional sources. The marginal farmers received a relatively smaller share even from cooperatives and had to depend more on private moneylenders. Sources of financing outstanding debt varied across the land holding size groups. The outstanding debt of the sub- marginal land holder (land possessed less than 0.40 hectares) households was financed mostly by non-institutional agencies (Table 5.6).

Table 5.5 Incidence, Amount and Source of Indebtedness by Size Class of Holding: 2003

Size class of land possessed (Hectares)	Total house-holds (%)	Total indebted house-holds (%)	Incidence of indebt-edness (%)	Amount outstanding per farmer Household (Rs)	Loans from	
					Institutional Agencies (%)	Non-Institutional Agencies (%)
<0.01	1.4	1.3	45.3	6121	22.6	77.4
0.01-0.40	32.8	30.0	44.4	6545	43.3	56.7
0.40-1.00	31.7	29.8	45.6	8623	52.8	47.2
1.01- 2.00	18.0	18.9	51.0	13762	57.6	42.3
Up to 2.00	83.9	79.9	46.3	8870	51.3	49.7
2.01-4.00	10.5	12.5	58.2	23456	65.1	35.0
4.01-10.00	4.8	6.4	65.1	42532	68.8	31.1
10.00+	0.9	1.2	66.4	76232	67.6	32.4
All size	100.0	100.0	48.6	12595	57.7	42.4

Source: NSSO, Situation Assessment Survey of Farmers, 2003.

Table 5.6 Non- Institutional Debt for each Size Class of Holding across States: 2003 (in percentages)

State/Region	Size class of land possessed							
	<0.01	0.01-0.40	0.40-1.00	1.01-2.00	2.01-4.00	4.01-10.00	10.00+	All sizes
A.P	83.1	80.7	74.9	73.4	58.5	51.4	50.5	68.6
Assam	100.0	70.9	62.2	54.8	53.6	77.0	100.0	62.5
Bihar	63.5	79.2	53.0	33.9	36.6	80.4	29.9	58.3
Chhattisgarh	52.9	73.4	49.9	19.6	29.3	11.5	0.0	27.6
Gujarat	89.9	65.2	59.3	34.8	15.1	19.8	0.0	30.5
Haryana	75.4	53.5	29.0	38.0	13.6	40.6	25.3	32.4
H.P	0.0	49.2	22.2	20.6	45.2	7.7	100.0	34.7
J & K	0.0	39.1	38.4	26.1	11.1	99.9	1..0	32.4
Jharkhand	35.5	29.2	65.5	12.4	39.5	2.0	0.0	35.9
Karnataka	84.4	66.6	37.9	41.3	26.6	13.0	3.0	31.1
Kerala	35.2	23.9	13.2	7.1	3.6	32.7	29.7	17.7
M. P	89.6	64.6	56.6	47.3	53.2	26.9	16.1	43.1
Maharashtra	41.7	16.8	19.8	21.2	16.2	11.3	8.9	16.2
Orissa	35.3	37.6	22.9	27.9	11.6	3.1	86.8	25.2
Punjab	75.2	70.8	34.4	50.9	38.8	52.5	69.9	52.1
Rajasthan	93.8	80.8	77.6	67.1	59.9	58.1	61.8	65.8
Tamil Nadu	80.9	62.6	54.0	38.5	34.8	25.7	17.1	46.6
Uttar Pradesh	79.8	70.2	43.3	31.5	20.2	11.5	1.8	39.7
Uttaranchal	100	21.3	27.1	23.3	92.7	100	100.0	23.9
West Bengal	76.6	57.3	36.9	19.9	24.6	78.7	100.0	42.0
All India	77.4	56.7	47.2	42.4	34.9	31.2	32.4	42.3

Source: NSSO: Situation Assessment Survey of Farmers, 2003

In majority of the states, more than 70 percent of their outstanding debt was from non-institutional agencies. In Andhra Pradesh and Rajasthan, non-institutional agencies accounted for as high as 80 percent of their outstanding debt. In Kerala and Maharashtra, dependent of very sub-marginal landholding households on non-institutional sources was much less. This could be attributed to the spread of commercial bank and cooperative banks/societies in the rural areas of these states.

Debt by Interest Rates:

The interest rates charged by non-institutional agencies were much higher than those charged by institutional agencies for the outstanding debt as on end June 2002 (Table 5.7). About 85 percent of outstanding debt of cultivator households from institutional agencies was in the interest range of 12 to 20 percent per annum. On the other hand, 36 per cent of cultivator households" outstanding debt from non-institutional agencies was at the interest rate of 20 to 25 percent and another 38 percent of outstanding debt at high interest rate of 30 percent and above. This shows the exploitative nature of non-institutional credit market.

Table 5.7 Distribution of Debt by Interest Rates and Source for Cultivator Households: 2002

	Institutional	Non- Institutional
Nil	0.5	17.4
0-6	1.8	2.3
6-10	3.0	0.3
10-12	7.4	0.6
12-15	50.0	1.6
15-20	34.8	2.7
20-25	1.4	36.2
25-30	0.0	0.3
>30	0.3	38.2
All	100.0	100.0

Source: NSSO, Household Indebtedness in India, All- India Debt and Investment Survey (Jan-Dec 2003), NSS 59th Round, Report No. 501, 2005.

Debt by Purpose

A significant proportion of cultivator households" debt was for productive purpose at the all India level (Table 5.8). However, debt for productive purposes as a percentage of total debt declined from 72 percent in 1981 to 63 per cent in 2002. Similarly the share of debt incurred for farm business declined from 64 per cent in 1981 to 53 per cent in 2002. Within farm business expenditure, the share of capital expenditure declined from 45.3 per cent to 34.3 per cent. The increase in capital expenditure for non-farm business could not fully compensate the fall in farm business expenditure, which resulted in a fall in the share of overall productive expenditure between 1981 and 2002. There were substantial inter-state variations in the purposes for which debt was incurred (Table 5.9 and Figure 5.4). Outstanding debt for productive purposes varied from 40 per cent in Assam, 44 per cent in Kerala and 47 per cent in Bihar to 80 per cent in Maharashtra, 78 per cent in Karnataka and 75 per in Gujarat. The outstanding debt in the states which reported suicides (AP, Karnataka, Maharashtra and Punjab) was incurred largely for productive purposes.

Table 5.8 Distribution of Debt by Purpose among Rural Cultivator Households: 1961-2002 (in percentages)

Purpose	1961	1971	1981	2002
Productive	40.1	54.0	71.6	62.9
Farm- Business	36.6	49.7	63.8	52.5
Capital Expenditure	26.8	34.7	45.3	34.3
Current Expenditure	9.8	15.0	18.5	18.2
Non -Farm- Business	3.5	4.3	7.8	9.4
Capital Expenditure	1.4	3.2	6.3	7.4
Current Expenditure	2.1	1.1	1.5	2.0
Non-Productive	60.0	46.0	28.4	38.1
Household Expenditure	49.2	37.8	20.0	27.7
Other purposes	10.8	7.2	8.4	10.4
Repayment of Debt	5.0	1.5	0.1	1.5
Expenditure on Litigation	1.8	0.7	0.8	0.3
Financial Investment	0.2	0.2	1.0	0.6
All purposes	100.0	100.0	100.0	100.0

Source: RBI, All- India Rural Debt and Investment survey, 1961-62 and NSSO, All- India Debt and Investment Surveys, 1971-72, 1981-82 and 2003.

Table 5.9 Distribution of Debt by Purpose across Major States: 2003 (in percentages)

States	Productive				Others					Total
	Farm business capital	Farm business current	Other	Total	Consumption	Marriages& ceremonies	Education	Medical	Others	
Andhra Pradesh	23.4	38.1	3.2	64.7	11.5	9.6	1.4	2.4	10.5	100.0
Assam	16.6	6.7	16.2	39.5	12.4	11.8	0.1	1.5	34.8	100.0
Bihar	30.8	8.6	7.6	47.0	6.4	22.9	2.3	10.2	11.2	100.0
Gujarat	20.3	50.3	3.9	74.5	6.3	10.2	0.5	3.0	5.6	100.0
Haryana	36.0	26.2	6.8	69.0	4.8	14.0	0.0	2.0	10.3	100.0
Himachal Pradesh	9.4	10.1	29.0	48.5	6.6	10.2	0.9	2.9	30.9	100.0
Jammu& Kashmir	26.0	3.2	24.1	53.3	18.3	9.3	0.0	2.0	17.1	100.0
Karnataka	30.7	37.5	9.8	78.0	5.6	7.4	0.6	0.2	8.1	100.0
Kerala	11.0	10.4	22.8	44.2	10.2	11.2	1.4	2.5	30.5	100.0
Madhya Pradesh	47.0	21.3	1.4	69.7	9.6	14.4	0.1	3.6	2.7	100.0
Maharashtra	37.9	37.5	4.8	80.2	4.2	4.9	0.9	1.5	8.3	100.0
Orissa	28.9	24.4	11.5	64.8	11.4	14.0	0.1	2.9	6.9	100.0
Punjab	26.4	36.0	4.4	66.8	8.5	10.2	0.0	2.6	12.0	100.0
Rajasthan	37.5	19.7	2.2	59.4	13.8	17.6	0.8	3.9	4.4	100.0
Tamil Nadu	24.3	25.1	5.5	54.9	13.1	8.7	2.6	4.1	16.6	100.0
Uttar Pradesh	40.3	20.6	7.0	67.9	6.8	11.8	0.2	6.1	7.1	100.0
West Bengal	24.4	21.3	10.3	56.0	7.2	11.1	0.5	5.1	20.1	100.0
All India	30.6	27.8	6.7	65.1	8.8	11.1	0.8	3.3	10.8	100.0

Source: NSSO: Situation Assessment Survey of Farmers, 2003

Figure 5.4 Distribution of Debt by Purpose across Major states 2003

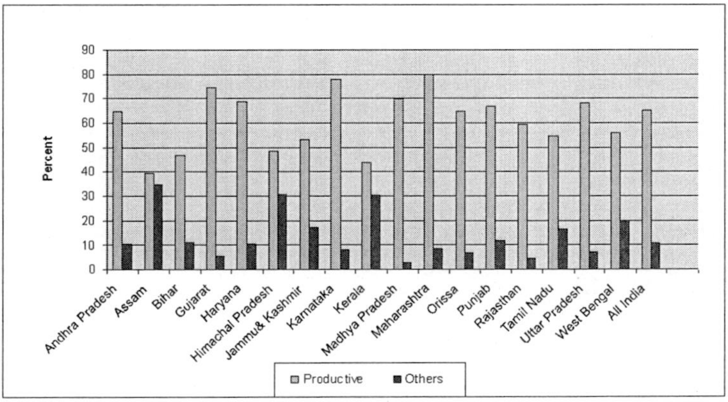

Sources: NSSO: Situation Assessment Survey of Farmers, 2003

Indebtedness for productive purpose was generally high in states with high incidence of indebtedness and low in states with low incidence of indebtedness (Table 5.9). Debt incurred by farmers for marriages and social ceremonies was also very significant in some states. Through Bihar had low level of debt per farmer household, 23 per cent of the outstanding debt was for marriages and ceremonies. This was much higher than the all India average of 11 per cent.

Household Borrowings and Repayments

The trends in annual borrowings are similar to those of outstanding debt. The proportion of households reporting borrowings and the extent of borrowings by occupational categories of households and assets holding classes are also discussed in this chapter. Table 5.10 presents the total amount of cash borrowings and percentage shares by occupational category of households during 1971-72, 1981-82, 1991-92 and 2002-2003 for rural households. The aggregate estimates given in this table are at current prices. The table shows that as per the results of the various rounds of AIDIS, the total amount of cash borrowings (TCB), at current prices, increased over three times during1970s and 1980s and about four times during 1990s in rural areas. The rise was sharper among non-cultivator households i.e., nearly 7 times in rural areas during the 1980s and slowed down to 5.5 times during 1990s.

Table 5.10 Amount of cash Borrowings by Occupational Category of Households (All-India) Rural

Year	Amount Borrowings (Rs. 00, 00, 000)		
	Cultivator	Non- Cultivator	All
1971-72(26th)	1155 (85.9)	190 (14.1)	1345 (100.0)
1981-82(37th)	3757 (89.8)	427 (10.2)	4185 (100.0)
1991-92(48th)	10636 (78.8)	2862 (21.2)	13498 (100.0)
2002-03(59th)	39294 (71.3)	15825 (28.7)	55119 (100.0)

Source: Household Borrowings and Repayments in India.2002 – 03, All -India Debt and Investment Survey NSS 59th Round Jan-Dec 2003 NSSO, January 2006.

Table 5.11 Amount of Repayments by Occupational Category of Households All- India Rural

Year	Amount of Repayment (Rs. 00, 00, 000)		
	Cultivator	Non- Cultivator	All
1971-72(26th)	1009 (87.4)	146 (12.6)	1155 (100.0)
1981-82(37th)	1899 (90.9)	193 (9.1)	20901(100.0)
1991-92(48th)	4070 (78.3)	1133 (21.7)	5203 (100.0)
2002-03(59th)	17729 (71.3)	7154 (28.7)	24883 (100.0)

Source: Household Borrowings and Repayments in India.2002 – 03, All- India Debt and Investment Survey NSS 59th Round Jan-Dec 2003, NSSO, January 2006

Table 5.11 reveals that the aggregate repayments of cash dues of households increased 1.8 times during the 1970s, 2.5 times during the 1980s and 4.9 times during the 1990s for rural households as a whole. However, the aggregate repayments of non-cultivator households reported a remarkable increase (nearly six times), though that of cultivator households reported a small increase (2.1 times) during the 1980s. The corresponding increase accelerated further during the 1990s, and became 6.3 times and 4.4 times, respectively.

Incidence of Borrowings and Repayments by Occupation Category:

Table 5.12 Percentage of Households Reporting cash Borrowings (IOB), cash Repayments (IOR) and Average amount of Borrowings (AOB), Repayments (AOR) per Household by Occupational Category of Households (2002-03) (All-India) Rural

Occupational Category of Households	Indebtedness		Borrowings		Repayments	
	IOI (%)	AOD (Rs.)	IOB (%)	AOB (Rs.)	IOR (%)	AOR (Rs.)
Cultivator	29.7	9261	22.4	4446	16.9	2006
Non-Cultivator	21.8	4991	18.4	2657	15.9	1202
All	26.5	7539	20.8	3726	16.5	1682

Source: Household Borrowings and Repayments in India.2002 - 03, All- India Debt and Investment Survey NSS 59th Round Jan-Dec 2003, NSSO, January 2006

Table 5.12 displays the incidence of cash borrowings (IOB), i.e. percentage of households reporting cash borrowings, along with the average amount of (cash) borrowings (AOB) per household by occupational categories, during the period of survey (AY 02-03). The table also displays side by side the incidence of cash repayments (IOR) per household and average amount of repayments (AOR) of cash borrowings during the period of survey. While the incidence of indebtedness (IOI) as on 30.6.02, in the rural areas, was about 27 per cent (NSS Report No.500), the incidence of cash borrowings was 21 percent during 2002-03. The average amount of cash borrowings per rural household was Rs. 3726. A comparison of IORs and AORs together with the IOB and AOB, perhaps, indicates that the incidence of indebtedness is likely to increase in the areas if the relationship between borrowings and repayments observed in the survey continues with same direction, i.e., IOR and AOR are less than the IOB and AOB, respectively in the future years.

Among the occupational categories, the incidences of borrowings as well as the average amount of borrowings are found to be higher for the cultivator households than that of the non-cultivator households in the rural areas. Moreover, the relationship between borrowings (IOB and AOB values) and repayments (IOR and AOR value) that was observed for the rural areas as a whole also holds the same in the case of both the cultivator and non-cultivator households.

Incidence of Borrowings and Repayments over Assets Holding Classes:

Table 5.13 Percentage of Households Reporting cash Borrowings (IOB), Cash Repayments (IOR) and Average amount of Borrowings (AOB), repayments (AOR) per Households by Household Asset holding class (AHC) (All-India) Rural

Assets holding class (Rs 000)	Indebtedness		Borrowings		Repayments	
	IOI (%)	AOB (Rs.)	IOI (%)	AOB (Rs.)	IOI (%)	AOB (Rs.)
less than 15	15.0	1423	14.7	663	10.3	278
15-30	19.0	2243	17.2	1161	12.2	471
30-60	25.2	3153	18.5	1294	14.1	564
60-100	26.5	4301	21.0	1907	16.2	739
100-150	28.9	5299	20.6	2552	16.2	974
150-200	28.7	5696	20.5	2981	18.5	1123
200-300	28.7	7058	21.0	3612	16.9	1494
300-450	28.7	9857	22.9	5243	18.7	2124
450-800	31.0	15090	24.2	6519	20.1	3387
800& above	32.9	33414	30.8	17909	25.0	9115
All	26.5	7539	20.8	3726	16.5	1682

Source: Household Borrowings and Repayments in India.2002 – 03, All -India Debt and Investment Survey NSS 59th Round Jan-Dec 2003, NSSO, January 2006

Table 5.13 gives the IOB, AOB, IOR and AOR by assets holding class separately for the rural areas of the country. If may be worth mentioning in this context that the incidence of indebtedness and average amount of cash debt as on 30.6.02 increased steadily with the increase of assets holdings of the households (NSS Report No. 500). A similar trend is also observed in the case of the indicators of cash borrowings and repayments among the households in the rural areas. The average amount of borrowing (AOB) of a household belonging to the highest assets holding class (Rs. 8 lakh and above) is Rs. 17909 which is about 27 times to that in the lowest assets holding class (less than Rs. 0.15 lakh) in the rural areas. In respect of AOR values, the households belonging to the lowest and top asset classes are separated by as high as 33 times and nearly 16 times in the rural areas.

Changes in Incidence of Borrowings and Repayments by Occupation Category

Table 5.14 IOB and IOR by Occupational Category of Households (All-India) Rural

Occupational	IOB (%)				IOR (%)			
Category	71-72	81-82	91-92	2002-03	71-72	81-82	91-92	2002-03
Cultivator	29.3	20.6	21.9	22.4	13.1	15.2	14.6	16.9
Non-Cultivator	23.4	16.7	15.9	18.4	10.4	10.9	12.9	15.9
All	27.7	19.7	19.9	20.8	12.2	14.2	14.0	16.5

Source: Household Borrowings and Repayments in India.2002 – 03, All -India Debt and Investment Survey NSS 59th Round Jan-Dec 2003 NSSO, January 2006

The incidence of borrowings (IOB), i.e. percentage of households reporting cash borrowings, by occupational categories, and the incidence of repayments (IOR), during the period of survey for the 26th (for rural only), 37th , 48th and 59th rounds at all India level are presented in Table 5.14. Very little change in the levels of IOB is noticed between 1981-82 and 1991-92 in rural areas. However, a perceptible fall is seen from 1971-71 to 1981-82 in rural areas – for cultivator as well as non-cultivator households. Further, throughout the 1970s, 1980s and 1990s, IOB for cultivator households was distinctly higher than that of non- cultivator households. About a fifth of the households- are they in rural India-reported some cash borrowings during 91-92. The proportion increased in the rural areas, but decreased by about 3 percentage points in the sample areas during the period 1991-92 to 2002-03. Table 5.14 also shows the incidence of repayments (IOR), i.e. percentage of households reporting repayments of loans, during 1971-72, 1981-82, 1991-92 and 2002-03 for the rural areas. During 2002-03, nearly 17 percent of the rural households were reported to have repaid some of their outstanding dues. Over the three decades ending 2002-03, the level of IOR is seen to have increased for both cultivator and non-cultivator households in rural areas. The results of the present survey and those of earlier AIDIS rounds are presented in Table 5.15.

Table 5.15 Percentage of Households Reporting cash Borrowings (IOB) Rural

Major states	1971-72	1981-82	1991-92	2002-03
Andhra Pradesh	26.5	29.2	34.7	33.2
Assam	11.0	4.8	11.1	12.4
Bihar	17.2	13.7	10.9	14.3
Chhattisgarh	-	-	-	16.3
Gujarat	25.1	14.0	13.6	16.1

Haryana	36.2	15.4	20.0	19.4
Himachal Pradesh	23.0	10.5	12.4	12.3
Jammu& Kashmir	34.3	15.6	8.1	2.6
Jharkhand	-	-	-	6.3
Karnataka	28.4	16.1	20.3	21.8
Kerala	23.8	33.7	25.8	35.9
Madhya Pradesh	30.5	17.6	18.1	17.9
Maharashtra	31.8	21.7	19.5	15.5
Orissa	17.6	13.6	9.4	14.8
Punjab	58.0	31.1	26.7	32.7
Rajasthan	49.5	18.5	25.0	16.2
Tamil Nadu	29.7	28.5	30.2	41.6
Uttaranchal	-	-	-	5.4
Uttar Pradesh	30.6	19.0	30.2	18.6
West Bengal	28.4	19.0	19.2	18.7
India	27.7	19.7	19.9	20.8

Source: Household Borrowings and Repayments in India.2002–03, All- India Debt and Investment Survey NSS 59th Round Jan-Dec 2003 NSSO, January 2006.

The table shows that IOB reported at the all India level during 2002-03 (20.8 percent), was close to that reported (19.9 percent) during 1991-92 and to that reported (19.7 percent) during 1981-82, but was much lower than that (27.7 percent) during 71-72. Tamil Nadu, Kerala and AP are the three top states, in the order of ranks, where the proportion of households reporting cash borrowings during 2002-03 was very high in the rural (varying between 42 to 33 percent). Similarly, in J&K, Uttaranchal, Delhi and

Jharkhand, the incidence of borrowings was very low- ranging from 3 to 6 per cent. Apparently, the trend in the change of IOB was neither similar nor definitive in the rural sectors of all the states. In fact, study of change for these indicators over time need to be done carefully keeping in mind the sample households reporting cash borrowings in the respective sectors of all these states.

The average values of borrowings per household in major states during 1971-72, 1981-82, 1991-92 and 2002-03 for the rural areas are presented in Table 5.16.

Table 5.16 Average Amount of cash Borrowings per Household (AOB) Rural

Major states	1971-72	1981-82	1991-92	2002-03
Andhra Pradesh	155	664	1894	5306
Assam	31	29	236	622
Bihar	62	113	305	1028
Chhattisgarh	-	-	-	1569
Gujarat	232	478	1222	270
Haryana	537	841	2430	9327
Himachal Pradesh	235	309	1288	3464
Jammu& Kashmir	175	392	774	1544
Jharkhand	-	-	-	1368
Karnataka	239	506	1285	4446
Kerala	136	919	2171	11066
Madhya Pradesh	180	349	1025	3288
Maharashtra	200	659	1522	3957
Orissa	53	194	269	1548
Punjab	723	1659	2868	13264
Rajasthan	380	639	1745	3435
Tamil Nadu	192	538	1870	7231
Uttaranchal	-	-	-	882
Uttar Pradesh	157	364	773	2227
West Bengal	100	196	615	1400
India	174	446	1160	3726

Source: Household Borrowings and Repayments in India.2002 – 03, All- India Debt and Investment Survey NSS 59th Round Jan-Dec 2003 NSSO, January 2006.

The Table reveals that generally, the states in the Eastern Region like Bihar, Jharkhand, West Bengal and (rural) Orissa including Assam reported much lower levels of AOB than those of other states throughout the three decades ending 2002-03. Among other states, Uttaranchal also reported low value of AOB. On the other hand, some of the Northern states like Punjab, Haryana and some of the Southern states like Kerala, Tamil Nadu and Andhra Pradesh reported high AOB throughout this period. Interestingly, in Kerala, Tamil Nadu, Andhra Pradesh, and rural Punjab AOB rose significantly throughout this period.

Share of Institutional Agencies in cash Borrowings of Households

The institutional agencies accounted for just about a fifth of cash borrowings during 1971-72. During 1981-82 and 1991-92, institutional agencies as a whole, showed a sharp rise in their share (Table 5.17). While their share in TCB exceeded 50 per cent during 1981-82, it remained almost at the same level during 1991-92 and then rose to 57 per cent during 2002-03. It may be noted that the commercial banks were nationalized in 1969. The impact of nationalization could only be felt subsequent to those periods only. While both cultivator and non-cultivator households exhibited the above pattern, in value terms, the share of institutional agencies in TCB for non-cultivator households rose from about 8 per cent during 1971-72 to 40 per cent during 1981-82, and further to 47 per cent during 1991-92 and 51per cent during 2002-03. The share of institutional borrowings of rural for the major states is presented in Table 5.18.

Table 5.17 Percentage Share of Institutional Agencies in cash Borrowings of Households by Occupational of Households (All-India) Rural

Occupation	1971-72	1981-82	1991-92	2002-03
Cultivator	21.7	56.2	55.0	59.5
Non- Cultivator	7.7	40.4	47.1	51.3
All	19.7	54.5	53.3	57.2

Source: Household Borrowings and Repayments in India.2002 – 03, All- India Debt and Investment Survey NSS 59th Round Jan-Dec 2003 NSSO, January 2006.

Table 5.18 Percentage Share of Institutional Agencies in cash Borrowings of the Households Rural

Major States	1981-82	1991-92	2002-03
Andhra Pradesh	40.9	23.9	37.6
Assam	22.6	44.7	46.5
Bihar	39.8	57.7	23.4
Chhattisgarh	-	-	57.9
Gujarat	65.8	71.9	75.7
Haryana	75.2	52.4	61.7
Himachal Pradesh	68.6	60.2	57.0
Jammu& Kashmir	48.4	42.8	82.7
Jharkhand	-	-	90.7
Karnataka	64.9	57.7	62.5
Kerala	68.6	77.2	81.6
Madhya Pradesh	45.8	58.7	62.6
Maharashtra	71.0	75.9	78.4
Orissa	69.2	68.5	69.6
Punjab	63.2	59.0	53.5
Rajasthan	36.8	26.6	38.6
Tamil Nadu	47.1	61.4	46.6
Uttaranchal	-	-	53.9
Uttar Pradesh	49.9	49.9	53.5
West Bengal	45.2	55.0	48.9
India	54.5	53.3	57.2

Source: Household Borrowings and Repayments in India.2002 – 03, All -India Debt and Investment Survey NSS 59th Round Jan-Dec 2003 NSSO, January 2006.

It would be of interest to examine the state-wise variations in the shares of institutional agencies after the impact of nationalization of banks began to be felt. Thus, the comparison has been limited to 1981-82, 1991-92 and 2002-03 in Table 5.18. The table shows that in Jharkhand, J&K, Kerala, Maharashtra and Gujarat, more than three- fourth of the TCB was accounted for by the institutional agencies. In contrast, not even 50 per cent of the borrowings were done through institutional agencies in Bihar (23 percent), AP, Assam, Tamil Nadu and West Bengal. Out of 20 major states considered in the rural areas, 3 states, viz., Chhattisgarh, Jharkhand and Uttaranchal were formed after 1991. For the remaining 17 major states, the picture relating to cash borrowings of households from institutional agencies turned somewhat different by 2002-03. Of these 17 states, 5 have shown a fall in the share for institutional agencies, notable among whom are Bihar, Himachal Pradesh, Punjab, Tamil Nadu and west Bengal where the decline in percentage share from their values 1991-92 was to the tune of 24,3,5,15 and 6 percentage points, respectively. With this fall, Bihar, with a share for institutional agencies of just 23 per cent, joined league with AP (37 per cent) and Rajasthan (39 per cent) as being the only three major states whose share for such agencies was below 40 per cent.

Share of Institutional Agencies in Cash Borrowings of Households by Assets Holding Class:

Table 5.19 Percentage share of Institutional and Non-Institutional Agencies in cash Borrowings of Households by Households assets holding class

Assets holding Class (Rs)	Institutional	Non-Institutional	All
less than 15	18.0	82.0	100.0
15-30	35.5	64.5	100.0
30-60	26.6	73.4	100.0
60-100	39.5	60.5	100.0
100-150	43.6	56.4	100.0
150-200	48.1	51.9	100.0
200-300	51.5	48.5	100.0
300-450	58.7	41.3	100.0
450-800	63.4	36.6	100.0
800& above	73.8	26.2	100.0
All	57.2	42.8	100.0

Source: Household Borrowings and Repayments in India.2002 – 03, All- India Debt and Investment Survey NSS 59th Round Jan-Dec 2003 NSSO, January 2006.

Table 5.19 displays the percentage distribution of TCB of rural households by assets holding class (AHC) at the all India level. It is clear from the table that households having assets valued up to Rs. 2 lakhs depended more on the non-institutional agencies for their cash borrowings. While households belonging to the second highest AHC viz., having assets valued between Rs. 2 lakhs and 3 lakhs borrowed almost equally from institutional agencies and non-institutional agencies. Among the "richest" households owning assets worth Rs 8 lakhs of more, share of institutional borrowings was much higher (74 per cent). The shares of different credit agencies, within the institutional and non-institutional types, in total cash borrowings of rural households, during 2002-03 are presented in Table 5.20.

Table 5.20 Percentage Share of Different credit Agencies in cash Borrowings of the Households by Occupational Category (2002-03) (All-India)

Credit agency	Cultivator	Non-Cultivator	All
Government	1.2	6.4	2.7
Co-op. society / bank	31.0	20.7	28.0
Commercial bank etc.	24.5	18.1	22.7
Insurance	0.3	0.3	0.3
Provident fund	0.4	2.3	1.0
Financial corpn /Institution	0.3	1.3	0.6
Financial company	0.9	0.6	0.8
Other institutional agencies	0.7	1.6	1.0
All institutional agencies	59.5	51.3	57.2
Landlord	0.6	0.7	0.6
Agriculturist moneylender	11.2	5.6	9.6
Professional moneylender	17.9	27.5	20.6
Traders	3.0	2.5	2.9
Relatives & friends	6.2	10.4	7.4
Doctors, lawyers etc.	0.2	0.3	0.2
Others	1.4	1.7	1.5
All non -instit. Agencies	40.5	48.7	42.8
All agencies	100.0	100.0	100.0

Source: Household Borrowings and Repayments in India.2002 – 03, All -India Debt and Investment Survey NSS 59th Round Jan-Dec 2003 NSSO, January 2006.

It is observed from the table that, at the all India level, among the institutional credit agencies, co-operative societies and commercial banks were the two most important agencies, in rural areas. For rural households, these two agencies, taken together, accounted for 50.7 per cent of the aggregate cash borrowings during 2002-03, with co-operative societies (28.0 per cent) having a larger share than commercial banks (22.7 per cent). Among the non-institutional credit agencies, money lenders both professional and agricultural and in that order, were found to be important sources for household borrowings in rural areas, their shares standing at 20.6 and 9.6 per cent, respectively. As seen from Table 5.20, for all the categories of household, the pattern of distribution in terms of the relative importance of the credit agencies is almost the same in the rural areas. Among the institutional agencies, the co-operative societies and commercial banks played a greater role as a credit agency for the cultivator households.

The shares of different credit agencies, with in the institutional and non-institutional types, in total cash borrowings for each size and class of assets of rural households, during 2002-03 is presented in Table 5.21.

Table 5.21 Percentage share of Different Credit Agencies in cash Borrowings of the Households by Household asset holding class (2002-03) (All India) Rural

Credit agency	Household asset holding class (Rs .000)			
	Less than100	100 -300	300 &above	All
Government	4.6	5.2	1.1	2.7
Co-op. society / bank	12.8	22.9	34.8	28.0
Commercial bank etc.	12.8	15.3	28.9	22.7
Insurance	0.0	0.5	0.3	0.3
Provident fund	0.5	1.4	0.9	1.0
Financial corporation/ Institution	0.3	1.0	0.6	0.6
Financial company	0.3	0.7	1.0	0.8
Other institutional agencies	1.8	1.1	0.8	1.0
All institutional agencies	33.2	48.0	68.2	57.2
Landlord	1.3	0.8	0.3	0.6
Agriculturist moneylender	13.0	10.8	8.1	9.6
Professional moneylender	35.0	27.0	13.6	20.6
Traders	3.1	2.9	2.8	2.9
Relatives & friends	11.2	8.5	5.8	7.4
Doctors, lawyers etc.	0.5	0.2	0.1	0.2
Others	2.9	1.9	0.9	1.5
All non -instit. Agencies	66.8	52.0	31.8	42.8
All agencies	100.0	100.0	100.0	100.0

Source: Household Borrowings and Repayments in India.2002 – 03, All -India Debt and Investment Survey NSS 59th Round Jan-Dec 2003, NSSO, January 2006.

A few important observations can be noted from the table. Firstly, the overall distribution patterns by type of credit agency observed for the rural or for the other areas are reflected for each asset class. That is, the co-operative societies and commercial banks, among the institutional agencies, played the dominant role in funding credit to the households belonging to any asset class, and among the non- institutional agencies, both professional and agricultural moneylenders acted as the principal agencies in funding credit to the households for all the assets holding classes. Secondly, as it appears from the inter-class comparison of the distributions, the co-operative societies and commercial banks have favored the rich households than the poor households, measured in respect of assets, in providing cash credit- as the poor households are, perhaps, unable to provide adequate security in terms of their assets in obtaining institutional credit. On the other hand, the Government has played a bigger role in providing cash credit to the poor households, as compared to the rich households. Among the non-institutional agencies, the share of cash borrowings from the agricultural and professional moneylenders, and traders was higher for the poor households than that of the rich households.

Changing Role of Credit Agencies:

Table 5.22 Percentage share of Different credit Agencies in cash Borrowings of the Households (All –India) Rural

Credit Agency	1971-72	1981-82	1991-92	2002-03
Government	3.1	4.2	3.9	2.7
Co-op. society / bank	14.9	26.3	25.7	28.0
Commercial bank etc.	1.7	23.1	20.7	22.7
Insurance	-	0.1	0.3	0.3
Provident fund	-	0.8	1.3	1.0
Financial corporation	-	-	-	0.6
Financial company	-	-	-	0.8
other institutional agencies	-	-	1.4	1.0
All institutional agencies	19.7	54.5	53.3	57.2
Landlord	6.4	3.8	3.9	0.6
Agriculturist moneylender	18.7	9.7	8.1	9.6
Professional moneylender	15.9	7.8	13.3	20.6
Traders	14.9	5.9	4.0	2.9
Relatives & friends	11.4	12.4	8.9	7.4
Other incl. doctor, Lawyers etc.	12.9	4.7	4.2	1.7
All non –instit. Agencies	80.3	44.3	42.3	42.8
Unspecified	-	1.2	4.4	0.0
All agencies	100.0	100.0	100.0	100.0

Source: Household Borrowings and Repayments in India.2002 – 03, All- India Debt and Investment Survey NSS 59th Round Jan-Dec 2003, NSSO, January 2006.

Table 5.22 reveals that throughout the last three decades, maximum amount of institutional borrowings of rural households were from "co-operative societies", although its share in TCB rose from 14.9 per cent during 1971-72 to 26.3 per cent during 1981-82 but fell marginally to 25.7 per cent during 1991-92 with a substantial rise thereafter to 28.1 per cent during 2002-03. "Commercial banks" closely followed the "co-operative societies", with its share in TCB soaring by 21 percentage points during the 1970s, the post-nationalization decade, to reach a significant 23.1 per cent during 1981-82, from where it fell to 20.7 per cent during 91-92. During the 1990s, however, the corresponding share gained by 2 percentage points. The share of government departments ranged between 2.7 per cent to 4.2 per cent throughout these three decades. Table 5.22 shows that the share of all non-institutional agencies sharply declined by about 36 percentage points during the period 1971-72 to 1981-82. During this period, the share of almost all categories of non-institutional agencies showed a fall – the decline being 8 percentage points or more for moneylenders (agricultural or professional) and traders. The decade ending 1991-92 also saw a marginal fall of about 2 percentage points in the combined share of the non-institutional agencies. However, there was a 9 percentage point increase in the combined share of professional and agricultural moneylenders during 2002-03. Among the non-institutional agencies, a significant rise of more than 7 percentage points in the share of professional moneylenders during the 1990s is worth noting. Relatives and friends accounted for about 7 per cent to 12 per cent of total household borrowings throughout the two decades under study.

Borrowings against Security:

Table 5.23 Percentage of Households Reporting Borrowings (P) and Percentage share in Total Borrowings (S) during 2002-03 by Type of Security and Occupational Category (All-India)

Type of security	Cultivator		Non-Cultivator		All	
	(P)	(S)	(P)	(S)	(P)	(S)
Personal security	15.1	44.6	14.7	59.7	14.9	49.0
Surely security etc.	1.1	6.9	1.1	11.0	1.1	8.1
Crop	1.4	7.2	0.0	0.1	0.9	5.1
First charge on immov. Property	1.9	12.5	0.4	7.1	1.3	10.9
Mortgage of immovable property	2.9	19.3	0.8	12.2	2.0	17.2
Bullion/ ornaments	1.3	3.0	1.9	6.2	1.5	3.9
Share of companies, etc.	0.1	0.6	0.1	0.7	0.1	0.6
Agricultural commodities	0.1	1.4	0.0	0.0	0.0	1.0
Other movable property	0.1	2.3	0.1	0.9	0.1	1.9
Other type of security	0.4	2.2	0.5	2.0	0.5	2.2
Total	22.4	100.0	18.4	100.0	20.8	100.0

Source: Household Borrowings and Repayments in India.2002 – 03, All- India Debt and Investment Survey NSS 59th Round Jan-Dec 2003, NSSO, January 2006.

Table 5.23 shows that percentage shares (S) of borrowings against different types of security follow almost the same order of priority as that observed earlier for the proportions reporting borrowings (P). Borrowings against "personal security" accounted for the largest share (49) of TCB, followed by those against "mortgage of immovable property" (17 percent) and against "first charge on immovable" (11 percent). There was hardly any difference between cultivator and non-cultivator households in this regard.

Borrowings by Purpose:

One of the important aspects of borrowings is the purpose for which it is made. This is because borrowings made and utilized for productive purposes such as capital or current expenditure in household enterprises (agricultural or non-agricultural) may be expected to accelerate the economic activity of the households.

Table 5.24 Percentage of Households Reporting Borrowings (P) and Percentage Share in Total Borrowings (S) during 1.7.02 to 30.6.03 by Purpose of Borrowing and Occupational Category of households (All-India)

Purpose of Borrowing	Cultivator		Non-Cultivator		All	
	P	S	P	S	P	S
Capital exp in farm business	3.3	20.0	0.6	4.5	2.2	15.6
Current exp in farm business	7.6	30.8	0.5	1.8	4.7	22.4
All exp in farm business	10.7	50.8	1.1	6.3	6.8	38.0
Capital exp in non-farm Business	0.7	8.1	1.0	13.7	0.8	9.7
Current exp in non-farm Business	0.5	3.0	1.0	7.6	0.7	4.3
All exp in non-farm business	1.2	11.1	1.9	21.3	1.5	14.1
Household expenditure	10.2	28.4	14.0	57.2	11.8	36.6
Expenditure on litigation	0.0	0.1	0.0	0.1	0.0	0.1
Repayment of debt	0.4	1.9	0.5	2.5	0.4	2.0
Financial investment	0.1	0.2	0.1	0.7	0.1	0.4
Expenditure others	1.5	7.5	1.4	12.0	1.4	8.8
All non-business expenditure in household	12.0	38.0	15.8	72.4	13.5	47.9
All	22.4	100.0	18.4	100.0	20.8	100.0

Source: Household Borrowings and Repayments in India.2002 – 03, All -India Debt and Investment Survey NSS 59th Round Jan-Dec 2003, NSSO, January 2006.

Table 5.24 shows that "household expenditure" was the most frequently reported reason for taking loans in the rural areas. It may be noted that the term "household expenditure" has been used above in a broad sense as it included expenditure on purchase of residential land, building, construction, renovation of building, etc. The second most frequently reported reason for borrowing money was "expenditure in farm business (including both capital and current)" (68 per cent) in the rural areas, incidence of borrowings for other specified reasons were insignificant in he rural areas- the proportion being less than or equal to 1 percent for each of the other reasons. It is necessary to mention here that these percentage figures should be assessed in relation to overall percentage of households reporting borrowings, which was 20.8 per cent in the rural areas. Although fewer borrowings may be made for a particular purpose, the average amount of borrowings may be large enough to affect the importance to that purpose, especially in the allocation of funds for advancing loans by the financial institutions. In this respect, the percentage shares of the amounts of borrowings by different purposes in the total volume of borrowings provide a measure of their relative importance. The estimates of these percentage shares (S) during 2002-03 by occupational categories have been presented in table 5.24 for the rural areas.

Shift in Borrowings According to Purposes:

In order to study the changes in the distribution of aggregate borrowings by purposes on the basis of results of different AIDIS rounds, the percentage shares of borrowings for different purposes during the four periods 1971-72, 1981-82, 1991-91 and 2002-03, have been presented for the rural areas in table 5.25.

Table 5.25 Percentage Share of Amount of Borrowings by Purpose (All India) Rural

Purpose of Borrowing	1971-72	1981-82	1991-92	2002-03
Farm Business:				
Capital exp	18.3	25.9	9.3	15.6
Current exp	15.1	25.5	3.6	22.4
Non-Farm Business:				
Capital exp	1.6	9.8	5.7	9.7
Current exp	2.0	3.7	1.7	4.3
Productive Purposes	37.0	64.9	20.3	52.1
Other purpose	63.0	35.1	79.7	47.9
All purpose	100.0	100.0	100.0	100.0

Source: Household Borrowings and Repayments in India.2002 – 03, All- India Debt and Investment Survey NSS 59th Round Jan-Dec 2003, NSSO, January 2006.

From the survey results, it appears that prominent change in the rural areas occurred in the share of borrowings made for productive purposes, which oscillated over the four points of time. The share which was 37 per cent in 1971-72, rose to the highest level of 64.9 per cent in 1981-82 and then, suffered drastically a fall of more than 44 percentage points in 1991-92 followed by a gain of nearly 32 percentage points in 2002-03. This could perhaps be due to the different procedure followed in the 48th round, from that in the earlier rounds, to record the different purposes for which loans were taken by households. Note that code structure used for collection of data on "purpose of loan" was exactly the same for the 26th, 37th & 59th rounds was arrived at by cross classifying data on "purpose of loan" (3 codes) and "type of expenditure" (14 codes) collected through two independent questions. The decline or rise appears to stem from a greater or smaller portion of TCB being used to meet all household expenditure, whose percentage shares at these points were 63, 35, 80 and 48, respectively.

SECTION-II
THEORY OF ASYMMETRIC INFORMATION

5.3 Theory of Asymmetric Information

An attempt to explain the puzzle of rural poor borrowing at very high rates of interest from the local moneylender rather than from the local bank at a much lower interest rate, led to the emergence of the theory of asymmetric information Hoff Karla and Joseph E. Stiglitz (1990). The theory of asymmetric information states that informal sector lending thrives due to the advantage it has over formal sector regarding the sources of information about its prospective clients and the credit worthiness of clients. As pointed out by Stiglitz and Weiss, due to asymmetric information, the targeted loans may fail to reach target households Stiglitz-Joseph E., and Anren Weiss, (1981). Therefore, financial institutions may need to address the concern of imperfect information to reach the rural poor. Financing through groups can be used by the formal credit market to overcome its informational disadvantage to lend successfully to the poor borrowers S. Madheswaran and Amita Dharmadhikary, (2001). Many microcredit programmes rely on group based lending to resolve the problem of imperfect information. Using a group-based approach to lending, the country's small-scale microcredit programs provide more credit than the traditional financial institutions in rural areas World Bank (1996).

Group lending may help to identify target households better than individual lending. Individual lending can "perpetuate and reinforce the existing socio-economic inequities and access to scarce financial resources" Yaron Jacob (1992). In contrast, group lending can help the poor self-select programs, making it a powerful instrument of identification and targeting Khandker Shahidur R, Baqui Khalily and Zahed Khar, (1995). In the available literature, it is well documented that many microcredit programs have attained the out reach objective of reaching a large number of clients with small amounts of resources Bernett Lynn, Mike Goldberg and Pamela Hunte, (1996); Dersing Maryket, (1990); Hossain Mahabub, (1988); Hulme David and Paul Mosely, (1996). Government-directed financial institutions have been developed in order to provide the poor with access to credit. One of the examples for this is SHG-Bank linkage programme sponsored by the NABARD. Hence, the pertinent questions are what type of information or what factors are crucial in order to provide the poor with access to credit from these sources? and who are really getting access to credit from group lending?

The factors, which will limit the access of the rural poor for formal credit, are well discussed from the angle of the rationing mechanism Manfred Zeller, (1994). The most important factor is the physical collateral such as land, which will be considered by the formal lender assessing the borrowers" credit worthiness. In other words, the demand for physical collateral limits the access of the rural poor like landless farmers, wage labourers, small holders and small-scale rural entrepreneurs to formal sources of credit. On the other hand, informal lenders substitute third-party guarantees, tied contracts, etc. for physical collateral. The rural poor due to their social contracts provide these substitutes which reflect easy access to informal sources. These collateral substitutes depend on the ability of the lender to obtain information about the creditworthiness of the borrower, at a lower cost. The recent innovative policy of group lending by the formal sources has taken into consideration the joint liability in place of physical collateral. Hence, the disadvantages of the poor i.e., lack of physical assets, has been overcome by the group lending.

Now, the interesting aspect is which factors influence the group member's access to the group loan? Can the microcredit be an alternative to informal credit in rural areas?

The above mentioned theoretical arguments are all related to the supply side of the credit. Coming to the demand side of the credit, the access of the rural poor is limited by the mismatch between the demand and supply of credit structures. The rural poor generally demand credit in small amounts for non-productive purposes like consumption, health, education, marriages, petty production, petty trade, etc. This does not match with the supply menu of banks, which consists of large amounts of loan for production purposes. It is not the rigidity of the banks but their constraints due to high transaction costs and risk because of asymmetric information that they cannot extent such credit to individual borrowers. Individual borrowers on the other hand, face the problems of absorbing large amounts of credit for some unwanted purpose. Loan contract therefore does not take place between an individual small borrower and a formal lender basically because of a mismatch between demand and supply of credit structure. Through group lending this mismatch between demand and supply is reduced because the bank extends credit in lump sum amounts and the group uses the amount according to its own needs Rajraram Dasgupta, (2001).

Therefore, the questions are: (i) which demand side factors will influence the access of the rural poor for the formal credit through groups? (ii) Has the microcredit increased access to institutional credit, thereby reducing borrowing from informal sources? And (iii) Can microcredit supplements the formal credit in meeting the credit needs of the rural poor? In the succeeding section, an attempt is made to answer the above questions by a comparative analysis between formal, informal and microcredit.

SECTION-III
STRUCTURE OF BORROWINGS OF THE SAMPLE HOUSEHOLDS

5.4.1 Structure of Borrowings of the Sample Households:

In this section, an attempt has been made to analyze the borrowings of sample households in the study area, with reference to the purpose of borrowing, agencies involved, rate of interest at which loans are borrowed and the nature of security offered. To know the factors influencing borrowings from different agencies, two groups of households (OSHG and NSHG) were selected from Visakhapatnam district in Andhra Pradesh. The major objective behind this classification is to assess whether access to microcredit has reduced the dependence of poor on informal credit agencies in rural areas.

Deficit of Income over Expenditure

To estimate the burden of debt, it is necessary to relate the incomes to the expenditure of the household. After arriving at the deficit of income over expenditure, one can estimate the burden of debt of the households. Where there is no deficit of income over expenditure, it doesn"t mean that these households are free from debt burden. Generally in poor families, the income-expenditure gap is a time-lagged phenomenon. Past expenditures and/or liabilities are met with the surplus of the present income. The borrowings will act as a bridge to meet this time-lagged gap between income and expenditure. To begin with, the distributions of households by levels of deficit have been worked out for all the sample households because it is the deficit of income over expenditure that largely reflects the need to borrow. The details are presented in table -5.26.

Table 5.26 Distribution of Households by Percentage of Deficit

Percentage of deficit	OSHG	NSHG	All
Nil	49.5	54.0	51.8
Below 15	22.0	15.5	18.7
15 to30	9.0	7.0	8.0
31 to 45	5.5	9.5	7.5
Above 45	14.0	14.0	14.0
Total	100.0 (200)	100.0 (200)	100.0 (400)

Source: Field survey

Figure - 5.5 Percentage of Deficit of Income over Expenditure among Rural Households

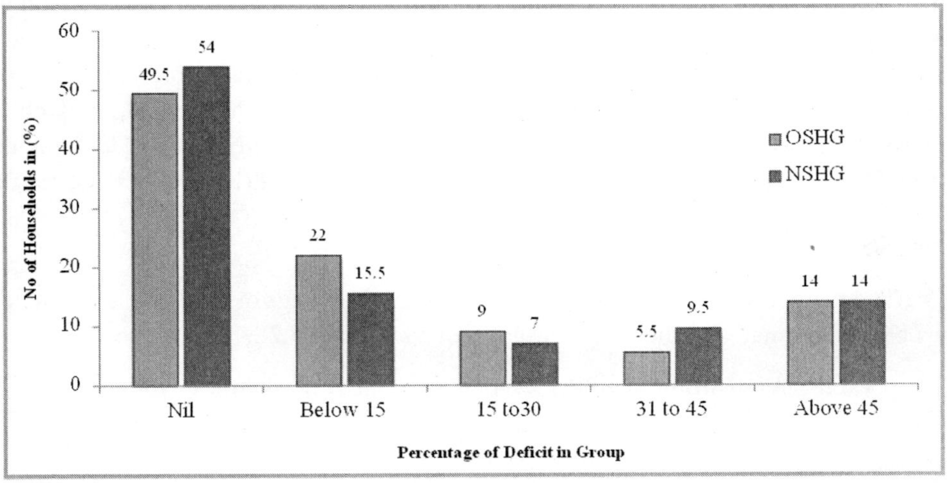

It could be observed from the above table that, the percentage of households without any deficit is 54 among the NSHG households and 49.5 in the OSHG households. Further, the proportion of households in the deficit range of below 15 is comparatively higher in OSHG (22) than NSHG (15.5) households.

Extent and Magnitude of Credit

Data regarding the borrowings of the sample households during the past three years, (from the beginning of the period of study) were collected to iron out the annual differences. The average amount of credit by the rural poor and the relative proportion of different sources are presented in Table -5.27.

Table 5.27 Distribution of the Average Amount of Borrowings by Source

Source of Credit	OSHG	NSHG	All
Micro Credit	65.7 (40,705)	61.8 (26,252)	63.8 (33,478)
Private Micro Credit	5.4 (2,655)	3.6 (1,750)	4.5 (2,202)
Formal Credit	6.9 (8,485)	6.7 (9,540)	6.8 (9,012)
Informal Credit	22.0 (16,665)	27.9 (18,650)	24.9 (17,657)
Total	100.0 (68,510)	100.0 (56,192)	100.0 (62,351)

Source: Field survey

Note: Figures in brackets are Average amount of Borrowing.

It is clear from the above table that average amount of credit per household was reported at Rs. 68,510/- for the OSHG households and Rs. 56,192/- for the NSHG households. In both the households more than 60 percent of the total credit was from microcredit sources. It can be inferred from the table that through the intervention of microcredit, the formal credit can reach the rural poor and also the demand for credit will increase when credit is made available. The SHG-Bank linkage programme will be a good supplementary to the existing formal credit services, which could do much to improve the welfare of the rural poor and their families. Not only that, prudent linking of SHGs with banks could also increase the demand for credit (Karmakar K.G, 1988).

Distribution of Borrowings by Agency:

The relative share of different agencies in the borrowings of rural poor households has been examined and the details are presented in table 5.28.

Table-5.28 Distribution of the Average Amount of Borrowings by Agency

Type of Credit	Commercial Bank	Co-operative Bank	Private Chit funds	Money Lender	Friends & Relatives	Private Micro finance	Total
			OSHG				
Micro Credit	100.0	-	-	-	-	-	100.0 (40,705)
Private Micro Credit	-	-	-	-	-	100.0	100.0 (2,655)
Formal Credit	76.1	23.9	-	-	-	-	100.0 (8,485)
Informal Credit	-	-	6.6	26.1	67.3	-	100.0 (16,665)
Total	68.9	3.0	1.6	6.4	16.5	3.9	100.0 (68,510)
			NSHG				
Micro Credit	100.0	-	-	-	-	-	100.0 (26,252)
Private Micro Credit	-	-	-	-	-	100.0	100.0 (1,750)
Formal Credit	44.4	55.6	-	-	-	-	100.0 (9,540)
Informal Credit	-	-	14.1	19.7	66.2	-	100.0 (18,650)
Total	54.3	9.4	4.7	6.5	22.0	3.1	100.0 (56,192)
			All				
Micro Credit	100.0	-	-	-	-	-	100.0 (33,478)
Private Micro Credit	-	-	-	-	-	100.0	100.0 (2,202)
Formal Credit	59.4	40.6	-	-	-	-	100.0 (9,012)
Informal Credit	-	-	10.6	22.7	66.7	-	100.0 (17,657)
Total	62.3	5.9	3.0	6.4	18.9	3.5	100.0 (62,351)

Source: Field survey
Note: Figures in brackets are Average amount of borrowings.

In both the households, in case of microcredit, commercial banks have provided the entire credit (100 percent). In formal credit also, commercial banks have provided the highest percentage of borrowings (around 60 percent). In informal sources of credit, friends and relatives have provided the highest percentage of borrowings. There are no significant differences observed between OSHG and NSHG.

Distribution of Borrowings by Purpose:

The excess of expenditure over income largely reflects the need for poor households to borrow. For this purpose, borrowings from microcredit, formal and informal credit sources are examined to bring out sharply the differences in their relative shares in total borrowings. They are shown in table - 5.29.

Table- 5.29 Distribution of the Average Amount of Borrowings by Purpose

Type of Credit	Agrl. Investment & livestock	Trade	Education	Health	H.C & Repair	Con Sump tion	Marriage & cere monies	Repay ment of old debt	Total
				OSHG					
Micro Credit	3.0	35.3	5.5	2.7	8.4	20.5	0.8	23.6	100.0 (40,705)
Private Micro Credit	-	12.2	10.4	7.5	44.3	21.8	3.8	-	100.0 (2,655)
Formal Credit	9.4	11.8	8.8	1.5	37.4	1.6	24.7	-	100.0 (8,485)
Informal Credit	-	19.2	18.0	4.8	18.8	16.3	21.3	1.5	100.0 (16,665)
Total	3.0	27.6	9.1	3.3	15.9	17.2	8.9	14.4	100.0 (68,510)
				NSHG					
Micro Credit	2.5	28.2	1.8	2.8	3.1	41.1	1.1	19.3	100.0 (26,252)
Private Micro Credit	-	44.3	8.6	11.4	5.7	30.0	-	-	100.0 (1,750)
Formal Credit	29.6	5.8	15.5	6.2	26.7	0.5	2.6	7.9	100.0 (9,540)
Informal Credit	3.1	14.7	17.3	6.2	21.2	19.6	18.0	-	100.0 (18,650)
Total	7.3	20.4	9.5	4.7	13.2	26.7	6.9	10.4	100.0 (56,192)
				All					
Micro Credit	2.8	32.4	4.0	2.8	6.3	28.6	0.9	21.9	100.0 (33,478)
Private Micro Credit	-	25.0	9.6	9.1	28.9	25.1	2.3	-	100.0 (2,202)
Formal Credit	20.2	8.6	12.3	4.0	31.8	1.0	13.0	4.2	100.0 (9,012)
Informal Credit	1.6	16.9	17.6	5.5	20.1	18.0	19.5	0.7	100.0 (17,657)
Total	4.9	24.3	9.3	3.7	14.7	21.5	8.0	12.6	100.0 (62,351)

Source: Field survey

Note: Figures in brackets are Average amount of borrowings.

An analysis of borrowings from microcredit and formal credit agencies shows that around 30 percent of borrowings by rural households are for productive purposes such as agriculture, livestock and trade. But in case of informal credit sources only 18.5 percent of borrowings are for productive purposes. There are no significant differences observed between OSHG and NSHG.

Distribution of Borrowings by Rate of Interest:

The present policy of providing microcredit to the poor households for productive purposes and for consumption purposes should have reduced the interest burden of SHG households. This aspect has been examined, taking into consideration the borrowings from formal and informal sources for the SHG groups. Table 5.30 presents the distribution of average amount of credit by rate of interest.

Table- 5.30 Distribution of the Average Amount by Borrowings by Rate of Interest

Source	Less than 12	12 -24	24 -36	36 & above	Total
OSHG					
Micro Credit	100.0	-	-	-	100.0 (40,705)
Private Micro Credit	-	100.0	-	-	100.0 (2,655)
Formal Credit	86.2	8.0	5.9	-	100.0 (8,485)
Informal Credit	2.5	74.5	19.9	3.1	100.0 (16,665)
NSHG					
Micro Credit	100.0	-	-	-	100.0 (26,252)
Private Micro Credit	-	100.0	-	-	100.0 (1,750)
Formal Credit	94.2	5.8	-	-	100.0 (9,540)
Informal Credit	1.9	82.5	13.2	2.4	100.0 (18,650)
ALL					
Micro Credit	100.0	-	-	-	100.0 (33,478)
Private Micro Credit	-	100.0	-	-	100.0 (2,202)
Formal Credit	90.4	6.8	2.8	-	100.0 (9,012)
Informal Credit	2.2	78.7	16.4	2.7	100.0 (17,657)

Source: Field survey

Note: Figures in brackets are Average Amount of Borrowings.

It could be seen from the above table that the entire microcredit borrowings in all rural households are at an interest rate of less than 12 per cent per annum. In the case of formal credit also, 90 per cent of the borrowings are at an interest rate of less than 12 per cent. While in the case of informal credit, around 75 per cent of the borrowings are at an interest rate of 12-24 per cent. There are no significant differences observed between households.

Distribution of Borrowings by Security:

While well-to-do farmers are able to raise funds from formal agencies, the poor find it difficult, as they do not possess any assets worth mentioning to offer as a security. This is evident from the table 5.31.

Table - 5.31 Distribution of Average Amount of Borrowings by type of Security

Type of Credit	Promissory Note	Group Security	Pledge of Gold	Pledge of Land	Pledge of House	Friends and Relatives	Total
OSHG							
Micro Credit		100.0					100.0 (40,705)
Private Micro Credit	5.6	94.4					100.0 (2,655)
Formal Credit			36.1	22.4	41.5		100.0 (8,485)
Informal Credit	84.2	0.2			9.4	6.3	100.0 (16,665)
Total	20.7	63.1	4.5	2.8	7.4	1.5	100.0 (68,510)
NSHG							
Micro Credit		100.0					100.0 (26,252)
Private Micro Credit		100.0					100.0 (1,750)
Formal Credit			25.1	59.7	15.2		100.0 (9,540)
Informal Credit	69.5	0.4		6.7	17.9	5.5	100.0 (18,650)
Total	23.3	48.1	4.8	12.4	9.6	1.8	100.0 (56,192)
All							
Micro Credit		100.0					100.0 (33,478)
Private Micro Credit	3.4	96.6					100.0 (2,202)
Formal Credit			30.2	42.2	27.2		100.0 (9,012)
Informal Credit	76.5	0.3		3.5	13.8	5.8	100.0 (17,657)
Total	21.9	56.3	4.6	7.1	8.4	1.6	100.0 (62,351)

Source: Field survey

Note: Figures in brackets are Average Amount of Borrowings.

It could be seen from the table that group security is the most important means for getting loan from microcredit. It is observed that securities like pledge of gold, land and house are the means for getting a loan from formal credit agencies. In informal credit, promissory note is the most important means for getting a loan.

5.4.2 Factors Influencing Borrowing and Indebtedness and Results of Regression Analysis

Regression methods may be used for time series data considering historical evidence or cross-section data representing the technological relationships. The purpose of regression model is to quantify the degree of effect of each of the variables under consideration, in explaining the variation in the dependent variable. Since our study is based on cross-section data, the regression analysis will help us to identify the significant factors that influence the dependent variable.

Specification of the Variables and Model:

In the study, total amount of borrowings of rural households is the relevant dependent variable. Accordingly, Y is the total borrowings of households. Borrowings include all loans by the households under the study. The following explanatory variables are considered as the important determinants. Age, Literacy level, Earner, Occupational pattern, Size of the family, Asset holdings, Income, Dependency Ratio, Recurring Expenditure and Non- Recurring Expenditure. By considering the above variables, the regression function is adopted and is specified as` under:

Age	=	Age of the respondent
Literacy level	=	Number of Years of Education of the Respondent.
Earner	=	Dummy variable, whether the respondent is working
Occupational pattern	=	Dummy variable, whether the respondent is employee
Size of the family	=	Family size of the house.
Asset holdings	=	Value of Assets owned by the household
Income	=	Income of the household
Dependency ratio	=	Dependency ratio of the household
Recurring Expenditure	=	Food and non food expenditure of the household
Non - Recurring Expenditure	=	Sickness of the family members, ceremonies, etc
Borrowings	=	Total loan amount borrowed (Dependent Variable)

Based on the above variables, a multiple linear regression model is presented as follows:

$$Borrowings\ (Y) = Y=a+ b_1x_1+ b_2x_2+ b_3x_3+ b_4x_4+b_5x_5+.....+b_nx_n+\mu$$

Results of Regression Analysis:

Impact of Microcredit Borrowings on Sample Rural Respondents

Independent variables	OSHG		NSHG		All	
	B	Sig.	B	Sig.	B	Sig.
(Constant)	39984.575* (4.310)	0.000	-3496.384 (-0.243)	0.808	16174.989*** (1.820)	0.069
Age	-161.954*** (-1.614)	0.100	168.433 (1.406)	0.161	105.742 (1.239)	0.216
Literacy level	50.663 (0.202)	0.840	497.432*** (1.835)	0.068	371.669*** (1.821)	0.069
Earner	-2663.321 -.388	0.699	14757.547 (1.258)	0.210	3472.409 (0.505)	0.614
Occupational pattern	1076.310 (0.532)	0.595	5124.571** (2.032)	0.044	3319.558*** (1.863)	0.063
Size of the family	-1162.817 (-1.072)	0.285	-2553.405 (-1.523)	0.129	-1869.916*** (-1.800)	0.073
Asset Holdings	.011 (1.285)	0.200	-.008 (-1.094)	0.275	-0.005 (-0.826)	0.409
Income	0.001 (0.053)	0.958	-0.025 (-0.710)	0.479	0.005 (0.236)	0.814
Dependency Ratio	-2999.023*** (-1.828)	0.069	1508.101 (0.859)	0.392	-34.910 (-0.027)	0.979
Recurring Expenditure	0.088 (0.682)	0.496	0.177 (1.165)	0.245	0.077 (0.728)	0.467
Non-Recurring Expenditure	0.227* (3.342)	0.001	0.177* (2.777)	0.006	0.217* (4.271)	0.000
Observations	200		200		400	
R2	0.157		0.152		0.108	
Adjusted R2	0.112		0.107		0.085	
F-value	3.509*(0.000)		3.367* (0.000)		4.718* (0.000)	

Source: Field survey

Note:* Significant at 1% level, ** Significant at 5% level & *** Significant at 10% level.

Figures in brackets are t –values.

Impact of Microcredit Borrowings on OSHG Households:

Age of the respondent is observed to have a positive relation at Microcredit Borrowings of the sample households. The hypothesis is younger individuals are borrowing more since they have more capacity to repay. The age of the respondent is turned out to be statistically significant with expected negative sign. Literacy level is a variable which is estimated by number of school going years and revealed the literacy status of the respondent and it is expected to have a positive relation. The hypothesis is that the Microcredit Borrowing is more where the literacy level is high and vice-versa. The literacy level is not significant with relation to Microcredit Borrowings among sample households. Earner is a dummy variable and specifies the working capacity of the respondent. It takes value 1 for worker and 0 for non-worker. It is expected to have a positive relation in Microcredit Borrowings since workers are expected to participate in borrowings as they have higher repayment capacity but it is insignificant.

Occupational pattern is a dummy variable and specify the employment status of the respondent. It takes value 1 for household in industry and trade and 0 for construction labour and others. It is expected to have a positive relation as households depending on industry and trade are having more Microcredit Borrowings as they have higher repayment capacity but it is not significant. Size of the Family is a variable considered as number of persons living in a family. The hypothesis indicates that if the family size is large the borrowings will increase and vice-versa. It is expected to have a positive relation in Microcredit borrowings but it indicates insignificant level. Asset holdings represent the value of assets (both fixed and durable property) of the households. It is a quantitative variable, which takes actual value of the asset holdings. It is expected to have a negative relation with the probability to borrow. As the value of asset holdings increases, the need for borrowing decreases but the variables" coefficient indicates positive sign which is contrary to the hypothesis and it is not significant. Income of the sample respondent is expected to have a negative relation with the probability to borrow. The hypothesis is that as the household income increases, the need for borrowing decreases but it is also found to have positive sign and indicates insignificant.

Dependency Ratio represents the ratio of non-working members to the working members and is expected to have positive relation in Microcredit borrowings. The hypothesis is that higher the dependency ratio higher will be the borrowings and vice- versa. The dependency ratio is turned out to be statistically significant with expected negative sign. Recurring Expenditure represents the expenditure on food and non-food items of the sample households, which is expected to have positive relation in Microcredit Borrowings. The identified expenditure on food and non-food items lead to Microcredit Borrowings but it indicates not at significant level. Non-Recurring Expenditure represents the number of events such as sickness of the family members, birth and death ceremonies, marriage functions, etc. occurred in the household. This variable takes a value according to the number of events happened in the household. If the identified incidents are more, expenditure increases which leads to more borrowings. The non-recurring expenditure is turned out to be statistically significant with expected positive sign.

The F-value (3.509) shows that the model is best fit and it is significant at 1 per cent level. The model explains 11.2 percentage of variation. In this model, three variables are found to be significant viz., age, dependency ratio and non-recurring expenditure.

Impact of Microcredit Borrowings on NSHG Households:

Age of the respondent is observed to have a positive relation at Micro credit borrowing of the sample respondent. The hypothesis is older individuals are more borrowing since they have less capacity to repay but this relation is not at significant level. Literacy level is a variable which is estimated by number of school going years and specify the literacy status of the respondent and it is expected to have a positive relation. It is expected that the Microcredit Borrowings are more where the literacy levels are high and vice-versa. The literacy status of the respondent is turned out to be significant with expected positive sign. Earner is a dummy variable and specifies the working capacity of the respondent. It takes value 1 for worker and 0 for non-worker. It is expected to have a positive relation in Microcredit Borrowings since workers are expected to participate in borrowings as they have higher repayment capacity but it indicates not significant.

Occupational pattern is a dummy variable and specifies the employment status of the respondent. It takes value 1 for household working in industry and trade and 0 for construction labour and others. It is expected to have a positive relation as households depending on industry and trade are having more Microcredit Borrowings as they have higher repayment capacity. The Occupational pattern is turned out to be significant with expected positive sign. Size of the Family is a variable considered as number of persons living in a family. The hypothesis indicates that if the family size is large the borrowings will increase and vice-versa. It is expected to have a positive relation in Microcredit borrowings but it has negative sign and indicates insignificant level. Asset holdings represent the value of assets (both fixed and durable property) of the household. It is a quantitative variable, which takes actual value of the asset holdings. It is expected to have a negative relation with the probability to borrow. As the value of asset holdings increases, the need for borrowing decreases. But it shows negative sign and not significant as expected. Income of the sample respondent is expected to have a positive relation with the probability to borrow. It indicates that as the household income increases, the need for borrowing decreases but the sign of the coefficient is negative and insignificant.

Dependency Ratio represents the ratio of non-working members to the working members and is expected to have positive relation in Microcredit borrowings. The hypothesis is higher the dependency ratio higher will be the borrowings and vice-versa but it indicates not significant level. Recurring Expenditure represents the expenditure on food and non-food items of the sample household, which is expected to have positive relation in Microcredit Borrowings. The more expenditure on food and non-food items leads to Microcredit Borrowings. As expected it has positive impact but not significant. Non-Recurring Expenditure represents the number of events such as sickness of the family members, birth and death ceremonies, marriage functions, etc. occurred in the household. This variable takes a value according to the number of events happened in the household. If the identified incidents are more, expenditure increases which leads to more borrowings. The non-recurring expenditure is turned out to be significant with expected positive sign.

The F-value is 3.367 which show that the model is best fit and it is significant at 1 per cent level. The model explains 10.7 percentage of variation. In this model, three variables are found to be significant viz., literacy level, occupational pattern and non- recurring expenditure.

Impact of Microcredit Borrowings on All Households

Age of the respondent is observed to have a positive relation at Microcredit Borrowing of the sample respondent. The hypothesis is older individuals are more Borrowings since they have less capacity to repay but this relation is not at significant level. Literacy level is a variable which is estimated by number of school going years and specify the literacy status of the respondent and it is expected to have a positive relation. It is expected that the Microcredit Borrowings are more where the literacy levels are high and vice-versa. The literacy status of the respondent is turned out to be significant with expected positive sign. Earner is a dummy variable and specifies the working capacity of the respondent. It takes value 1 for worker and 0 for non-worker. It is expected to have a positive relation in Microcredit Borrowings since workers are expected to participate in borrowings as they have higher repayment capacity but this relation is not at significant level.

Occupational pattern is a dummy variable and specifies the employment status of the respondent. It takes value 1 for household working in industry and trade and 0 for construction labour and others. It is expected to have a positive relation as households depending on industry and trade are having more Microcredit Borrowings as they have higher repayment capacity. The Occupational pattern is turned out to be significant with expected positive sign. Size of the Family is a variable considered as number of persons living together in a family. It is expected to have a positive relation in Microcredit borrowings. The hypothesis indicates that if the family size is large the borrowings will increase and vice-versa. The size of the family is turned out to be significant with expected negative sign. Asset holdings represent the value of assets (both fixed and durable property) of the household. It is a quantitative variable, which takes actual value of the asset holdings. It is expected to have a negative relation with the probability to borrow. As the value of asset holdings increases, the need for borrowing decreases. But it has negative impact and insignificant. Income of the sample respondent is expected to have a negative relation with the probability to borrow. The hypothesis is that as the household income increases, the need for borrowing decreases but it shows positive sign and it indicates not significant.

Dependency Ratio represents the ratio of non-working members to the working members and is expected to have positive relation in Microcredit borrowings. The hypothesis is higher the dependency ratio higher will be the borrowings and vice-versa but it indicates not significant. Recurring Expenditure represents the expenditure on food and non-food items of the sample household, which is expected to have positive relation in Microcredit Borrowings. The increasing expenditure on food and non-food items lead to more Microcredit Borrowings but it has positive impact and not significant. Non- Recurring Expenditure represents the number of events such as sickness of the family members, birth and death ceremonies, marriage functions, etc. occurred in the household. This variable takes a value according to the number of events happened in the household. If the identified incidents are more the expenditure increase which leads to more borrowings. The non-recurring expenditure is turned out to be significant with expected positive sign.

The F-value is 4.718 and indicates that the model is best fit and it is significant at 1 per cent level. The model explains 8.5 percentage of variation. In this model, four variables are found to be significant viz., literacy level, occupational pattern, size of the family and non-recurring expenditure.

Impact of Formal Credit Borrowings on Rural Sample Respondents

Independent variables	OSHG		NSHG		All	
	B	Sig.	B	Sig.	B	Sig.
(Constant)	55380.869*** (1.932)	0.060	39531.108 (0.654)	0.519	24722.465 (0.468)	0.641
Age	96.273 (0.325)	0.747	-960.403 (-0.771)	0.448	-225.573 (-0.447)	0.656
Literacy level	203.706 (0.281)	0.780	1624.282 (0.664)	0.513	121.861 (0.118)	0.906
Earner	-2663.321 (-0.335)	0.739	omitted	omitted	-2273.409 (-0.054)	0.957
Occupational pattern	737.403 (0.127)	0.900	-43528.181*** (-1.727)	0.097	-8380.442 (-0.834)	0.407
Size of the family	-6151.181*** (-1.927)	0.061	1522.530 (0.123)	0.903	3184.299 (0.629)	0.531
Asset Holdings	0.008 (0.313)	0.756	-0.025 (-0.452)	0.655	0.018 (0.651)	0.517
Income	0.124 (1.364)	0.180	-0.256 (-0.892)	0.381	0.028 (0.216)	0.830
Dependency Ratio	-1023.293 (-0.212)	0.833	8280.844 (0.406)	0.688	-3574.258 (-0.463)	0.644
Recurring Expenditure	-0.817** (-2.434)	0.019	1.384 (1.299)	0.206	-0.096 (-0.223)	0.824
Non-Recurring Expenditure	0.419** (2.207)	0.033	0.569*** (1.792)	0.086	0.394** (2.119)	0.037
Observations	51		34		85	
R2	0.333		0.346		0.133	
Adjusted R2	0.167		0.101		0.016	
F-value	2.000** (0.059)		1.412 (0.238)		1.136 (0.348)	

Source: Field survey

Note:* Significant at 1% level, ** Significant at 5% level & *** Significant at 10% level.

Figures in brackets are t -values.

Impact of Formal Credit Borrowings on OSHG Households

Age of the respondent is expected to have a positive relation with formal credit borrowings. The hypothesis is that the older individuals are borrowing less since they have less capacity to repay but it indicates not significant. Literacy level is a variable which is estimated by number of school going years and specifies the literacy status of the respondent and it is expected to have a positive relation. It is expected that the formal credit Borrowing are more where the literacy levels are high and vice-versa but it is not significant. Earner is a dummy variable and specifies the working capacity of the respondent. It takes value 1 for worker and 0 for non-worker. It is expected to have a positive relation in formal credit Borrowings since workers are expected to participate in borrowings as they have higher repayment capacity but it indicates not at significant level.

Occupational pattern is a dummy variable and specifies the employment status of the respondent. It takes value 1 for household who are working in industry and trade and 0 for construction labour and others. It is expected to have a positive relation as households depending on industry and trade are having more Formal credit Borrowings as they have higher repayment capacity but it indicates not significant. Size of the Family is a variable considered as number of persons living together in a family. The hypothesis indicates that if the family size is large the borrowings will increase and vice- versa. It is expected to have a positive relation in formal credit borrowings and is turned out to be significant with negative sign. Asset holdings represent the value of assets (both fixed and durable property) of the households. It is a quantitative variable, which takes actual value of the asset holdings. It is expected to have a negative relation with the probability to borrow but it indicates not at significant level. Income of the sample respondent is expected have a negative relation with the probability to borrow. It indicates that as the household income increases the need for borrowing decreases but it indicates not at significant level.

Dependency Ratio represents the ratio of non-working members to the working members and is expected to have positive relation in formal borrowings. It indicates that higher the dependency ratio higher will be the borrowings and vive-versa but it shows positive sign and not significant. Recurring Expenditure represents the expenditure on food and non-food items of the sample household, which is expected to positive relation with formal borrowing of the respondents. It indicates that more expenditure leads to more borrowings. The recurring expenditure is turned out to be significant with expected negative sign. Non- Recurring Expenditure represents the number of events such as sickness of the family members, birth and death ceremonies, marriage functions, etc. in the household. This variable takes a value according to the number of events happened in the household. If the existence of incidents is more, expenditure increases which leads to more borrowings. The non-recurring expenditure is turned out to be significant with expected positive sign.

The F-vale (2.000) shows that the model is best fit which is significant at 5 per cent level. The model explains 16.7 percentage of variation. In this model, three variables are found to be significant viz., Size of the Family, recurring expenditure and non-recurring expenditure.

Impact of Formal Credit Borrowings on NSHG Households

Age of the respondent is expected to have a positive relation with formal credit borrowings. The hypothesis is that the older individuals are borrowing less since they have less capacity to repay but it indicates not significant. Literacy level is a variable which is estimated by number of school going years and specifies the literacy status of the respondent and it is expected to have a positive relation. It is expected that the formal credit Borrowing are more where the literacy levels are high and vice-versa but it shows insignificant.

Occupational pattern is a dummy variable and specifies the employment status of the respondent. It takes value 1 for household working in industry and trade and 0 for construction labour and others. It is expected to have a positive relation as households depending on industry and trade are having more Formal credit Borrowings as they have higher repayment capacity. The Occupational pattern is turned out to be significant with expected negative sign. Size of the Family is a variable considered as number of persons living together in a family. The hypothesis indicates that if the family size is large the borrowings will increase and vice-versa. It is expected to have a positive relation in Formal credit borrowings. Even though the sign of the coefficient is as expected but it is not significant. Asset holdings represent the value of assets (both fixed and durable property) of the households. It is a quantitative variable, which takes actual value of the asset holdings. It is expected to have a negative relation with the probability to borrow. As the value of asset holdings increases, the need for borrowing decreases but the sign of the coefficient is negative and it is insignificant. Income of the sample respondent is expected to have a negative relation with the probability to borrow. It indicates that as the household income increases the need for borrowing decreases but it indicates insignificant level.

Dependency Ratio represents the ratio of non-working members to the working members and is expected to have positive relation in formal borrowings. It indicates that higher the dependency ratio higher will be the borrowings and vice-versa but it reveal not significant. Recurring Expenditure represents the expenditure on food and non-food items of the sample households, which is expected to have positive relation with formal borrowing of the respondents. Though it indicates that more expenditure leads to more borrowings, it is not significant. Non-Recurring Expenditure represents the number of events such as sickness of the family members, birth and death ceremonies, marriage functions, etc. in the households. This variable takes a value according to the number of events happened in the household. The identified incidents occurred more than expenditure increases which lead to more borrowings. The non-recurring expenditure is turned out to be significant with expected positive sign.

In this model the F value is 1.412. The model explains 10.1 percentage of variation. In this model, two variables are found to be significant viz., occupational pattern and non-recurring expenditure.

Impact of Formal Credit Borrowings on All Households

Age of the respondent is expected to have a positive relation with formal credit borrowings. The hypothesis is that the older individuals are borrowing less since they have less capacity to repay but it indicates not at significant level. Literacy level is a variable which is estimated by number of school going years and specifies the literacy status of the respondent and it is expected to have a positive relation. Though, it is expected that the formal credit Borrowing are more where the literacy levels are high and vice-versa, it insignificant. Earner is a dummy variable and specifies the working capacity of the respondent. It takes value 1 for worker and 0 for non-worker. It is expected to have a positive relation in formal credit Borrowings since workers are expected to participate in borrowings as they have higher repayment capacity but it specifies not significant.

Occupational pattern is a dummy variable and specifies the employment status of the respondents. It takes value 1 for household working in industry and trade and 0 for construction labour and others. It is expected to have a positive relation as household working in industry and trade are having more Formal credit Borrowings as they have higher repayment capacity than the others but it shows insignificant. Size of the Family is a variable considered as number of persons living together in a family. The hypothesis indicates that if the family size is large the borrowings will increase and vice-versa. It is expected to have a positive relation in Formal credit borrowings but it is not significant. Asset holdings represent the value of assets (both fixed and durable property) of the households. It is a quantitative variable, which takes actual value of the asset holdings. It is expected to have a negative relation with the probability to borrow. As the value of asset holdings increases, the need for borrowing decreases but the sign of the coefficient turns out to be positive and not significant. Income of the sample respondent is expected to have a negative relation with the probability to borrow. It indicates that as the household income increases the need for borrowing decreases, but it indicates not at significant level.

Dependency Ratio represents the ratio of non-working members to the working members and is expected to have a positive relation in formal borrowings. It indicates that higher the dependency ratio higher will be the borrowings and vice-versa but it indicates not significant. Recurring Expenditure represents the expenditure on food and non-food items of the sample households, which is expected to have a positive relation with formal borrowing of the respondents. It indicates that more expenditure leads to more borrowings. The identified expenditure on food and non-food items lead to Formal credit Borrowings but it indicates not significant. Non-Recurring Expenditure represents the number of events such as sickness of the family members, birth and death ceremonies, marriage functions, etc. in the households. This variable takes a value according to the number of events happened in the household. If the identified incidents are more, expenditure increases which leads to more borrowings. The non-recurring expenditure is turned out to be significant with expected positive sign.

In this model the F value is 1.136. The model explains 1.6 percentage of variation. In this model, only one variable is found to be significant viz., non-recurring expenditure.

Impact of Informal credit Borrowings on Sample Rural Respondents

Independent Variables	OSHG		NSHG		All	
	B	Sig.	B	Sig.	B	Sig.
(Constant)	13531.442 (0.331)	0.742	-40048.968 (-1.270)	0.207	-1415.085 (-0.056)	0.956
Age	-151.607 (-0.434)	0.665	222.250 (0.743)	0.459	-110.050 (-0.480)	0.632
Literacy level	-50.421 (-0.058)	0.954	-127.873 (-0.191)	0.849	-439.149 (-0.801)	0.424
Earner	1711.249 (0.046)	0.963	14009.360 (0.585)	0.560	6534.327 (0.311)	0.756
Occupational pattern	4116.689 (0.591)	0.555	-3108.648 (-0.510)	0.611	2274.002 (0.478)	0.633
Size of the family	1385.343 (0.347)	0.729	-4879.662 (-1.174)	0.243	3184.299 (0.629)	0.837
Asset Holdings	-0.018 (-0.671)	0.503	0.077* (2.983)	0.003	0.018 (0.651)	0.114
Income	0.191*** (1.644)	0.103	0.066 (0.781)	0.436	0.028 (0.216)	0.351
Dependency Ratio	228.900 (0.044)	0.965	817.241 (0.180)	0.858	-3574.258 (-0.463)	0.790
Recurring Expenditure	-0.647 (-1.530)	0.129	-0.373 (-0.946)	0.346	-0.096** (-0.223)	0.042
Non-Recurring Expenditure	0.438** (2.044)	0.043	1.332* (6.723)	0.000	0.394* (2.119)	0.000
Observations	123		125		248	
R^2	0.089		0.355		0.169	
Adjusted R^2	0.008		0.407		0.134	
F-value	1.098 (0.370)		7.823* (0.000)		4.817* (0.000)	

Source: Field survey

Note:* Significant at 1% level, ** Significant at 5% level & *** Significant at 10% level.

Figures in brackets are t -values.

Impact of Informal Credit Borrowings on OSHG Households

Age of the respondent is observed to have a negative relation with Informal credit borrowings of the sample respondent. The hypothesis is older individuals are borrowing less since they have less capacity to repay but it indicates not significant. Literacy level is a variable which is estimated by number of school going years and specifies the literacy status of the respondent. The literacy level is expected to have a negative relation to borrowings. It indicates that the Informal credit Borrowings are less where the literacy level is high and vice-versa but it indicates insignificant. Earner is a dummy variable and specifies the working capacity of the respondent. It takes value 1 for worker and 0 for non-worker. It is expected to have a positive relation in Informal credit borrowings since earners are expected to participate in borrowings as they have higher repayment capacity but it shows insignificant level.

Occupational pattern is a dummy variable and specifies the employment status of the respondents. It takes value 1 for household working in industry and trade and 0 for construction labour and others. Though, it is expected to have a positive relation as households engaging in industry and trade are having more repayment capacity than the others, it indicates not significant. Size of the Family is a variable considered as number of persons living together in a family. It is expected to have a positive relation in informal credit borrowings. It indicates that if the family size is large the borrowings will increase and vice-versa but it reveal that it is not significant. Asset holdings represent the value of assets (both fixed and durable property) of the households. It is a quantitative variable, which takes actual value of the asset holdings. It is expected to have a negative relation with the probability to borrow. As the value of asset holdings increases, the need for borrowing decreases but it specifies insignificant. Income of the sample respondent is expected to have a negative relation with the probability to borrow. It indicates that as the household income increases, the need for borrowing decreases. The income of the sample respondent is turned out to be significant with negative sign which is contrary to hypothesis.

Dependency Ratio represents the ratio of non-working members to the working members and is expected to have positive relation on Informal credit Borrowings. It indicates that higher the dependency ratio higher will be the borrowings and vice-versa but it indicates not significant. Recurring Expenditure represents the expenditure on food and non-food items of the sample households and is expected to have a positive relation in Informal credit Borrowings. The identified incident of recurring expenditure lead to Informal credit borrowings turns out to be negative and it is not at significant relation. Non-Recurring Expenditure represents the number of events such as sickness of the family members, birth and death ceremonies, marriage functions, etc. occurred in the households and is expected to have positive relation in Informal credit borrowings. The identified incident of non-recurring expenditure leads to more Informal credit borrowing and it indicates significant with expected positive sign.

In this model the F value is 1.098. The model explains 0.08 percentage of variation. In this model, two variables are found to be significant viz., income and non- recurring expenditure.

Impact of Informal Credit Borrowings on NSHG Households:

Age of the respondent is observed to have a negative relation with Informal credit borrowings of the sample respondents. The hypothesis is older individuals are borrowing less since they have less capacity to repay but it indicates not significant. Literacy level is a variable which is estimated by number of school going years and specifies the literacy status of the respondent.The literacy level is expected to have a negative relation to borrowings. It indicates that the Informal credit Borrowings are less where the literacy level is high and vice-versa but it shows insignificant. Earner is a dummy variable and specifies the working capacity of the respondent. It takes value 1 for worker and 0 for non-worker. It is expected to have a positive relation in Informal credit borrowings since earners are expected to participate in borrowings as they have higher repayment capacity. Though the coefficient sign is as expected but it indicates not significant.

Occupational pattern is a dummy variable and specifies the employment status of the respondents. It takes value 1 for household working in industry and trade and 0 for construction labour and others. It is expected to have a positive relation as households engaging in industry and trade are having more repayment capacity than the others. The sign of the coefficient is not as expected and also it is not significant. Size of the Family is a variable considered as number of persons living together in a family. It is expected to have a positive relation in informal credit borrowings. It indicates that if the family size is large the borrowings will increase and vice-versa but it indicates negative sing as well as it is not significant. Asset holdings represent the value of asset holdings (both fixed and durable property) of the sample household. It is a quantitative variable, which takes actual value of the asset holdings of the sample households. It is expected to have a negative relation with the probability to borrow. As the value of asset holdings increases, the need for borrowing decreases. Though, the coefficient of asset holding of the sample respondent is turned out to be significant but it has negative sign which is contrary to hypothesis. Income of the sample respondent is expected to have a negative relation with the probability to borrow. It indicates that as the household income increases, the need for raising credit decreases but it indicates positive sign and also not significant.

Dependency Ratio represents the number of household members who are depending on the other members earnings, which is expected to have positive effect on Informal credit Borrowing. It indicates that higher the dependency ratio higher will be the borrowings and vice-versa but it indicates positive sign and not significant. Recurring Expenditure represents the expenditure on food and non-food items of the sample households, and is expected to have positive relation in Informal credit Borrowings. The identified incident of recurring expenditure lead to Informal credit borrowings but it has negative sing and also not significant relation. Non-Recurring Expenditure represents the number of events such as sickness of the family members, birth and death ceremonies, marriage functions, etc. occurred in the households and is expected to have positive relation in Informal credit borrowings. The identified incident of non-recurring expenditure leads to more Informal credit borrowing and it indicates positive sign and significant.

This F-value (7.823) of the model shows that it is best fit which is significant at 1 per cent level. The model explains 40.7 percentage of variation. In this model two variables are found to be significant viz., asset holdings and non-recurring expenditure.

Impact of Informal Credit Borrowings on All Households:

Age of the respondent is observed to have a negative relation with Informal credit borrowings of the sample respondents. The hypothesis is older individuals are borrowing less since they have less capacity to repay but it indicates not significant. Literacy level is a variable which is estimated by number of school going years and specifies the literacy status of the respondent. The literacy level is expected to have a negative relation to borrowings. It indicates that the Informal credit Borrowings are less where the literacy level is high and vice-versa. The coefficient sign is as expected but not significant. Earner is a dummy variable and specifies the working capacity of the respondent. It takes value 1 for worker and 0 for non-worker. It is expected to have a positive relation in Informal credit borrowings since earners are expected to participate in borrowings as they have higher repayment capacity. Though the coefficient sign is expected it is not significant.

Occupational pattern is a dummy variable and specifies the employment status of the respondent. It takes value 1 for household working in industry and trade and 0 for construction labour and others. It is expected to have a positive relation as households engaging in industry and trade are having more repayment capacity than the others but it indicates not at significant level. Size of the Family is a variable considered as number of persons living together in a family. It is expected to have a positive relation in informal credit borrowings. It indicates that if the family size is large the borrowings will increase and vice-versa. The coefficient sign is as expected and it indicates not significant. Asset holdings represent the value of assets (both fixed and durable property) of the households. It is a quantitative variable, which takes actual value of the asset holdings. It is expected to have a negative relation with the probability to borrow. As the value of asset holdings increases, the need for borrowing decreases but it shows positive sign and it is not significant. Income of the sample respondent is expected to have a negative relation with the probability to borrow. It indicates that as the household income increases, the need for raising credit decreases but it indicates positive sign and not significant.

Dependency Ratio represents the number of household members who are depending on the other members earnings, which is expected to have positive effect on Informal credit Borrowing. It indicates that higher the dependency ratio higher will be the borrowings and vice-versa but it indicates negative sign and not significant. Recurring Expenditure represents the expenditure on food and non-food items of the sample households, which is expected to have positive relation in Informal credit Borrowings. The identified incident of expenditure on food items lead to increase in informal credit borrowing, in the case of rural respondents but it indicates significant with negative sign. Non-Recurring Expenditure represents the number of events such as sickness of the family members, birth and death ceremonies, marriage functions, etc. occurred in the households and is expected to have positive relation in Informal credit borrowings. The identified incident of non-recurring expenditure leads to more Informal credit borrowing and it indicates significant with expected positive sign.

The F-value (4.817) shows that the model is best fit which is significant at 1 per cent level. The model explains 13.4 percentage of variation. In this model two variables are found to be significant viz., recurring expenditure and non-recurring expenditure.

SECTION IV
REPAYMENT PERFORMANCE OF THE LOANS

5.5.1 Repayment Performance of the Loans:

In this section the repayment performance of households towards microcredit, formal and informal credit sources are examined. An attempt is also made in this section to study the factors influencing repayment performance of borrowers through regression analysis. In general, the formal loan repayments are postponed in preference to the informal loans. This is attributable to the proximity between the lender and the borrower in respect of informal loans compared to the formal loans. The proximity between the lender and the borrower was also noticed in respect of microcredit. In group-lending programmes, the functions of screening, monitoring and enforcement of repayment are to a large extent transferred from the formal lender to the borrowers i.e., the group members themselves.

In this context, the repayment pattern of micro, formal and informal credit by sample households was studied and is shown in table 5.32. It may be observed from the table that the repayment performance in respect of microcredit and private microcredit accounted for 57.58 percent and 52.40 percent. In respect of formal credit the repayment is only 30.29 percent. In informal credit source also the repayment is low i.e., 37.27 percent in all households.

Table 5.32 Repayment Performance of Borrowers

Amount Borrowed (Rs.)					Amount Repaid (Rs.)					Amount Outstanding (Rs.)			
Micro Credit	Private Micro Credit	Formal Credit	Informal Credit	Total	Micro Credit	Private Micro Credit	Formal Credit	Informal Credit	Total	Micro Credit	Formal Credit	Informal Credit	Total
OSHG													
8141000	531000	1697000	3333000	13702000	4731900	276300	597000	1574500	7179700	3409100	1100000	1758500	6522300
(100.00)	(100.00)	(100.00)	(100.00)	(100.00)	(58.12)	(52.03)	(35.18)	(47.24)	(52.40)	(41.88)	(64.82)	(52.76)	(47.60)
NSHG													
5250500	350000	1908000	3730000	11238500	2978700	185350	495000	1057550	4716600	2271800	1413000	2672450	6521900
(100.00)	(100.00)	(100.00)	(100.00)	(100.00)	(56.73)	(52.96)	(25.94)	(28.35)	(41.97)	(43.27)	(74.06)	(71.65)	(58.03)
ALL													
13391500	881000	3605000	7063000	24940500	7710600	461650	1092000	2632050	11896300	5680900	2513000	4430950	13044200
(100.00)	(100.00)	(100.00)	(100.00)	(100.00)	(57.58)	(52.40)	(30.29)	(37.27)	(47.70)	(42.42)	(69.71)	(62.73)	(52.30)

Source: Field survey

Note: Figures in brackets indicate percentages.

Repayment of Loans by Source of Finance:

Repayment of loan is a problem for the poor largely because of their deficit budgets. Accordingly, the repayment of loans by source towards microcredit, private micro credit, formal and informal credit and the relative share of these sources for all households are studied and presented in table-5.33.

Table - 5.33 Percentage Distribution of Repayment of Loans: Source-wise

Source of Income	Micro Credit	Private Micro Credit	Formal Credit	Informal Credit	Total
OSHG					
Wage Income	37.7	43.9	38.5	38.0	38.1
Crop Income	1.0	-	1.9	-	0.8
Salary	19.0	22.0	19.2	15.7	18.4
Household industry	31.2	20.0	29.4	27.3	31.9
Trade	11.1	14.1	11.0	19.1	10.6
Total	100.0 (47,31,900)	100.0 (2,76,300)	100.0 (5,97,000)	100.0 (15,74,500)	100.0 (71,79,700)
NSHG					
Wage Income	31.2	25.9	12.0	43.5	33.1
Crop Income	7.0	-	58.0	2.9	9.0
Salary	22.4	18.5	14.0	12.6	19.0
Household industry	21.3	34.6	9.5	19.0	21.5
Trade	18.1	21.0	6.5	22.1	17.4
Total	100.0 (2978700)	100.0 (1,85,350)	100.0 (4,95,000)	100.0 (10,57,550)	100.0 (47,16,600)
ALL					
Wage Income	34.6	36.8	25.5	41.0	35.6
Crop Income	3.9	-	29.4	1.6	4.9
Salary	20.6	20.6	16.7	13.9	18.7
Household industry	25.5	26.6	19.2	27.5	29.6
Trade	15.4	16.0	9.2	15.9	11.2
Total	100.0 (77,10,600)	100.0 (4,61,650)	100.0 (10,92,000)	100.0 (26,32,050)	100.0 (1,18,96,300)

Source: Field survey

Note: Figures in brackets indicate amount in Rupees

It can be observed from the table that in all households, in respect of microcredit, private microcredit, formal and informal credit, income from household industry and trade is the major source of repayment of loans borrowed, followed by income from wage. There are no significant differences between OSHG and NSHG.

Repayment of Loans by Purpose of Borrowing:

The repayment performance of a borrower depends largely upon the purpose for which the loan is contracted. Loans taken for productive purposes usually generate additional income thereby enhancing the repaying capacity of the borrowers. The loans taken for unproductive purposes, on the other hand, do not generate any income and result in debt burden. Keeping in view the above aspects, the repayment performance of all households from microcredit, private microcredit, formal and informal credit sources has been examined with reference to purpose of borrowing and is presented in tables - 5.34 A, B & C.

Table – 5.34A Repayment of Loans by Purpose of Borrowing (OSHG)

Purpose	Micro Credit		Private Micro Credit		Formal Credit		Informal Credit	
	Amount Borrowed	Amount Repaid	Amount Borrowed	Amount Repaid	Amount Borrowed	Amount Repaid	Amount Borrowed	Amount Repaid
Agrl. Investment	80000	55000 (68.75)	-	-	160000	40000 (25)	-	-
Consumption Purpose	1668500	1395900 (83.66)	116000	84300 (72.67)	27000	27000 (100)	544000	354500 (65.17)
Sickness	445000	169000 (37.98)	55000	10000 (18.18)	150000	35000 (23.33)	601000	380000 (63.23)
Marriage	66000	42000 (63.64)	20000	20000 (100.00)	420000	150000 (35.71)	710000	260000 (36.62)
To clear private loan	1918000	689800 (35.96)	-	-	-	-	50000	-
Education	198000	99600 (50.30)	40000	20000 (50.00)	25000	2000 (8.00)	160000	67000 (41.88)
Land Development	25000	14000 (56.00)	-	-	80000	61000 (76.25)	-	-
H.C & Repair	680000	304800 (44.82)	235000	93000 (39.57)	635000	163000 (25.67)	628000	165000 (26.27)
Livestock	162500	129000 (79.38)	-	-	-	-	-	-
Trade	2873000	1812800 (63.10)	65000	49000 (75.38)	200000	119000 (59.50)	640000	368000 (57.50)
Total	8141000	4731900 (58.12)	531000	276300 (52.03)	1697000	597000 (35.18)	3333000	1574500 (47.24)

Table - 5.34B Repayment of Loans by Purpose of Borrowing (NSHG)

Purpose	Micro Credit		Private Micro Credit		Formal Credit		Informal Credit	
	Amount Borrowed	Amount Repaid	Amount Borrowed	Amount Repaid	Amount Borrowed	Amount Repaid	Amount Borrowed	Amount Repaid
Agrl. Investment	55000	30000 (54.55)	-	-	455000	220000 (48.35)	70000	-
Consumption Purpose	2159000	1748950 (81.01)	105000	78500 (74.76)	10000		730000	388750 (53.25)
Sickness	96000	67600 (70.42)	30000	22000 (73.33)	295000	15000 (5.08)	645000	263000 (40.78)
Marriage	56000	54500 (97.32)	-	-	50000		670000	40000 (5.97)
To clear private loan	1015000	144500 (14.24)	-	-	150000	30000 (20.00)	-	-
Education	120000	41550 (34.63)	40000	14400 (36.00)	118000	45000 (38.14)	220000	57500 (26.14)
Land Development	-	-	-	-	100000	-	-	-
H.C & Repair	25000	1000 (4.00)	-	-	-	-	-	-
Livestock	165000	92000 (55.76)	20000	12000 (60.00)	510000	155000 (30.39)	790000	168300 (21.30)
Trade	1478500	753850 (50.99)	155000	58450 (37.71)	110000	10000 (9.09)	550000	110000 (20.00)
Total	5250500	2978700 (56.73)	350000	185350 (52.95)	1908000	495000 (25.94)	3730000	1057550 (28.35)

Source: Field survey

Note: Figures in brackets indicate percentage.

Table - 5.34C Repayment of Loans by Purpose of Borrowing (All)

Purpose	Micro Credit		Private Micro Credit		Formal Credit		Informal Credit	
	Amount Borrowed	Amount Repaid	Amount Borrowed	Amount Repaid	Amount Borrowed	Amount Repaid	Amount Borrowed	Amount Repaid
Agrl. Investment	135000	85000 62.96)	-	-	615000	260000	70000	-
Consumption Purpose	3827500	3144850 (82.16)	221000	162800 (73.67)	37000	27000 (72.97)	1274000	743250 (58.34)
Sickness	541000	236600 (43.73)	85000	32000 (37.65)	445000	50000 (11.23)	1246000	643000 (51.61)
Marriage	122000	96500 (79.10)	20000	20000 (100.00)	470000	150000 (31.91)	1380000	300000 (21.74)
To clear private loan	2933000	834300 (28.45)	-	-	150000	30000 (20.00)	50000	0 0.00)
Education	318000	141150 (44.39)	80000	34400 (43.00)	143000	47000 (32.86)	380000	124500 (32.76)
Land Development	25000	14000 (56.00)	-	-	180000	61000 (33.88)	10000	10000 (100.0)
H.C & Repair	845000	396800 (46.96)	255000	105000 (41.18)	1145000	318000 (27.77)	1418000	333300 (23.50)
Livestock	243500	173750 (71.36)	-	-	110000	20000 (18.18)	45000	20000 (44.44)
Trade	4351500	2566650 (58.98)	220000	107450 (48.84)	310000	129000 (41.61)	1190000	458000 (38.49)
Total	13391500	7710600 (57.58)	881000	461650 (52.40)	3605000	1092000 (30.29)	7063000	2632050 (37.27)

Source: Field survey

Note: Figures in brackets indicate percentage.

As observed from the tables, the repayment performance in respect of loans contracted from microcredit sources for all purposes is found to be better in both the households. The analysis further has shown that in the case of loans contracted from informal sources, very poor repayment was reported in both the households. This may be because of group based approach adopted by the microcredit programme.

Repayment of Loans by Rate of Interest:

In general the loans carrying higher rates of interest are repaid first in preference to those with lower rates of interest. It is examined and is shown in table 5-35.

It can be observed from the table that in respect of microcredit, the repayment performance is better. However, in informal credit sources, there is no specific trend regarding the repayment performance of borrowers.

Table - 5.35 Repayments of Loans by Rate of Interest

Rate of Interest Group	Micro Credit		Private Micro Credit		Formal Credit		Informal Credit		Total	
	Amount Bor-rowed	Amount Repaid	Amount Borrowed	Amount Repaid	Amount Borrowed	Amount Repaid	Amount Borrowed	Amount Repaid	Amount Bor-rowed	Amount Repaid
OSHG										
Below 12	8141000	4731900 (58.12)	15000	7000 (46.67)	1462000	537000 (36.73)	83000	52500 (63.25)	9701000	5328400 (54.93)
12-24	-	-	516000	269300 (52.19)	135000	60000 (44.44)	2483000	1199000 (48.29)	3134000	1528300 (48.77)
24-36	-	-	-	-	100000	-	664000	297000 (44.73)	764000	297000 (38.87)
Above 36	-	-	-	-	-	-	103000	26000 (25.24)	103000	26000 (25.24)
Total	8141000	4731900 (58.12)	531000	276300 (52.03)	1697000	597000 (35.18)	3333000	1574500 (47.24)	13702000	7179700 (52.40)
NSHG										
Below 12	5250500	2978700 (56.73)	35000	31000 (88.57)	1798000	485000 (26.97)	70000	25000 (35.71)	7153500	3519700 (49.20)
12-24	-	-	315000	154350 (49.00)	110000	10000 (9.09)	3076000	736450 (23.94)	3501000	900800 (25.73)
24-36	-	-	-	-	-	-	494000	269600 (54.57)	494000	269600 (54.57)
Above 36	-	-	-	-	-	-	90000	26500 (29.44)	90000	26500 (29.44)
Total	5250500	2978700 (56.73)	350000	185350 (52.96)	1908000	495000 (25.94)	3730000	1057550 (28.35)	11238500	4716600 (41.97)
ALL										
Below 12	13391500	7710600 (57.58)	50000	38000 (76.00)	3260000	1022000 (31.35)	153000	77500 (50.65)	16854500	8848100 (52.50)
12-24	-	-	831000	423650 (50.98)	245000	70000 (28.57)	5559000	1935450 (34.82)	6635000	2429100 (36.61)
24-36	-	-	-	-	100000	-	1158000	566600 (48.93)	1258000	566600 (45.04)
Above 36	-	-	-	-	-	-	193000	52500 (27.20)	193000	52500 (27.20)
Total	13391500	7710600 (57.58)	881000	461650 (52.40)	3605000	1092000 (30.29)	7063000	2632050 (37.27)	24940500	11896300 (47.70)

Source: Field survey

Note: Figures in brackets indicate percentage.

5.5.2 Factors Influencing Repayment of Loans and Results of Regression Analysis:

An attempt is made to examine the factors influencing repayment of loans by using multiple regression analysis. Regression methods may be used for the time series data considering historical evidence or cross-section data representing the technological relationships. Since our study is based on cross-section data, the regression analysis will help us to identify the factors that influencing the dependent variable.

Specification of the Variables and Model:

In this study, total amount of repayment of loans of households is the relevant dependent variable. Accordingly, Y is the total repayment of loans of households. Repayment of loans includes all loans by the households during the year under the study. The following explanatory variables are considered as the important determinants. Age, Literacy level, Earner, Occupational pattern, Size of the Family, Asset holdings, Income, Dependency Ratio, Recurring Expenditure and Non-Recurring Expenditure. By considering the above variables, the regression function adopted in this study is specified as under:

Age	=	Age of the respondent
Literacy level	=	Number of Years of Education of the Respondent.
Earner	=	Dummy variable, whether the respondent is working
Occupational pattern	=	Dummy variable, whether the respondent is employee
Size of the family	=	Family size of the house.
Asset holdings	=	Value of Assets owned by the household
Income	=	Income of the household
Dependency ratio	=	Dependency ratio of the household
Recurring Expenditure	=	Food and non-food expenditure of the household
Expenditure	=	Sickness of the family members, ceremonies, etc.
Repayment	=	Repayment of loans taken (Dependent Variable)

Based on the above given variables, a multiple linear regression model is presented as follows:

Repayments (Y) = $Y=a+ b_1x_1+ b_2x_2+ b_3x_3+ b_4x_4+b_5x_5+.....+b_nx_n+\mu$

Results of Regression Analysis:

Impact of Microcredit Repayments on Sample Rural Respondents

Independent variables	OSHG		NSHG		All	
	B	Sig.	B	Sig.	B	Sig.
(Constant)	17835.315* (3.480)	0.001	4247.711 (0.605)	0.546	9930.841** (2.107)	0.036
Age	52.284 (0.943)	0.347	53.507 (0.915)	0.361	96.146** (2.124)	0.034
Literacy level	346.394** (2.501)	0.013	187.001 (1.412)	0.160	290.715* (2.683)	0.008
Earner	-1499.628 (-0.395)	0.693	5065.732 (0.885)	0.377	742.475 (0.204)	0.839
Occupational pattern	-370.992 (-0.332)	0.740	1851.316 (1.497)	0.136	872.996 (0.922)	0.357
Size of the family	803.793 (1.341)	0.181	506.845 (0.616)	0.539	685.056 (1.241)	0.215
Asset Holdings	0.007 (1.626)	0.106	-0.002 (-.482)	0.630	7.956 (0.024)	0.981
Income	-0.023*** (-1.894)	0.060	-0.023 (-1.331)	0.185	-0.017 (-1.478)	0.140
Dependency Ratio	-1973.410** (-2.178)	0.031	-273.989 (-0.319)	0.750	-914.043 (-1.312)	0.190
Recurring Expenditure	0.067 (0.938)	0.349	-0.014 (-0.189)	0.850	-0.009 (-0.167)	0.868
Non-Recurring Expenditure	0.011 (0.291)	0.772	0.068** (2.176)	0.031	0.063** (2.350)	0.019
Observations	200		198		398	
R^2	0.101		0.078		0.061	
Adjusted R^2	0.053		0.028		0.036	
F-value	2.117** (0.025)		1.575 (0.117)		2.501* (0.006)	

Source: Field survey

Note:* Significant at 1% level, ** Significant at 5% level & *** Significant at 10% level.

Figures in brackets are t -values.

Impact of Microcredit Repayments on OSHG Households:

Age of the respondent is observed to have a positive relation at Microcredit Repayments. The hypothesis is younger individuals are repaying better since they have better repayment capacity but this relation is not at significant level. Literacy level is a variable which is estimated by number of school going years and specifies the literacy status of the respondent. The literacy level is expected to have a positive relation in Microcredit Repayments among sample respondents. The literacy level is turned out to be significant with expected positive sign. Earner is a dummy variable and specifies the working capacity of the respondent. It takes value 1 for worker and 0 for non-worker and is expected to have a positive relation in Microcredit Repayments among sample households but the sign of the coefficient is turned out to be negative and it is not significant.

Occupational pattern is a dummy variable and specifies the employment status of the respondent. It takes value 1 for household working in industry and trade and 0 for wage and others. It is expected to have a positive relation as households depending on industry and trade are having more Microcredit Repayments as they have better repayment capacity but this relation is not significant and it has negative impact. Size of the Family is a variable considered as number of persons living in a single family. The hypothesis indicates that if the family size is large the repayment will be less and vice- versa but it is not found at any significant level. Asset holdings represent the value of assets (both fixed and durable property) of sample household. It is a quantitative variable, which takes actual value of the assets of the sample household. It is expected to have a negative relation in Microcredit Repayments but it is found to be positive and insignificant. Income of the sample respondent is expected to have positive relation with Microcredit Repayments. The hypothesis is that higher the income higher will be the Microcredit Repayments of the households in the study area. It is found that the sign of the coefficient is negative and significant.

Dependency Ratio represents the ratio of non-working members to the working members and is expected to have a negative relation in Microcredit Repayments. The hypothesis is higher the dependency ratio lower will be the Microcredit repayments and vice-versa. The dependency ratio is turned out to be significant with expected negative sign. Recurring Expenditure represents the expenditure on food and non-food items of the household which is expected to have negative relation in Microcredit Repayments of the respondent. If the expenditure on food and non-food items are higher, lower will be Microcredit Repayments but the coefficient sign is positive and insignificant.Non-Recurring Expenditure represents the number of household events such as sickness of the family members, marriage and other ceremonies occurred in the household which is expected to have negative relation in Microcredit Repayments of the respondent. If the identified incidents are higher in relation to the non-recurring expenditure lower will be Microcredit Repayments. The non-recurring expenditure coefficient sign is turned out to be positive and insignificant.

The F value is 2.117 which is significant at 5 per cent level and shows that the model is best fit. The model explains 5.3 percentage of variation. In this model three variables are found to be significant viz., literacy level, income and dependency ratio.

Impact of Microcredit Repayments on NSHG Households:

Age of the respondent is observed to have a positive relation at Microcredit Repayments. The hypothesis is younger individuals are repaying better since they have better repayment capacity but this relation is not at significant level. Literacy level is a variable which is estimated by number of school going years and specifies the literacy status of the respondent. The literacy level is expected to have a positive relation in Microcredit Repayments among sample respondents but this relation is not at significant level. Earner is a dummy variable and specifies the working capacity of the respondent. It takes value 1 for worker and 0 for non-worker and is expected to have a positive relation in Microcredit Repayments among sample households but this relation is not at significant level.

Occupational pattern is a dummy variable and specifies the employment status of the respondent. It takes value 1 for household working in industry and trade and 0 for wage and others. It is expected to have a positive relation as households depending on industry and trade are having more Microcredit Repayments as they have better repayment capacity but this relation is not at significant level. Size of the Family is a variable considered as number of persons living in a single family. The hypothesis indicates that if the family size is large the repayment will be less and vice-versa but it is not found at any significant level. Asset holdings represent the value of assets (both fixed and durable property) of sample household. It is a quantitative variable, which takes actual value of the assets of the sample household. It is expected to have a positive relation in Microcredit Repayments but it is turned out to be negative and not significant. Income of the sample respondent is expected to have positive relation with Microcredit Repayments. The hypothesis is that higher the income, higher will be the Microcredit Repayments of the households in the study area but this relation is not significant and the sign of the coefficient is negative.

Dependency Ratio represents the ratio of non-working members to the working members and is expected to have a negative relation in Microcredit Repayments. The hypothesis is higher the dependency ratio lower will be the Microcredit repayments and vice-versa but this relation is not significant with negative sign. Recurring Expenditure represents the expenditure on food and non-food items of the household which is expected to have a negative relation in Microcredit Repayments of the respondent. If the expenditure on food and non-food items are higher, lower will be Microcredit Repayments and it has negative sign and not significant. Non-Recurring Expenditure represents the number of household events such as sickness of the family members, marriage and other ceremonies occurred in the household which is expected to have a negative relation in Microcredit Repayments of the respondent. If the identified incidents are higher, the non-recurring expenditure increases which leads to lower Microcredit Repayments. The non-recurring expenditure is turned out to be significant with negative sign.

In this model the F value is 1.575. The model explains 2.8 percentage of variation. In this model one variable are found to be significant viz., non-recurring expenditure.

Impact of Microcredit Repayments on All Households

Age of the respondent is observed to have a positive relation at Microcredit Repayments. The hypothesis is younger individuals are repaying better since they have better repayment capacity. The age is turned out to be significant with expected positive sign. Literacy level is a variable which is estimated by number of school going years and specifies the literacy status of the respondent. The literacy level is expected to have a positive relation in Microcredit Repayments among sample respondents. The literacy level is turned out to be significant with expected positive sign. Earner is a dummy variable and specifies the working capacity of the respondent. It takes value 1 for worker and 0 for non-worker and is expected to have a positive relation in Microcredit Repayments among sample households but this relation is not at significant level though it is having positive sign.

Occupational pattern is a dummy variable and specifies the employment status of the respondent. It takes value 1 for household working in industry and trade and 0 for wage and others. It is expected to have a positive relation as households depending on industry and trade are having more Microcredit Repayments as they have better repayment capacity but this relation is not at significant level though it has positive sign. Size of the Family is a variable considered as number of persons living in a single family. The hypothesis indicates that if the family size is large the repayment will be less and vice-versa but it is turned out to be positive and not significant.Assetholdings represent the value of assets (both fixed and durable property) of sample household. It is a quantitative variable, which takes actual value of the assets of the sample household. It is expected to have a negative relation in Microcredit Repayments but it has positive sign and not found to be significant. Income of the sample respondent is expected to have positive relation with Microcredit Repayments. The hypothesis is that higher the income higher will be the Microcredit Repayments of the households in the study area but it is turned out to be negative and not significant.

Dependency Ratio represents the ratio of non-working members to the working members and is expected to have a negative relation in Microcredit Repayments. The hypothesis is higher the dependency ratio, lower will be the Microcredit repayments and vice-versa but it is not significant. Recurring Expenditure represents the expenditure on food and non-food items of the household which is expected to have a negative relation in Microcredit Repayments of the respondent. If the expenditure on food and non-food items are higher, lower will be Microcredit Repayments and it is not significant though it has expected sign. Non-Recurring Expenditure represents the number of household events such as sickness of the family members, marriage and other ceremonies occurred in the household which is expected to have a negative relation in Microcredit Repayments of the respondent. If the identified incidents are higher in relation to the non-recurring expenditure, lower will be Microcredit Repayments. The non-recurring expenditure is turned out to be significant with positive sign.

The F-value is 2.501 which show that the model is best fit and it is significant at 1 percent level. The model explains 3.6 percentage of variation. In this model three variables are found to be significant viz., age, literacy level and non-recurring expenditure.

Impact of Formal Credit Repayments on Sample rural respondents

Independent variables	OSHG		NSHG		All	
	B	Sig.	B	Sig.	B	Sig.
(Constant)	3980.433 (0.182)	0.857	-32625.736 (-0.469)	0.649	-23026.889 (-1.062)	0.294
Age	440.701 (1.590)	0.125	-1294.038 (-1.284)	0.228	-327.835 (-1.189)	0.241
Literacy level	1749.202** (2.433)	0.023	806.142 (0.421)	0.683	197.884 (0.336)	0.738
Earner	-10376.980*** (-1.783)	0.087	-11295.477 (-1.124)	0.287	-10806.650** (-2.123)	0.039
Occupational pattern	934.864 (0.197)	0.846	-31792.802** (-2.403)	0.037	-9075.856*** (-1.784)	0.081
Size of the family	-3563.272 (-0.700)	0.491	18763.468** (2.745)	0.021	12900.426* (3.232)	0.002
Asset Holdings	-0.046 (-1.611)	0.120	0.005 (0.163)	0.874	0.011 (0.610)	0.545
Income	0.227** (2.254)	0.034	-0.120 (-1.107)	0.294	-0.025 (-0.372)	0.712
Dependency Ratio	-1204.068 (-0.358)	0.723	7093.901 (0.895)	0.392	2221.641 (0.666)	0.509
Recurring Expenditure	-0.155 (-0.559)	0.581	-0.032 (-0.267)	0.795	-0.048 (-0.841)	0.405
Non-Recurring Expenditure	0.062 (0.195)	0.847	0.731 (1.735)	0.113	0.089 (0.397)	0.693
Observations	35		21		56	
R^2	0.307		0.691		0.309	
Adjusted R^2	0.018		0.382		0.156	
F-value	1.061 (0.427)		2.237(0.110)		2.017**(0.054)	

Source: Field survey

Note:* Significant at 1% level, ** Significant at 5% level & *** Significant at 10% level.

Figures in brackets are t –values.

Impact of Formal Credit Repayments on OSHG Households:

Age of the respondent is observed to have a positive relation at Formal credit Repayments. The hypothesis is younger individuals are repaying better since they have better repayment capacity but this relation is not at significant level. Literacy level is a variable which is estimated by number of school going years and specifies the literacy status of the respondent. The literacy level is expected to have a positive relation in Formal credit Repayments among sample respondents. The literacy level is turned out to be significant with expected positive sign. Earner is a dummy variable and specifies the working capacity of the respondent. It takes value 1 for worker and 0 for non-worker and is expected to have a positive relation in Formal credit Repayments among sample households. The Earner is turned out to be significant with negative sign.

Occupational pattern is a dummy variable and specifies the employment status of the respondent. It takes value 1 for household working in industry and trade and 0 for wage and others. It is expected to have a positive relation as households depending on industry and trade are having more Formal credit Repayments as they have better repayment capacity but this relation is not at significant level. Size of the Family is a variable considered as number of persons living in a single family. The hypothesis indicates that if the family size is large the repayment will be less and vice-versa but it is not found at any significant level with negative sign. Asset holdings represent the value of assets (both fixed and durable property) of sample household. It is a quantitative variable, which takes actual value of the assets of the sample household. It is expected to have a positive relation in Formal credit Repayments but it is not found at any significant level with negative sign. Income of the sample respondent is expected to have a positive relation with Formal credit Repayments. The hypothesis is that higher the income, higher will be the Formal credit Repayments of the households in the study area. The Income is turned out to be significant with expected positive sign.

Dependency Ratio represents the ratio of non-working members to the working members and is expected to have a negative relation in Formal credit Repayments. The hypothesis is higher the dependency ratio, lower will be the Microcredit repayments and vice-versa but it is not found at any significant level with expected negative sign. Recurring Expenditure represents the expenditure on food and non-food items of the household which is expected to have negative relation in Formal credit Repayments of the respondent. If the expenditure on food and non-food items increases, lower will be Formal credit Repayments but it is not found at any significant level with expected negative sign. Non-Recurring Expenditure represents the number of household events such as sickness of the family members, marriage and other ceremonies occurred in the household which is expected to have a negative relation in Formal credit Repayments of the respondent. If the identified incidents are higher, lower will be Formal credit Repayments but it is not found at any significant level with positive sign.

In this model the F value is 1.061. The model explains 1.8 percentage of variation. In this model three variables are found to be significant viz., literacy level, earner and income.

Impact of Formal Credit Repayments on NSHG Households:

Age of the respondent is observed to have a positive relation at Formal credit Repayments. The hypothesis is younger individuals are repaying better since they have better repayment capacity but it is not found at any significant level negative sign. Literacy level is a variable which is estimated by number of school going years and specifies the literacy status of the respondent. The literacy level is expected to have a positive relation in Formal credit Repayments among sample respondents but it is not found at any significant level though the sign of the coefficient turned out to be positive. Earner is a dummy variable and specifies the working capacity of the respondent. It takes value 1 for worker and 0 for non-worker and is expected to have a positive relation in Formal credit Repayments among sample households but it has negative sign and not found at any significant level.

Occupational pattern is a dummy variable and specifies the employment status of the respondent. It takes value 1 for household working in industry and trade and 0 for wage and others. It is expected to have a positive relation as households depending on industry and trade are having more Formal credit Repayments as they have better repayment capacity. The Occupational pattern is turned out to be significant with negative sign. Size of the Family is a variable considered as number of persons living in a single family. The hypothesis indicates that if the family size is large the repayment will be less and vice-versa. The Size of the Family is turned out to be significant with positive sign. Asset holdings represent the value of assets (both fixed and durable property) of sample household. It is a quantitative variable, which takes actual value of the assets of the sample household. It is expected to have a positive relation in Formal credit Repayments but it is not found at any significant level with expected positive sign. Income of the sample respondent is expected to have a positive relation with Formal credit Repayments. The hypothesis is that higher the income, higher will be the Formal credit Repayments of the households in the study area but it has negative impact and not found at any significant level.

Dependency Ratio represents the ratio of non-working members to the working members and is expected to have a negative relation in Formal credit Repayments. The hypothesis is higher the dependency ratio lower will be the Formal credit repayments and vice-versa but it is not found at any significant level with positive sign. Recurring Expenditure represents the expenditure on food and non-food items of the household which is expected to have a negative relation in Formal credit Repayments of the respondent. If the expenditure on food and non-food items increases, lower will be Formal credit Repayments but it is not found at any significant level with negative sign. Non-Recurring Expenditure represents the number of household events such as sickness of the family members, marriage and other ceremonies occurred in the household which is expected to have a negative relation in Formal credit Repayments of the respondent. If the identified incidents are higher, lower will be Formal credit Repayments but it is not found at any significant level with positive sign.

In this model the F value is 2.237. The model explains 38.2 percentage of variation. In these model two variables is found to be significant viz., occupational pattern and size of the family.

Impact of Formal Credit Repayment on All Households:

Age of the respondent is observed to have a positive relation at Formal credit Repayments. The hypothesis is younger individuals are repaying better since they have better repayment capacity but this relation is not at significant level with negative sign. Literacy level is a variable which is estimated by number of school going years and specifies the literacy status of the respondent. The literacy level is expected to have a positive relation in Formal credit Repayments among sample respondents but this relation is not at significant level with positive sign. Earner is a dummy variable and specifies the working capacity of the respondent. It takes value 1 for worker and 0 for non-worker and is expected to have a positive relation in Formal credit Repayments among sample households. The Earner coefficient is turned out to be significant with negative sign.

Occupational pattern is a dummy variable and specifies the employment status of the respondent. It takes value 1 for household working in industry and trade and 0 for wage and others. It is expected to have a positive relation as households depending on industry and trade are having more Formal credit Repayments as they have better repayment capacity. The Occupational pattern is turned out to be significant with negative sign.

Size of the Family is a variable considered as number of persons living in a single family. The hypothesis indicates that if the family size is large the repayment will be less and vice-versa. The Size of the Family is turned out to be significant with positive sign. Asset holdings represent the value of assets (both fixed and durable property) of sample household. It is a quantitative variable, which takes actual value of the assets of the sample household. It is expected to have a positive relation in Formal credit Repayments but it is not found at any significant level with expected positive sign. Income of the sample respondent is expected to have a positive relation with Formal credit Repayments. The hypothesis is that higher the income, higher will be the Formal credit Repayments of the households in the study area but it has negative sign and not significant.

Dependency Ratio represents the ratio of non-working members to the working members and is expected to have a negative relation in Formal credit Repayments. The hypothesis is higher the dependency ratio lower will be the Formal credit repayments and vice-versa but it is not significant with positive sign. Recurring Expenditure represents the expenditure on food and non-food items of the household which is expected to have a negative relation in Formal credit Repayments of the respondent. The expenditure on food and non-food items increases, lower will be Formal credit Repayments. The coefficient is having negative sign and not significant. Non-Recurring Expenditure represents the number of household events such as sickness of the family members, marriage and other ceremonies occurred in the household which is expected to have a negative relation in Formal credit Repayments of the respondent. If the identified incidents are higher, lower will be Formal credit Repayments but it is not found significant with positive sign.

The F-value (2.017) is significant at 5 per cent level and show that it is best fit. The model explains 15.6 percentage of variation. In this model three variables are found to be significant viz., Earner, Occupational pattern and Size of the family.

Impact of Informal Credit Repayments on sample rural respondents

Independent variables	OSHG		NSHG		All	
	B	Sig.	B	Sig.	B	Sig.
(Constant)	-5930.962 (-0.328)	0.744	-3665.476 (-0.646)	0.520	-5764.758 (-0.601)	0.548
Age	51.956 (0.217)	0.829	52.694 (0.748)	0.456	106.685 (0.875)	0.383
Literacy level	780.516 (1.200)	0.234	-277.395 (-1.454)	0.149	204.276 (0.606)	0.546
Earner	3479.467 (0.514)	0.609	416.509 (0.149)	0.882	1618.207 (0.394)	0.694
Occupational pattern	1607.275 (0.329)	0.743	163.548 (0.100)	0.920	2296.095 (0.837)	0.404
Size of the family	3513.115 (1.282)	0.204	182.559 (0.186)	0.853	1537.294 (0.979)	0.329
Asset Holdings	-0.009 (-1.370)	0.174	0.004** (2.308)	0.023	0.001 (0.464)	0.643
Income	0.070* (4.619)	0.000	0.004 (1.567)	0.121	0.015* (2.988)	0.003
Dependency Ratio	-75.434 (-0.089)	0.930	-293.672 (-0.302)	0.763	-168.686 (-0.272)	0.786
Recurring Expenditure	-.562** (-2.245)	0.027	0.176*** (1.666)	0.099	-0.317** (-2.025)	0.044
Non-Recurring Expenditure	.320** (2.164)	0.033	0.113*** (1.830)	0.071	0.330* (3.682)	0.000
Observations	93		101		194	
R2	0.311		0.294		0.129	
Adjusted R2	0.227		0.216		0.082	
F-value	3.707*(0.000)		3.755*(0.000)		2.718*(0.004)	

Source: Field survey

Note:* Significant at 1% level, ** Significant at 5% level & *** Significant at 10% level.

Figures in brackets are t -values.

Impact of Informal Credit Repayments on OSHG Households

Age of the respondent is observed to have a positive relation at Informal credit Repayments. The hypothesis is younger individuals are repaying better since they have better repayment capacity but this relation is not at significant level with positive sign. Literacy level is a variable which is estimated by number of school going years and specifies the literacy status of the respondent. The literacy level is expected to have a positive relation in Informal credit Repayments among sample respondents but this relation is not at significant level with positive sign. Earner is a dummy variable and specifies the working capacity of the respondent. It takes value 1 for worker and 0 for non-worker and is expected to have a positive relation in Informal credit Repayments among sample households but this relation is not at significant level with expected positive sign.

Occupational pattern is a dummy variable and specifies the employment status of the respondent. It takes value 1 for household working in industry and trade and 0 for wage and others. It is expected to have a positive relation as households depending on industry and trade are having more Informal credit Repayments as they have better repayment capacity but this relation is not at significant level with expected positive sign. Size of the Family is a variable considered as number of persons living in a single family. The hypothesis indicates that if the family size is large the repayment will be less and vice-versa but it is not found at any significant level with positive sign. Asset holdings represent the value of assets (both fixed and durable property) of sample household. It is a quantitative variable, which takes actual value of the assets of the sample household. It is expected to have a positive relation in Informal credit Repayments but it has negative sign and it is not significant. Income of the sample respondent is expected to have a positive relation with Informal credit Repayments. The hypothesis is that higher the income higher will be the Informal credit Repayments of the households in the study area. The Income is turned out to be significant with expected positive sign.

Dependency Ratio represents the ratio of non-working members to the working members and is expected to have negative relation in Informal credit Repayments. The hypothesis is higher the dependency ratio, lower will be the Informal credit repayments and vice-versa but it is not found at any significant level with expected negative sign. Recurring Expenditure represents the expenditure on food and non-food items of the household which is expected to have a negative relation in Informal credit Repayments of the respondent. The expenditure on food and non-food items increases, lower will be Informal credit Repayments. The Recurring Expenditure is turned out to be significant with expected negative sign. Non-Recurring Expenditure represents the number of household events such as sickness of the family members, marriage and other ceremonies occurred in the household which is expected to have a negative relation in Informal credit Repayments of the respondent. The identified incidents are higher in relation to the non-recurring expenditure lower will be Informal credit Repayments. The Non-Recurring Expenditure is turned out to be significant with positive sign.

The F-value 3.707 which is significant at 1 per cent level and show that the model is best fit. The model explains 22.7 percentage of variation. In this model three variables are found to be significant viz., Income, Recurring Expenditure and Non- recurring Expenditure.

Impact of Informal Credit Repayments on NSHG Households:

Age of the respondent is observed to have a positive relation at Informal credit Repayments. The hypothesis is younger individuals are repaying better since they have better repayment capacity but this relation is not at significant level with positive sign. Literacy level is a variable which is estimated by number of school going years and specifies the literacy status of the respondent. The literacy level is expected to have a positive relation in Informal credit Repayments among sample respondents but this relation is not at significant level with negative sign. Earner is a dummy variable and specifies the working capacity of the respondent. It takes value 1 for worker and 0 for non-worker and is expected to have a positive relation in Informal credit Repayments among sample households but this relation is not at significant level with expected positive sign.

Occupational pattern is a dummy variable and specifies the employment status of the respondent. It takes value 1 for household working in industry and trade and 0 for wage and others. It is expected to have a positive relation as households depending on industry and trade are having more Informal credit Repayments as they have better repayment capacity but this relation is not at significant level with expected positive sign. Size of the Family is a variable considered as number of persons living in a single family. The hypothesis indicates that if the family size is large the repayment will be less and vice-versa but it is not found at any significant level with positive sign. Asset holdings represent the value of assets (both fixed and durable property) of sample household. It is a quantitative variable, which takes actual value of the assets of the sample household. It is expected to have a positive relation in Informal credit Repayments. The Asset holding is turned out to be significant with expected positive sign. Income of the sample respondent is expected to have a positive relation with Informal credit Repayments. The hypothesis is that higher the income, higher will be the Informal credit Repayments of the households in the study area but this relation is not at significant level though it has expected positive sign.

Dependency Ratio represents the ratio of non-working members to the working members and is expected is have a negative relation in Informal credit Repayments. The hypothesis is higher the dependency ratio lower will be the Informal credit repayments and vice-versa but it is not found at any significant level with expected negative sign. Recurring Expenditure represents the expenditure on food and non-food items of the household which is expected to have a negative relation in Informal credit Repayments of the respondent. The higher the expenditure on food and non-food items, lower will be Informal credit Repayments. The Recurring expenditure is turned out to be significant with positive sign. Non-Recurring Expenditure represents the number of household events such as sickness of the family members, marriage and other ceremonies occurred in the household which is expected to have a negative relation in Informal credit Repayments of the respondent. The identified incident of higher the non-recurring expenditure lower will be Informal credit Repayments. The non-recurring expenditure is turned out to be significant with positive sign.

The F-value is 3.755 which is significant at 1 per cent level and show that it is best fit. The model explains 21.6 percentage of variation. In this model three variables is found to be significant viz., Asset holdings, Recurring expenditure and Non-recurring expenditure.

Impact of Informal Credit Repayments on All Households:

Age of the respondent is observed to have a positive relation at Informal credit Repayments. The hypothesis is younger individuals are repaying better since they have better repayment capacity but this relation is not at significant level with expected positive sign. Literacy level is a variable which is estimated by number of school going years and specifies the literacy status of the respondent. The literacy level is expected to have a positive relation in Informal credit Repayments among sample respondents but this relation is not at significant level with expected positive sign. Earner is a dummy variable and specifies the working capacity of the respondent. It takes value 1 for worker and 0 for non-worker and is expected to have a positive relation in Informal credit Repayments among sample households but this relation is not at significant level with expected positive sign.

Occupational pattern is a dummy variable and specifies the employment status of the respondent. It takes value 1 for household working in industry and trade and 0 for wage and others. It is expected to have a positive relation as households depending on industry and trade are having more Informal credit Repayments as they have better repayment capacity but this relation is not at significant level with expected positive sign. Size of the Family is a variable considered as number of persons living in a single family. The hypothesis indicates that if the family size is large the repayment will be less and vice-versa but it is not found at any significant level with positive sign. Asset holdings represent the value of assets (both fixed and durable property) of sample household. It is a quantitative variable, which takes actual value of the assets of the sample household. It is expected to have a positive relation in Informal credit Repayments but it is not found at any significant level with expected positive sign.

Income of the sample respondent is expected to have a positive relation with Informal credit Repayments. The hypothesis is that higher the income higher will be the Informal credit Repayments of the households in the study area. The Income is turned out to be significant with expected positive sign.

Dependency Ratio represents the ratio of non-working members to the working members and is expected is have a negative relation in Informal credit Repayments. The hypothesis is higher the dependency ratio lower will be the Informal credit repayments and vice-versa but it is not found at any significant level with expected negative sign. Recurring Expenditure represents the expenditure on food and non-food items of the household which is expected to have negative relation in Informal credit Repayments of the respondent. The higher the expenditure on food and non-food items, lower will be Informal credit Repayments. The Recurring expenditure is turned out to be significant with expected negative sign. Non-Recurring Expenditure represents the number of household events such as sickness of the family members, marriage and other ceremonies occurred in the household which is expected to have a negative relation in Informal credit Repayments of the respondent. The identified incidents are higher, lower will be Informal credit Repayments. The non-recurring expenditure is turned out to be significant with positive sign.

The F-value is 2.718 which show that the model is best fit and significant at 1 per cent level. The model explains 8.2 percentage of variation. In this model three variables are found to be significant viz., Income, Recurring Expenditure and Non-recurring Expenditure.

5.6 Summary

The analysis of indebtedness among rural households shows that about half of them were in debt and three-fifths of their debt was owed to institutional sources. Of the total debt of about Rs.1.12 lakh crore in 2003, Rs.48,000 Crore was sourced from non- institutional agencies. Of which Rs. 18,000 crore of debt carried an interest rate greater than 30 per cent. There is a need to relieve the farmers from private debt carrying high interest rate by transferring it to institutional agencies. Farmers" indebtedness was strikingly a regional phenomenon; it was low in less developed states. In all states which had reported suicides among farmers, the incidence as well as debt per farmer household was high. However, sources of debt varied. For example, in Maharashtra, the major source was institutional agencies, whereas in AP, non-institutional agencies accounted for bulk of the debt. This suggests that while formalization of informal debt is an important step in reducing debt burden of farmers, other measures to ensure assured income from farm and non-farm sources are equally essential.

The analysis shows that, through microcredit intervention the formal credit can reach the rural poor. In both OSHG and NSHG households more than 60 percent of the total borrowings was from microcredit sources. But the SHG households are still depend upon the informal sources for supplementing the productive activities which reflects the inadequacy of microcredit. An analysis of borrowings from microcredit shows that only 30 percent of borrowings by rural households are used for productive purposes. An analysis of borrowings by rate of interest has clearly shown that microcredit is available for the members, at lower interest rates than formal and informal credit. An analysis of borrowings by nature of security has brought out that it is the personal security in the form of promissory note which replaced the collateral, in informal credit sector. In case of microcredit, the personal security took another form as group security which replaced the collateral security. Therefore, the poor are getting access to formal credit through microcredit sources.

In the regression model for microcredit borrowings for OSHG, three variables are found to be significant viz., age, dependency ratio and non-recurring expenditure and for NSHG, three variables viz., literacy level, occupational pattern and non-recurring expenditure are found to be significant. In formal credit borrowings for OSHG, three variables are found to be significant viz., Size of the Family, recurring expenditure and non-recurring expenditure, for NSHG two variables are found to be significant viz., occupational pattern and non-recurring expenditure. In informal credit borrowings for OSHG, two variables - income and non- recurring expenditure are significant and for NSHG, two variables are viz., asset holdings and non-recurring expenditure found to be significant.

In microcredit borrowings the regression model is best fit because F value is 4.718 which is significant at 1 percent level. The model explains 8.5 percentage of variation. In this model, four variables are found to be significant viz., literacy level, occupational pattern, size of the family and non-recurring expenditure. In Formal credit borrowings also the regression model is used. The F value is 1.136. The model explains 1.6 percentage of variation. In this model one variable is found to be significant viz., non-recurring expenditure. In Informal credit borrowings, the regression model is best fit because F value is 4.817 which is significant at 1 percent level. The model explains 13.4 percentage of variation. In this model, two variables are found to be significant viz., recurring expenditure and non-recurring expenditure.

The analysis of repayment of loans has shown that repayment of microcredit is better (around 60 per cent) compared to informal credit (around 40 per cent) in OSHG and NSHG households. This may be due to the intimacy of the lender and the borrower in respect of microcredit. In case of microcredit, household industry and trade are found to be the major means of repayment while wage income, household industry and trade are the major means of repayment of informal credit in both the households. The repayment performance in respect of loans contracted from microcredit sources for all purposes is found to be better where as in informal sources very poor repayment was reported in both the households. Repayments of loans by rate of interest show that in respect of microcredit, the repayment performance is better. However, in informal credit sources, there is no specific trend regarding the repayment performance of borrowers.

In the regression model for microcredit Repayments for OSHG, three variables are found to be significant viz., literacy level, dependency ratio and income. For NSHG, non-recurring expenditure is found to be significant. In formal credit Repayments for OSHG, three variables are found to be significant viz., literacy level, earner and income, for NSHG two variables are found to be significant viz., occupational pattern and size of the family. In informal credit Repayments for OSHG, three variables are - Income, Recurring Expenditure and Non-recurring Expenditure significant and for NSHG, three variables are viz., Asset holdings, Recurring expenditure and Non-recurring expenditure found to be significant.

In microcredit repayments the regression model is best fit because F value is 2.501 which is significant at 1 percent level. The model explains 3.6 percentage of variation. In this model three variables are found to be significant viz., age, literacy level and non-recurring expenditure. In formal credit repayments the regression model is best fit because F value is 2.017 which is significant at 5 per cent level. The model explains 15.6 percentage of variation. In this model three variables are found to be significant viz., earner, occupational pattern and size of the family. In Informal credit repayments too the regression model is best fit because the F value is 2.718 which is significant at 1 per cent level. The model explains 8.2 percentage of variation. In this model three variables are found to be significant viz., Income, Recurring Expenditure and Non-recurring Expenditure. Therefore, efforts should be made by the Government to provide gainful employment opportunities, which will help in improving the repayment performance of rural households.

References:

Bennett, L., Goldberg, M., & Hunte, P. (1996), "Ownership and sustainability: Lessons on group-based financial services from South Asia", *Journal of International Development*, *8*(2):271-288.

Dasgupta, R. (2001), "An Informal Journey through Self-Help Groups", *Indian Journal of Agricultural Economics*, 56(3): 370-386.

Dessing, M. (1990), "Support for microenterprises: lessons for sub-Saharan Africa", Vol. 122, World Bank, Washington D.C.

Gothoskar, S. P. (1988), On some estimates of rural indebtedness, *Reserve Bank of India Occasional Papers*, 9(4), 299-325.

Hossain, M. (1988), "Credit for alleviation of rural poverty: The Grameen Bank in Bangladesh", working paper No. 65, *Intl Food Policy Res Inst.*

Hulme, D., & Mosley, P. (1996), *Finance against poverty: Volume 1*, New York Routledge publishing.

Karnakar K.G. (1988), *Rural Credit and Self-Help Groups-Microfinance needs and Concepts in India*, Sage publications, New Delhi, pp.234-236

Khandker, S.R. & Khalily, B. & Khan, Z. (1995), Grameen Bank Performance and Sustainability, *World Bank, Discussion Paper 306*,Washington D.C.

Madheswaran, S. & Dharmadhikari, A. (2001), "Empowering Rural Women through Self-Help Groups", *Indian Journal of Agricultural Economics*, 56 (3): 427-43. NSSO (2003), Debt & Investment: NSS 59th Round, Government of India.

NSSO (2003), Situation Assessment Survey of Formers: NSS 59th Round, Government of India. NSSO (2006), Household Borrowings and Repayments in India: NSS 59th Round, Government of India.

Prabhu, K. S., Nadkarni, A., & Achuthan, C. V. (1988), "Rural credit: mystery of the missing households", *Economic and Political Weekly*, 23(50): 2642-2646.

Radhakrishna, R. (2007), "Report and Expert Group on Agricultural Indebtedness", Department of Economic Affairs Ministry of Finance, Government of India.

Stiglitz, E. Joseph (1990), "Peer Monitoring and Credit Markets" *The World Bank Economic Review*, 4 (3): 351-66.

Stiglitz, J. E., & Weiss, A. (1981), "Credit Rationing in Markets with Imperfect Information", *American Economic Review*, 71 (3): 393-410.

World Bank (1996): "Bangladesh: Poverty Alleviation Microfinance Project" Staff Appraisal Report South Asia Region, Country Department-1, Private Sector Development and Finance Division, Washington

Yaron, J. (1992), Assessing Development Finance Institutions. *World Bank Discussion Paper 174*, Washington D.C., p.12.

Zeller, M. (1994), "Determinants of credit rationing: A study of informal lenders and formal credit groups in Madagascar", *World Development*, 22(12): 1895-1907.

6

The Economic Impact on SHG Members, Women's Empowerment and Gender Relations

6.1 Introduction

The unique feature of microfinance is that it focuses on women for development. More than 90 per cent clients under microfinance are women. The basic idea is to empower women by providing them financial assistance and allowing them to earn an independent income, contribute financially to their household and generate self-employment. This economic independence is expected to generate increased self-respect, self-confidence and other forms of empowerment for women. The process of empowerment of the beneficiaries under microfinance is not automatic, but depends upon many factors. These factors may be abilities, environment, initiative and status of women as group. There are no dearth of studies which show that with the help of microfinance the status of a woman improves in the family than before; she participates in the decision-making and community meetings; and she gets freedom to move for the betterment of the business (Deepty Bansal, 2010). The present chapter studies the economic impact of microfinance on women empowerment. This chapter has been divided into three sections. The first section deals with the concept, measurement and indicators of women empowerment. The second section deals with the economic impact of microfinance on women empowerment and the third section explains the determinants of women empowerment.

SECTION-I
CONCEPT AND INDICATORS OF WOMEN EMPOWERMENT

6.2 Concept and Indicators of Women Empowerment: Concept of Empowerment:

There is no consensus on the concept of empowerment. It may be because of the fact that different experts use this concept differently. Empowerment is an intrinsic quality of a person, which cannot be bestowed by a third party. It is considered that an empowered person's behavior undergoes a change. In a nutshell, empowerment is a process which enables one to gain power, authority and influence over others. In the literature published on the subject, the empowerment is considered to be matching with the following traits (Deepty Bansal, 2010).

- Having decision-making power of one's own
- Having access to information and resources for taking proper decision
- Having a range of options from which one can make choices
- Ability to exercise assertiveness in collective decision-making
- Having positive thinking about the ability to make change
- Ability to learn skills for improving one's personal or group power
- Ability to change others" perceptions by democratic means
- Involving in the growth process

Empowerment helps the person concerned to exploit the economic environment in increasing the productivity of self, family and the society. Recently, the World Bank has made gender mainstreaming a priority in development assistance. In a policy research report, World Bank (2001) identified both gender equality and women empowerment as development objectives and means to promote growth, reduce poverty and support better governance. In the literature available on women empowerment, some of the concepts like gender equality, female autonomy or women status etc. are referring to as either similar or different concepts.

According to Kabeer's (2001) understanding there are two essential elements of women empowerment, i.e., process and agency. A process is defined as the series of events that produce gradual change. The process of women empowerment leads to expansion in their ability to have resources and to make strategic life choices. The agency element of women empowerment describes that women themselves are the significant actors in the process of change. Kabeer (1999) explained that women's empowerment refers to the process by which those who have been denied the ability to make strategic life choices, acquire such ability. The ability to exercise choices incorporates three inter-related dimensions: Resources, which include access as well as future claims to both material and social resources; Agency, which includes the process of decision-making, negotiation, deception and manipulation; and achievements. Kabeer's (2001) understanding of agency is mainly based upon Sen's study. Agency is defined as an actor's ability and involvement to make meaningful choices. It encompasses the ability to formulate strategic choices, to control resources and decisions that affect important life outcomes.

Longwe and Clarke (1994) explained women empowerment as an on-going cyclical process having five stages. The first stage is welfare stage and at this stage the women's resources are not fully recognized and met. The second is access stage, where women recognise it and take action to gain access to these resources. The third stage is the conscientisation level stage, where women realise that their lack of access to resources and their general subordinate status are due to socially constructed beliefs and phenomena. The fourth stage is participation level stage, where women become actively involved in decision-making processes within their households, communities and societies. The final stage is control stage, in which women get control over access tore sources and distribution of benefits by increasing their participation. This control increases women's power and respect within their households and societies at large.

Measurement of Women Empowerment:

The measurement aspect can differentiate between the aspects of customs, traditions and natural behavior of women and the change in behavior after intervention and emerge as subservient to the existing norms (Deepty Bansal, 2010). Malhotra et al., (2002) emphasized that measurement of empowerment is a primary development issue and so far neither the World Bank nor any other credible agency has given a rigorous methodology for measuring the changes in level of women empowerment.

The main problems in measuring empowerment are: (a) the measurement of women empowerment involves both quantitative as well as qualitative data such as access to financial resources, participation in household decision-making, change in the level of self-confidence, mobility, level of awareness etc. It is difficult to measure the qualitative indicators of empowerment. (b) Empowerment is an ongoing process and to measure the changes in a process, data is to be collected for at least two points in time.

But this method is further restricted as it is difficult to decide the time gap over which the changes are to be measured because some signs of empowerment can be seen in a short time period of 2 to 3 years while for others a longer time period may be required. There may be a shift in the relevance of empowerment indicators over time.

Due to the complexity of defining and measuring women empowerment, only a few empirical studies on the subject have tried to examine the impact of microfinance on women empowerment. The Human Development Report (1995) introduced two complementary indexes: the Gender-related Development Index (GDI) and the Gender Empowerment Measure (GEM). The GDI indicator measures the inequalities between men and women in terms of access to basic needs, whereas GEM evaluates women's access to political and economic posts, i.e., share of women seats in parliament/assemblies, the share of supervisory, administrative and technical posts. The GDI focuses on the extension of capabilities, whereas the GEM is concerned with the use of those capabilities to take advantage of the opportunities of life.

Most of the studies have measured the women empowerment with the help of an index. Mizan's (1994) study uses an index named "Household Decision Making (HHDM)" index to explore the impact of micro-credit on women's empowerment. She uses a number of indicators such as women's role in household decision-making, their control over fertility decisions, uses of healthcare services for self and the family and participation in voting. Goetz and Gupta (1996) hypothesised that control over loan activity is, in fact, a critical control point in the process by which access to loans translates into a range of valued achievements, and then managerial control can serve as an indicator of empowerment. They build an index of managerial control in order to classify the borrowers into five categories ranging from no control to full control over the entire productive process, including marketing.

Some of the researchers raised doubts about the appropriateness of the construction of indices for measurement of women empowerment. According to them assigning equal weights to various indicators of empowerment is not appropriate. For example, decision of visiting a nearby market and participation in a decision to buy a piece of land, both these decisions have different implications and magnitude of impact on women empowerment. Assigning equal weights to these different types of decisions may lead to inaccurate results. Thus, there cannot be a universal theory for measurement of empowerment. However, it depends upon the researcher to select representative indicators of women empowerment. The researcher should have good knowledge of social, economic and political environment of the area of study while choosing empowerment indicators and assigning weights to them. The present study also uses an index for measuring women empowerment. The index comprises of various indicators which determine women empowerment.

Indicators of Women Empowerment

One can judge empowerment through indicators. These indicators can be given values, based on the judgment of the researcher. Some of the studies assign weights to the indicators, which are mostly arbitrary. However, there cannot be any measure of empowerment because the nature of the concept is such that it is multifaceted concept which is not readily quantifiable. It can be said that empowerment is context and region specific which implies that there cannot be some standard indicators of women empowerment, applicable to all times and places. So, the measurement of empowerment through indicators can only be in a given socio-economic and political context where an intervention is made. There have been several efforts to devise indicators of empowerment. The table 6.1 shows the six domains of empowerment as suggested by the John Snow Inc. (1990).

Table 6.1: JSI Domains of Empowerment

Domain	Expressions
1. Sense of Self & vision of a future	Assertiveness, plans for the future, future-oriented actions, relative freedom from threat of physical violence, awareness of own problems and options, actions indicating sense of security.
2. Mobility & visibility	Activities outside of the home, relative freedom from harassment in public spaces, interaction with men.
3. Economic Security	Property ownership, new skills and knowledge and increased income, engaged in new/non-traditional types of work.
4. Status & Decision - making power within the household	Self-confidence, controlling spending money, enhanced Status in the family, controls/spends money, participation in decisions on allocation of resources, not dominated by others.
5. Ability to interact effectively in the public sphere	Awareness of legal status and services available, ability to get access to social services, political awareness, participation in credit program, provider of service in community.
6. Participation in non-family groups	Identified as a person outside the family, forum for creating sense of solidarity with other women, self-expression and articulation of problems, participating in a group with autonomous structure.

Source: John Snow Inc. (JSI) 1990:

Mostly, indicators of empowerment are proxy variables. During the field survey a number of questions were asked to capture the process of decision-making, control, choice etc. Such questions are observed as most effective representations of the process of empowerment. The indicators of empowerment based on field survey questions are specific and relevant within a particular social context. However, it points towards the impact of intervention in case of microfinance on the condition and process of the empowerment of women. The present study takes into consideration five indicators to measure economic empowerment. Table 6.2 shows these sixteen indicators of women empowerment. In order to quantify the impact of microfinance on women empowerment an Economic Empowerment Index is prepared. The scores assigned to different indicators are given in the Appendix- 6.1.

Table 6.2: Indicators of Economic Empowerment

Domain	Indicators
Economic Empowerment	1. Access to control over Family Resources 2. Credit worthiness 3. Freedom from money lenders 4. Bargaining power 5. Self-employment potential 6. Banking habits 7. Aware of property rights 8. Marketing skills 9. Productive skills 10. Household occupation 11. Reduction in wasteful expenditure 12. Food habits 13. Minor repairs to house 14. Reduction in consumption expenditure 15. Loan repayments 16. Purchase of household durables

Source: Own Compilation

The economic impact of the above indicators on the level of women empowerment is measured in the next section.

SECTION-II
THE ECONOMIC IMPACT OF MICRO FINANCE ON WOMEN EMPOWERMENT

6.3 The Economic Impact of Microfinance on Women Empowerment:

The economic impact of microfinance on women empowerment has been measured as discussed below. Microfinance through SHGs has linked poor women with formal credit delivery system, provided micro-loans and has encouraged them to start microenterprises. This programme has helped in increasing self-employment as well as income of the members and helped them to become economically more empowered than non-members.

Women's Access to Employment:

Traditionally, the women are capable of performing domestic chores only. But, employed women, wage or self-employed, discard this social belief. Employment provides them an opportunity to come out of the four walls of their house. Employment leads to possession over income, knowledge, awareness and self-confidence. Employment gives exposure to the outside world. Therefore, women's access to employment is an important indicator of empowerment. The study shows that the microfinance has helped the members in increasing employment (table 6.3).

Table 6.3 Employment

Category of Members	Un-employed	Below 80	80-160	160-240	Above 240	Total
OSHG	19 (9.5)	15 (7.5)	42 (21.0)	95 (47.5)	29 (14.5)	200 (100.0)
NSHG	30 (15.0)	20 (10.0)	45 (22.5)	72 (36.0)	33 (16.5)	200 (100.0)
ALL	49 (12.2)	35 (8.8)	87 (21.8)	167 (41.8)	62 (15.5)	400 (100.0)

Source: Field Survey

Note: the figures in brackets indicate percentages of OSHG and NSHG members.

Chi-square ($\chi 2$) = 6.713, df = 4, p-value =5.587

Women's contribution to Household Income

The increased household income improves the status of woman within her family. This increases her recognition, power and control over the family. The contribution to household income helps women to become economically independent and decision-maker in the household expenditure. The Microfinance has helped women participants to increase their contribution to the household income. Chi-square test shows that these differences between the OSHG and NSHG are significant at 1 percent level.

Table 6.4 Income

Category of Members	Up to3000	3001-5000	5001-10000	Above 10000	Total
OSHG	36 (43.9)	102 (52.3)	57 (50.8)	5 (45.5)	200 (100.0)
NSHG	46 (56.1)	93 (47.7)	55 (49.2)	6 (54.5)	200 (100.0)
ALL	82 (100.0)	195 (100.0)	112 (100.0)	11 (100.0)	400 (100.0)

Source: Field Survey

Note: the figures in brackets indicate percentages of OSHG and NSHG members.

Chi-square ($\chi 2$) = 1.762, df = 3, p-value = 0.623

Women's Access to Control over Household Resources:

Women's access to control over household resources has been considered as the possession of house, land, gold and jewellery, etc. If a woman owns the house/ land, she gets more respect and feels more control over the family. The possession of gold and jewellery leads to economic security. Microfinance increases the economic prospectus of the SHG members, which helps them to have access to and control over the household economic resources. Data was collected regarding the women's ownership of house, land, gold and jewellery (table 6.5).

Table 6.5 Access to and Control over Family Resources

Indicator		OSHG	NSHG	All	Chi-square ($\chi 2$)
Ownership of House	yes	152 (76.0)	157 (78.5)	309 (77.2)	0.356 (0.550)
	no	48 (24.0)	43 (21.5)	91 (22.8)	
Ownership of Land	yes	4 (2.0)	19 (9.5)	23 (5.8)	10.379* (0.001)
	no	196 (98.0)	181 (90.5)	377 (94.2)	
Possession of Gold and Jewellery	yes	170 (85.0)	176 (88.0)	346 (86.5)	0.771 (0.379)
	no	30 (15.0)	24 (12.0)	54 (13.5)	

Source: Field Survey

Note: the figures in brackets indicate percentages of OSHG and NSHG members.

*Significant at 1% level.

The results presented in Table 6.5 show that just 76 per cent of the OSHG households and 78.5 per cent of the NSHG households own house in their name and just 2 per cent of the OSHG households and 9.5 per cent of the NSHG households own land. The respondents were also asked about their possession of gold and jewellery. It is found that 85 per cent of the OSHG households and 88 per cent of the NSHG households possess some gold and jewellery. One of the reasons of large number of the households having possession of gold may be their economic prosperity. Chi-square test shows that these differences between the OSHG and NSHG are significant at 1 percent level.

Role of Women in Household Financial Decision-making:

Women involved in the household financial decision-making are definitely more empowered because generally male members of the family dominate in financial decision-making. The respondents were asked about their independence and contribution in making financial decisions like budget allocation, when to get a loan, amount and source of loan, buying and selling of household durables etc. Table 6.6 shows the role of women in the household financial decision-making.

Table 6.6 Role of Women in Household Financial Decision-Making

Category of Members	No Change	Little Improvement	Moderate Improvement	Good Improvement	Total
OSHG	15 (7.5)	20 (10.0)	64 (32.0)	101 (50.5)	200 (100.0)
NSHG	27 (13.5)	79 (39.5)	55 (27.5)	39 (19.5)	200 (100.0)
ALL	42 (10.5)	99 (24.8)	119 (29.8)	140 (35.0)	400 (100.0)

Source: Field Survey

Note: the figures in brackets indicate percentages of OSHG and NSHG members.

Chi-square ($\chi 2$) = 66.728, df = 3, p-value = 0.000

The table shows that around 60 per cent of the OSHG and NSHG households are expressing moderate and good improvement in financial decisions. In this way, microfinance raises the economic status of women. Chi-square test shows that these differences between the OSHG and NSHG are significant at 1 per cent level.

Saving in Bank Account

If a woman having a savings bank account, deposits money regularly in the account in her individual capacity, she is considered to have more foresightedness and economically aware as compared to those who do not take this initiative. Here, the amount of deposit, which is necessary for SHG to get microfinance benefit, may develop the banking habits of SHG members. This develops the habit of thrift and banking.

Economic Empowerment Index

The sixteen indicators of women empowerment discussed above are both quantitative as well as qualitative in nature. These indicators represent the economic empowerment of women. In order to quantify the level of women empowerment an

Economic Empowerment Index (EEI) is prepared. The indicators influencing women empowerment are assigned arbitrary scores as shown in Appendix-6.1 and then the scores of these indicators are added together. The respondents who score between 0-0.25, 0.25-0.50, 0.50-0.75 and 0.75-1.0 are classified as less, medium, high and very high empowered respectively. Andhra Pradesh is one of the prosperous states; and women residents of this state are relatively more empowered as compared to their counterparts living in other states. So, index score of 0.25 is assumed to be the minimum expected score from the respondents surveyed. The results of the EEI are exhibited in Table 6.7

$$\text{Economic Empowerment Index (EEI)} = \frac{\text{Actual Score Obtained}}{\text{Maximum Score Obtained}}$$

Table 6.7 Economic Empowerment Index of Respondents

Level of Empowerment	EEI Score	OSHG	NSHG	ALL
Less Empowered	(0-0.25)	3 (1.5)	11 (5.5)	14 (3.5)
Medium Empowered	(0.25-0.50)	11 (5.5)	113 (56.5)	124 (31.0)
High Empowered	(0.50-0.75)	119 (59.5)	76 (38.0)	195 (48.8)
Very High Empowered	(0.75-1.0)	67 (33.5)	0 (0.0)	67 (16.8)
Total		200 (100.0)	200 (100.0)	400 (100.0)

Source: Field Survey.

Note: the figures in brackets indicate percentages of OSHG and NSHG members.

Chi-square ($\chi 2$) =164.957, df = 3, p-value 0.000 at 1 percent significant level.

It is observed from the table that only 93 per cent of the OSHG and 38 percent of the NSHG are found to be empowered. Only 5.5 per cent of the OSHG and as high as 56.5 per cent of the NSHG fall in the medium empowered category. However, a very few per cent of both the households fall in the less empowered category.

SECTION-III
DETERMINANTS OF ECONOMIC IMPACT ON WOMEN EMPOWERMENT

6.4 Determinants of Economic Impact on Women Empowerment

The field survey and the review of literature give an idea that amount of group loans used for income generating activities, age of the SHG members their income, level of employment, assets, household income and their confidence in moving out of their houses may be the significant determinants of economic empowerment of the members. The present study finds out the impact of these variables on the level of economic empowerment. The following tables explain how the change in these variables affects the level of women empowerment.

Age of the Member and Economic Empowerment:

Table 6.8 Age of the Members and Economic Empowerment

Level of Empowerment	19-39	40-49	50-59	above 60
OSHG				
Less Empowered	2 (1.9)	1 (2.5)	0 (0.0)	0 (0.0)
Medium Empowered	5 (4.7)	3 (7.5)	3 (7.7)	0 (0.0)
High Empowered	67 (63.2)	20 (50.0)	23 (59.0)	9 (60.0)
Very High Empowered	32 (30.2)	16 (40.0)	13 (33.3)	6 (40.0)
Total	106 (100.0)	40 (100.0)	39 (100.0)	15 (100.0)
NSHG				
Less Empowered	6 (4.8)	0 (0.0)	1 (4.3)	4 (33.3)
Medium Empowered	70 (56.5)	26 (63.4)	12 (52.2)	5 (41.7)
High Empowered	48 (38.7)	15 (36.6)	10 (43.5)	3 (25.0)
Very High Empowered	-	-	-	-
Total	124 (100.0)	41 (100.0)	23 (100.0)	12 (100.0)

Source: Field Survey.

Note: The figures in brackets indicate percentages of OSHG and NSHG members employed their respective categories.

Table 6.8 shows the impact of age of the SHG members on the level of women empowerment. The table provides that 67.9 per cent and 57.5 per cent of the OSHG members and 95.2 percent and 100 percent of the NSHG members in the age groups of 19-39 and 40-49 years are in the medium and high empowered categories respectively. In the age group of above 60 years, all the OSHG members are high and very high empowered but in case of NSHG members 75 per cent are less and medium empowered, and the remaining 25 per cent are high empowered. Therefore, there exists no particular relation between age and empowerment. In this way, it can be said that the age of members is not a significant determinant of women empowerment.

Educational status and Economic Empowerment:

Table 6.9 Educational status and Economic Empowerment

Level of Empowerment	Illiterate	Primary	Secondary	Post-Secondary
OSHG				
Less Empowered	2 (3.3)	0 (0.0)	1 (2.1)	0 (0.0)
Medium Empowered	7 (11.5)	2 (2.5)	2 (4.2)	0 (0.0)
High Empowered	39 (63.9)	50 (63.3)	24 (50.0)	6 (50.0)
Very High Empowered	13 (21.3)	27 (34.2)	21 (43.8)	6 (50.0)
Total	61 (100.0)	79 (100.0)	48 (100.0)	12 (100.0)
NSHG				
Less Empowered	5 (6.8)	3 (4.5)	2 (4.9)	1 (5.3)
Medium Empowered	36 (49.3)	46 (68.7)	21 (51.2)	10 (52.6)
High Empowered	32 (43.8)	18 (26.9)	18 (43.9)	8 (42.1)
Very High Empowered	-	-	-	-
Total	73 (100.0)	67 (100.0)	41 (100.0)	19 (100.0)

Source: Field Survey.

Note: The figures in brackets indicate percentages of OSHG and NSHG members employed their respective categories.

Table 6.9 reflects the impact of educational status of the SHG members on their empowerment. It is revealed that an increase in the level of education results in increasing the level of empowerment and the members move from the less empowered category to medium, high and very high empowered categories. The table reveals that there is no impact of educational status of the SHG members on their empowerment.

Employment Status and Economic Empowerment:

Table 6.10 Level of Employment and Economic Empowerment (in days per annum)

Level of Empowerment	Un-employed	Below 80 days	80-160 days	160-240 days	Above 240 days
OSHG					
Less Empowered	2 (10.5)	0 (0.0)	1 (2.4)	0 (0.0)	0 (0.0)
Medium Empowered	2 (10.5)	4 (26.7)	2 (4.8)	2 (2.1)	1 (3.4)
High Empowered	9 (47.4)	11 (73.3)	31 (73.8)	53 (55.8)	15 (51.7)
Very High Empowered	6 (31.6)	0 (0.0)	8 (19.0)	40 (42.1)	13 (44.8)
Total	19 (100.0)	15 (100.0)	42 (100.0)	95 (100.0)	29 (100.0)
NSHG					
Less Empowered	4 (13.3)	5 (25.0)	1 (2.2)	1 (1.4)	0 (0.0)
Medium Empowered	24 (80.0)	11 (55.0)	33 (73.3)	31 (43.1)	14 (42.4)
High Empowered	2 (6.7)	4 (20.0)	11 (24.4)	40 (55.6)	19 (57.6)
Very High Empowered	-	-	-	-	-
Total	30 (100.0)	20 (100.0)	45 (100.0)	72 (100.0)	33 (100.0)

Source: Field Survey.

Note: The figures in brackets indicate percentages of OSHG and NSHG members employed their respective categories.

Table 6.10 reveals the impact of employment on the level of women empowerment. The table reflects that an increase in the number of employment days results in increasing the level of empowerment in the SHG women. An increase in the employment days shifts the SHG households from the less and medium empowered categories to high and very high empowered categories. The table brings out that 98 percent and 96 per cent of the OSHG members and 55 percent and 57 percent of the NSHG members employed for, 160-240 and above 240 days per annum are high empowered. In this way, the employment level of the SHG members is significantly influencing their level of empowerment.

Household Income and Economic Empowerment

Table 6.11 Household Income and Economic Empowerment (Income in Rs. per month)

Level of Empowerment	Up to3000	3001-5000	5001-10000	Above 10000
		OSHG		
Less Empowered	28 (77.8)	62 (60.8)	0 (0.0)	0 (0.0)
Medium Empowered	5 (13.9)	2 (2.0)	3 (5.3)	1 (20.0)
High Empowered	3 (8.4)	1 (1.0)	27 (47.4)	2 (40.0)
Very High Empowered	0 (0.0)	37 (36.3)	27 (47.4)	2 (40.0)
Total	36 (100.0)	102 (100.0)	57 (100.0)	5 (100.0)
		NSHG		
Less Empowered	6 (13.0)	3 (3.2)	2 (3.6)	0 (0.0)
Medium Empowered	29 (63.0)	57 (61.3)	24 (43.6)	3 (50.0)
High Empowered	11 (23.9)	33 (35.5)	29 (52.7)	3 (50.0)
Very High Empowered	-	-	-	-
Total	46 (100.0)	93 (100.0)	55 (100.0)	6 (100.0)

Source: Field Survey.

Note: The figures in brackets indicate percentages of OSHG and NSHG members employed their respective categories.

Table 6.11 measures the impact of household income of the SHG members on their empowerment. The table shows that the SHG members with higher levels of family income are more empowered as compared to the SHG members whose household income is comparatively less. The table provides that 91.7, and 62.8 per cent of the OSHG members and 76.0 and 64.5 per cent of the NSHG members with the respective household income up to Rs. 3,000 and 3,000-5,000 per month are less empowered and medium empowered. None of the participants in the household income group of up to Rs. 3,000 is found to be in the very high empowered category. The table provides that as the household income increases the level of empowerment also increases. In this way, household income is significantly influencing the level of women empowerment.

Loans used for Productive Purposes and Economic Empowerment:

Table 6.12 Loans Used for Productive Purposes and Economic Empowerment

(in Rupees)

Level of Empowerment	Nil	Up to 10000	10001 - 20000	20001-30000	Above 30000
			OSHG		
Less Empowered	20 (45.5)	3 (75.0)	0 (0.0)	0 (0.0)	0 (0.0)
Medium Empowered	4 (9.0)	0 (0.0)	4 (7.7)	1 (1.4)	2 (2.9)
High Empowered	20 (45.5)	1 (25.0)	16 (50.0)	43 (60.6)	39 (56.5)
Very High Empowered	0 (0.0)	0 (0.0)	12 (23.1)	7 (38.0)	28 (40.6)
Total	44 (100.0)	4 (100.0)	32 (100.0)	51 (100.0)	69 (100.0)
		NSHG			
Less Empowered	36 (33.6)	9 (33.3)	11 (45.8)	0 (0.0)	0 (0.00)
Medium Empowered	45 (42.0)	12 (44.4)	0 (0.0)	12 (36.4)	3 (33.3)
High Empowered	12 (11.2)	3 (11.1)	5 (20.8)	18 (54.5)	4 (44.5)
Very High Empowered	14 (13.1)	3 (11.1)	8 (33.3)	3 (9.1)	2 (22.2)
Total	107 (100.0)	27 (100.0)	24 (100.0)	33 (100.0)	9 (100.0)

Source: Field Survey.

Note: The figures in brackets indicate percentages of OSHG and NSHG members employed their respective categories.

Table 6.12 explains the level of empowerment of the SHG members who utilize different sums of group loans for income generating activities. The table provides that as the members utilize large amount of loans for productive purposes, they become more empowered. The table shows that more than half of the members who do not utilize loans for productive purposes are less and medium empowered. However, none of the participants who utilize above Rs. 30,000 for productive purposes is in the less empowered category. 97 per cent of the OSHG members and 66 percent of the NSHG members who use above Rs. 30,000 for productive purposes belong to high and very high categories of empowerment. In this way, the loans used for productive purposes also influence the women empowerment.

Level of Mobility and Economic Empowerment:

Table 6.13 Level of Mobility and Economic Empowerment

Level of Empowerment	Can"t Go Outside	Can Visit Another Village	Can Visit Nearest Town	Can Visit City
OSHG				
Less Empowered	2 (40.0)	8 (42.1)	3 (14.3)	0 (0.0)
Medium Empowered	2 (40.0)	8 (42.1)	4 (19.0)	3 (1.9)
High Empowered	1 (20.0)	3 (15.8)	11 (52.4)	98 (63.2)
Very High Empowered	0 (00.0)	0 (0.00)	3 (14.3)	54 (34.8)
Total	5 (100.0)	19 (100.0)	21 (100.0)	155 (100.0)
NSHG				
Less Empowered	1 (12.5)	2 (6.9)	7 (7.6)	1 (1.4)
Medium Empowered	5 (62.5)	24 (82.8)	64 (69.6)	20 (28.2)
High Empowered	2 (25.0)	3 (10.3)	21 (22.8)	50 (70.4)
Very High Empowered	-	-	-	-
Total	8 (100.0)	29 (100.0)	92 (100.0)	71 (100.0)

Source: Field Survey.

Note: The figures in brackets indicate percentages of OSHG and NSHG members employed their respective categories

.Table 6.13 highlights the level of mobility of the participants on their empowerment. The table depicts that 40 and 40 per cent of the OSHG members and 12.5 and 62.5 percent of the NSHG members who cannot go out of their houses independently fall in the less and medium empowered categories respectively. However, 15.8, 66.7 and 98 per cent of the OSHG members and 10.3, 22.8 and 70.4 per cent of the NSHG members having confidence to visit another village, nearest town and a city fall in the high empowered category. It establishes that women empowerment is directly influenced by their level of mobility.

Regression Analysis:

A multiple linear regression is used to statistically measure the impact of all these determinants on the level of Economic Empowerment Index (EEI). The following regression equation is used to measure the effect of key indicators on EEI.

$$EEI\ (Y) = b_0 + b_1AGE + b_2EDU + b_3EMPL + b_4HHINC + b_5PROLOAN + b_6ASSETS + b_7MOBLITY + ... + u$$

Where:

EEI	=	Economic Empowerment Index (Dependent variable)
AGE	=	Age of the members in years
EDU	=	Education level of the members
EMPL	=	Employment in person days in Post SHG
HHINC	=	Household income of the members in rupees
PROLOAN	=	Amount of loan used for productive purposes in rupees
ASSETS	=	Assets (house + land +jewellery)
MOBLITY	=	Level of mobility of the members

Table 6.14 Results of Regression Analysis

Variables	OSHG		NSHG	
	B	Sig.	B	Sig.
Constant	0.450* (10.234)	.000	0.489* (11.202)	.000
AGE	0.001** (2.190)	.030	-0.001*** (-1.748)	.082
EDU	0.002 (1.170)	.243	-0.004** (-2.394)	.018
PROLOAN	0.025* (6.286)	.000	0.007* (2.627)	.009
EMPL	-.010*** (-1.858)	.065	0.003 (0.507)	.613
HHINC	0.004 (0.687)	.493	0.002 (0.245)	.807
MOBLITY	0.015*** (1.954)	.052	0.049* (6.389)	.000
ASSETS	0.030* (3.249)	.001	-0.001 (-0.104)	.917
Observations	200		200	
R2	0.270		0.261	
Adjusted R2	0.244		0.235	
F-value	10.170* (0.000)		9.710*(0.000)	

*significant at 1 percent level. ** significant at 5 percent level. ***significant at 10 percent level. Note: The figures given in parentheses indicate t-values.

Table 6.14 highlights the coefficients of these variables. The regression results show that all the coefficients have positive values except variables viz., employment in OSHG and age, education and assets in NSHG. The coefficients of regression variables, e.g. age, amount of loans used for productive purposes, employment, spatial mobility and assets of the OSHG members and the coefficients of regression variables age, education, amount of loans used for productive purposes and mobility of the NSHG members are playing a significant role in women empowerment.

6.5 Summary

It can be concluded that microfinance is helpful in empowering women economically. The education, skill and training provided by microfinance lead to the development of the overall personality of the members. The SHG members have higher levels of employment, income and participation in household financial decision-making. It is also found that the members are more confident while travelling, visiting market for the purchase of household goods, and dealing with other members of the society. Members of the microfinance are able to raise their voice against various social exploitations more confidently. The regression results show that all the coefficients have positive values except variables viz., employment in OSHG and age, education and assets in NSHG. The coefficients of regression variables, e.g. age, amount of loans used for productive purposes, employment, spatial mobility and assets of the OSHG members and the coefficients of regression variables age, education, amount of loans used for productive purposes and mobility of the NSHG members are playing a significant role in women empowerment. In this way, microfinance has contributed a lot in the empowerment of women.

References

Bansal, D. (2010), "Impact of Microfinance on Poverty, Employment and Women Empowerment in Rural Punjab", unpublished thesis, *Punjabi University*, Bathinda.

Goetz, A. M., & Gupta, R. S. (1996), "Who takes the credit? Gender, power, and control over loan use in rural credit programs in Bangladesh", *World development*, 24(1): 45-63.

UNDP (1995), Human Development Report, Oxford University Press, New York.

Kabeer, N. (1999), "The Conditions and Consequences of Choice: Reflections on the Measurement of Women"s Empowerment", Discussion Paper, No. 108, *United Nations Research Institute for Social Development,* Geneva.

Kabeer, N. (2001), "Conflict over Credit: Re-evaluating the Empowerment Potential of Loans to Women in Rural Bangladesh", *World Development*, 29(1): 63-84.

Longwe, S. H.; and Clarke, R. (1994), "Women in Development, Culture and Youth: Workshop Readings", *Longwe Clarke and Associates*, Lusaka, Zambia.

Malhotra, A.; Schuler, S.R.; and Boender, C. (2002), Measuring Women"s Empowerment as a Variable in International Development, World Bank, Washington, DC.

Mizan, A.N. (1994), *In Quest of Empowerment: The Grameen Bank Impact on Women's Power and Status*, University Press Limited, Dhaka.

World Bank (2001), *Engendering Development: Through Gender Equality in Rights, Resources and Voice*, World Bank Policy Research Report, Oxford University Press, Oxford.

7

The Social Impact on SHG Members, Women's Empowerment and Gender Relations

7.1 Introduction

One of the most essential features of development is the transformation of society, which embraces the movement from traditional relations, socials norms and traditional ways of health care, education and methods of production to more modern ones. However, change from old to new is not an end in itself, but only a means to achieve the end. The changes associated with development provide societies as well as the individuals more control and influence over their own destiny. Development enriches the lives of individuals by widening horizons of the choices and freedoms and at the same time by reducing their sense of isolation. Hence, the development strategy must be aimed at facilitating the transformation of society in identifying the potential catalysts and barriers to change. The SHG programme is an attempt, which provides enough opportunities to women to participate in the affairs of the family as well as in the society. The SHG programme provides adequate scope for the rural households, especiallywomen, to develop their self-confidence and social behavior through a series of training programmes and group meetings organized by the NGOs and the banks. An assessment of the social impact of the SHGs on its members is attempted in this chapter. This chapter has been divided into two sections. The first section deals with the social impact of microfinance on women empowerment and the second section explains the determinants of social impact on women empowerment.

SECTION-I
THE SOCIAL IMPACT OF MICRO FINANCE ON WOMEN EMPOWERMENT

7.2 The Social Impact of Microfinance on Women Empowerment

The present study takes into consideration twenty seven indicators to measure social empowerment under four domains of women empowerment which measure socio- cultural, political and education, skill and training and health empowerment. Table 7.1 shows these four domains and twenty seven indicators of women empowerment. In order to quantify the impact of microfinance on women empowerment a social empowerment index is prepared. The scores assigned to different indicators are given in the Appendix-7.1.

Table 7.1: Indicators of Women Empowerment

Domain	Indicators
1. Socio-cultural Empowerment	1. Self-confidence 2. Reduction in alcoholic habits 3. Attitude towards the education of daughters 4. Attitude towards the education of sons 5. Mobility 6. Access to markets 7. Adoption of small family norm 8. Discontinuation of early marriages 9. Reduction in domestic violence 10. Decision making in the family 11. Decision making in the group 12. Child labour discontinuation 13. Status in the family 14. Status in the society 15. Clothing 16. Social functions/marriages 17. Aware of rights of women
2. Political Empowerment	1. Access to public participation 2. Access to information on Government programmes 3. Participation in Development programmes 4. Ability to meet Government officials 5. Ability to meet Non- officials
3. Education, Skill Development Empowerment	1. Communication skills
4. Health Empowerment	1. Sanitation status 2. Personal hygiene 3. Nutritional status 4. Visiting hospital

Source: Own Compilation

The impact of these indicators on the level of women empowerment is measured below:

Socio-Cultural Empowerment

Microfinance programme pursued through SHGs is a collective effort of group members. The members co-operate one another, deal with other members of the society, and meet the members of other groups in their joint group meetings. In this way, they develop a social behaviour. Women are given an opportunity to come out of the four walls of their houses and meet other members of the society, which leads to their socio-cultural empowerment.

Women's Freedom Self-confidence

The traditional social norms restrict women's freedom and self confidence. But if a woman becomes able to attain such freedom she is considered to be more empowered. SHG activates encourage and ager an opportunity to their members to visit other places for acquiring skills, training and exhibiting their products in various fairs and exhibitions. Exposure of the members in the programme increases their confidence in travelling to other places. Table 7.2 shows the freedom and confidence of SHG members.

Table 7.2 Women's Freedom and Self Confidence

Category of Members	No Change	Little Improvement	Moderate Improvement	Good Improvement	Total
OSHG	2 (1.0)	4 (2.0)	92 (46.0)	102 (51.0)	200 (100.0)
NSHG	8 (4.0)	50 (25.0)	80 (40.0)	62 (31.0)	200 (100.0)
ALL	10 (2.5)	54 (13.5)	172 (43.0)	164 (41.0)	400 (100.0)

Source: Field survey.

Note: The figures in brackets indicate percentages of OSHG and NSHG members.

Chi-square ($\chi 2$) = 53.378, d.f =3, p-value is 0.000, at 1 % significant level.

It has been observed that 97 per cent of the OSHG members and 71 per cent of the NSHG members are more confident. Chi-square test shows that these differences between the selected sample groups are significant at 1 per cent level.

Visiting Market for Purchase of Household Goods

Visiting market increases the ability of a woman in various ways. Her self confidence increases because she travels bargains and reports complaints of defective products etc. Her decision-making capacity is increased because she plans her visit and uses her choice to select a product. During the visit and meeting with other people, helps to increase her motivation, social relations and knowledge. The women starting their business under the microfinance are often required to visit the market for the purchase of raw materials or selling their products. It results in enhancing their self-confidence and they feel no hesitation to visit the market for the purchase of goods.

Table 7.3 Ability to Visit Market

Category of Members	No Change	Little Improvement	Moderate Improvement	Good Improvement	Total
OSHG	0 (0.0)	9 (4.5)	127 (63.5)	64 (32.0)	200 (100.0)
NSHG	5 (2.5)	90 (45.0)	70 (35.0)	35 (17.5)	200 (100.0)
ALL	5 (1.2)	99 (24.8)	197 (49.2)	99 (24.8)	400 (100.0)

Source: Field survey.

Note: The figures in brackets indicate percentages of OSHG and NSHG members.

Chi-square ($\chi 2$) = 96.260 , d.f = 3, P-value 0.000 at 1 % significant level.

Table 7.3 shows that 95 per cent of the OSHG members and 52.5 per cent of the NSHG members are more confident to visit the market for the purchase of the goods. Chi-square test shows that these differences between OSHG and NSGH are significant at 1 percent level.

Ability to Raise Voice against Social Exploitation

This indicator represents the awareness and self-confidence of a woman. She is able to raise her voice in the village Panchayat meetings against the common problems and exploitation of any kind. SHG members visit other villages; interact with important local people; go to the banks; and meet various government officials. This helps to increase their level of confidence in dealing with officials, group members and other members of the community. The SHG members arrange weekly or fortnightly meetings where they discuss their personal as well as social problems. These activities enable them not only to find solution of their personal problems in their households but also to take up the common issues in the Panchayat meetings.

Table 7.4A Reduction in alcoholic habits

Category of Members	No Change	Little Improvement	Moderate Improvement	Good Improvement	Total
OSHG	10 (5.0)	96 (48.0)	65 (32.5)	29 (14.5)	200 (100.0)
NSHG	39 (19.5)	95 (47.5)	45 (22.5)	21 (10.5)	200 (100.0)
ALL	49 (12.2)	191 (47.8)	110 (27.5)	50 (12.5)	400 (100.0)

Source: Field survey.

Note: The figures in brackets indicate percentages of OSHG and NSHG members.

Chi-square ($\chi 2$) = 22.085, d.f =3, p-value is 0.000, at 1 % significant level.

Table 7.4B Reduction in domestic violence

Category of Members	No Change	Little Improvement	Moderate Improvement	Good Improvement	Total
OSHG	3 (1.5)	12 (6.0)	118 (59.0)	67 (33.5)	200 (100.0)
NSHG	22 (11.0)	103 (51.5)	37 (18.5)	38 (19.0)	200 (100.0)
ALL	25 (6.2)	115 (28.8)	155 (38.8)	105 (26.2)	400 (100.0)

Source: Field survey.

Note: The figures in brackets indicate percentages of OSHG and NSHG members. Chi-square ($\chi2$) = 136.787, d.f =3, p-value is 0.000, at 1 % significant level.

Table 7.4 C Discontinuation of early marriages

Category of Members	No Change	Little Improvement	Moderate Improvement	Good Improvement	Total
OSHG	12 (6.0)	35 (17.5)	70 (35.0)	83 (41.5)	200 (100.0)
NSHG	6 (3.0)	51 (25.5)	87 (43.5)	56 (28.0)	200 (100.0)
ALL	18 (4.5)	86 (21.5)	157 (39.2)	139 (34.8)	400 (100.0)

Source: Field survey.

Note: The figures in brackets indicate percentages of OSHG and NSHG members.

Chi-square ($\chi2$) = 12.062, d.f =3, p-value is 0.000, at 1 % significant level.

Table 7.4D Awareness of rights of women

Category of Members	No Change	Little Improvement	Moderate Improvement	Good Improvement	Total
OSHG	1 (0.5)	22 (11.0)	123 (61.5)	54 (27.0)	200 (100.0)
NSHG	23 (11.5)	96 (48.0)	43 (21.5)	38 (19.0)	200 (100.0)
ALL	24 (6.0)	118 (29.5)	166 (41.5)	92 (23.0)	400 (100.0)

Source: Field survey.

Note: The figures in brackets indicate percentages of OSHG and NSHG members.

Chi-square ($\chi2$) = 107.910, d.f =3, p-value is 0.000, at 1 % significant level.

Tables 7.4 (A,B,C and D) show that 47 per cent of the OSHG members and only 33 per cent of the NSHG members are more confident in reduction in alcoholic habits and 92.5 per cent of the OSHG members and only 37.5 per cent of the NSHG members are more confident in reduction in domestic violence. The table further shows that 76.5 per cent of the OSHG members and 71.5 per cent of the NSHG members are more confident in discontinues of early marriages and 88.5 per cent of the OSHG members and only 40.5 per cent of the NSHG members are more confident in the awareness of rights of women. Chi-square test shows that there are significant differences among sample groups regarding their confidence in raising voice against social exploitation.

Attitude towards the Education of Daughters:

This indicator represents the thinking, awareness, psychology and authority of a woman. The sense of gender equality in a woman advocates the idea to send her girl child to a school. She will be considered socially empowered if she takes a decision for the well-being of her family against the general social customs. Both the members are found to be aware of the importance of education for their girl child.

Table 7.5 Girl child education

Category of Members	No Change	Little Improvement	Moderate Improvement	Good Improvement	Total
OSHG	4 (2.0)	8 (4.0)	101 (50.5)	87 (43.5)	200 (100.0)
NSHG	7 (3.5)	27 (13.5)	78 (39.0)	88 (44.0)	200 (100.0)
ALL	11 (2.8)	35 (8.8)	179 (44.8)	175 (43.8)	400 (100.0)

Source: Field surbrackets indicate percentages of OSHG and NSHG members.
Chi-square ($\chi 2$) = 14.093, d.f =3, p-value is 0.000, at 1 % significant level.

Table 7.5 shows that 94 per cent of the OSHG members and 83 per cent of the NSHG members are more confident in girl child education. Chi-square test shows that these differences between OSHG and NSHG are significant at 1 per cent level.

Political Empowerment

It has been observed that microfinance has empowered the women participants socio-economically as well as politically. The impact is measured by comparing the level of political awareness among the participants and non-participants as well as the interest taken by them to participate in the village political affairs.

Able to Meet Government Officials

Able to meet Government officials is one of the main indicators of empowerment. Able to meet Government officials develops different types of abilities in a person and broadens her outlook. Table 7.6 shows that 80.5 per cent of the OSHG members and 54.5 per cent of the NSHG members are more confident in meeting government officials. Chi-square test shows that the differences between the groups are significant at 1 per cent level.

Table 7.6 Able to meet Government officials

Category of Members	No Change	Little Improvement	Moderate Improvement	Good Improvement	Total
OSHG	0 (0.0)	39 (19.5)	128 (64.0)	33 (16.5)	200 (100.0)
NSHG	22 (11.0)	69 (34.5)	56 (28.0)	53 (26.5)	200 (100.0)
ALL	22 (5.5)	108 (27.0)	184 (46.0)	86 (21.5)	400 (100.0)

Source: Field survey.

Note: The figures in brackets indicate percentages of OSHG and NSHG members.

Chi-square ($\chi 2$) = 63.158, d.f =3, p-value is 0.000, at 1 % significant level.

Able to Meet Non-officials

Able to meet Non-officials is also one of the main indicators of empowerment. Able to meet Non-officials develops abilities in a person and broadens her outlook. Table 7.7 shows that 63 per cent of the OSHG members and only 38 per cent of the NSHG members are more confident in meeting Non-officials. Chi-square test shows that the differences are significant at 1 per cent level.

Table 7.7 Able to meet Non-officials

Category of Members	No Change	Little Improvement	Moderate Improvement	Good Improvement	Total
OSHG	4 (2.0)	70 (35.0)	105 (52.5)	21 (10.5)	200 (100.0)
NSHG	43 (21.5)	81 (40.5)	26 (13.0)	50 (25.0)	200 (100.0)
ALL	47 (11.8)	151 (37.8)	131 (32.8)	71 (17.8)	400 (100.0)

Source: Field survey.

Note: The figures in brackets indicate percentages of OSHG and NSHG members.

Chi-square ($\chi 2$) = 92.649, d.f =3, p-value is 0.000, at 1 % significant level.

Public Participation:

Public participation leads to acquisition knowledge and development of new skills. Public participation develops abilities in a person and broadens her outlook. Table 7.8 shows that 93.5 per cent of the OSHG members and 54 per cent of the NSHG members are more confident in public participation. Chi-square test shows that the differences are significant at 1 per cent level.

Table 7.8 Public participation

Category of Members	No Change	Little Improvement	Moderate Improvement	Good Improvement	Total
OSHG	2 (1.0)	11 (5.5)	116 (58.0)	71 (35.5)	200 (100.0)
NSHG	12 (6.0)	80 (40.0)	71 (35.5)	37 (18.5)	200 (100.0)
ALL	14 (3.5)	91 (22.8)	187 (46.8)	108 (27.0)	400 (100.0)

Source: Field survey.

Note: The figures in brackets indicate percentages of OSHG and NSHG members.

Chi-square ($\chi 2$) = 80.994, d.f =3, p-value is 0.000, at 1 % significant level.

Access to Information on Government Programmes

Access to information on Government programmes is one of the main indicators of empowerment. Access to information on Government programmes develops different types of abilities in a person and broadens her outlook. Table 7.9 shows that 88.5 per cent of the OSHG members and 55 per cent of the NSHG members are more confident in access to information on Government programmes. Chi-square test shows that the differences are significant at 1 per cent level.

Table 7.9 Access to information on Government programmes

Category of Members	No Change	Little Improvement	Moderate Improvement	Good Improvement	Total
OSHG	4 (2.0)	19 (9.5)	134 (67.0)	43 (21.5)	200 (100.0)
NSHG	11 (5.5)	79 (39.5)	58 (29.0)	52 (26.0)	200 (100.0)
ALL	15 (3.8)	98 (24.5)	192 (48.0)	95 (23.8)	400 (100.0)

Source: Field survey.

Note: The figures in brackets indicate percentages of OSHG and NSHG members.

Chi-square ($\chi 2$) = 70.937, d.f =3, p-value is 0.000, at 1 % significant level.

Participation in Development Programmes:

Participation in development programmes leads to acquisition knowledge and development of new skills. Participation in development programmes develops abilities in a person and broadens her outlook. Table 7.10 shows that 83 per cent of the OSHG members and 53 per cent of the NSHG members are more confident in participating in development programmes. Chi-square test shows that the differences between the sample groups are significant at 1 per cent level.

Table 7.10 Participation in Development programmes

Category of Members	No Change	Little Improvement	Moderate Improvement	Good Improvement	Total
OSHG	4 (2.0)	30 (15.0)	134 (67.0)	32 (16.0)	200 (100.0)
NSHG	23 (11.5)	71 (35.5)	58 (29.0)	48 (24.0)	200 (100.0)
ALL	27 (6.8)	101 (25.2)	192 (48.0)	80 (20.0)	400 (100.0)

Source: Field survey.

Note: The figures in brackets indicate percentages of OSHG and NSHG members. Chi-square ($\chi2$) = 63.297, d.f =3, p-value is 0.000, at 1 % significant level.

Education, Skill and Training Empowerment

Besides the socio-economic and political empowerment of the members, microfinance also develops the overall personality of its members. The group activities lead to the development of basic skills like writing their name, reading numbers, doing basic arithmetic, filling bank forms, etc. SHGs influence the level of comfort and confidence of its members by developing these basic skills in them. All this generates knowledge and self-confidence which are the indicators of their empowerment. Education is one of the main indicators of empowerment.

Table 7.11 Communication skills

Category of Members	No Change	Little Improvement	Moderate Improvement	Good Improvement	Total
OSHG	1 (0.5)	7 (3.5)	117 (58.5)	75 (37.5)	200 (100.0)
NSHG	26 (13.0)	92 (46.0)	44 (22.0)	38 (19.0)	200 (100.0)
ALL	27 (6.8)	99 (24.8)	161 (40.2)	113 (28.2)	400 (100.0)

Source: Field survey.

Note: The figures in brackets indicate percentages of OSHG and NSHG members.

Chi-square ($\chi2$) = 141.342, d.f =3, p-value is 0.000, at 1 % significant level.

The Communication skills are one of the main indicators of empowerment. Communication skills develop different types of abilities in a person and broaden her outlook. Table 7.11 shows that 96 per cent of the OSHG members and 41 per cent of the NSHG members are more confident in communication skills. Chi-square test shows that the differences between OSHG and NSHG are significant at 1 per cent level.

Health Empowerment

Microfinance develops the health status of its members. The group activities lead to the development of basic knowledge in health empowerment. SHGs influence the level of comfort and confidence of its members by developing this basic knowledge in them. All this generates knowledge and self confidence which are the indicators of their empowerment.

Sanitation Status

Sanitation status is one of the main indicators of health empowerment. Table 7.12 shows that 72 per cent of the OSHG members and 42 per cent of the NSHG members are more confident in sanitation status. Chi-square test shows that the differences between the sample groups are significant at 1 per cent level.

Table 7.12 Sanitation status

Category of Members	No Change	Little Improvement	Moderate Improvement	Good Improvement	Total
OSHG	2 (1.0)	54 (27.0)	83 (41.5)	61 (30.5)	200 (100.0)
NSHG	19 (9.5)	97 (48.5)	35 (17.5)	49 (24.5)	200 (100.0)
ALL	21 (5.2)	151 (37.8)	118 (29.5)	110 (27.5)	400 (100.0)

Source: Field survey.

Note: The figures given in brackets indicate percentages of OSHG and NSHG members.

Chi-square ($\chi2$) = 46.841, d.f =3, p-value is 0.000, at 1 % significant level.

Personal Hygiene

The Personal hygiene is one of the main indicators of empowerment. Table 7.13 shows that 88.5 per cent of the OSHG members and 41.5 per cent of the NSHG members are more confident in Personal hygiene. Chi-square test shows that the differences between OSHG and NSHG are significant at 1 per cent level.

Table 7.13 Personal hygiene

Category of Members	No Change	Little Improvement	Moderate Improvement	Good Improvement	Total
OSHG	2 (1.0)	21 (10.5)	114 (57.0)	63 (31.5)	200 (100.0)
NSHG	24 (12.0)	93 (46.5)	50 (25.0)	33 (16.5)	200 (100.0)
ALL	26 (6.5)	114 (28.5)	164 (41.0)	96 (24.0)	400 (100.0)

Source: Field survey.

Note: The figures given in brackets indicate percentages of OSHG and NSHG members.

Chi-square ($\chi2$) = 98.440, d.f =3, p-value is 0.000, at 1 % significant level.

Nutritional Status:

Nutritional status is one of the main indicators of empowerment. Table 7.14 shows that 89.5 per cent of the OSHG members and 63 per cent of the NSHG members are more confident in Nutritional status. Chi-square test shows that these differences between the sample groups are significant at 1 per cent level.

Table 7.14 Nutritional status

Category of Members	No Change	Little Improvement	Moderate Improvement	Good Improvement	Total
OSHG	5 (2.5)	16 (8.0)	136 (68.0)	43 (21.5)	200 (100.0)
NSHG	19 (9.5)	55 (27.5)	51 (25.5)	75 (37.5)	200 (100.0)
ALL	24 (6.0)	71 (17.8)	187 (46.8)	118 (29.5)	400 (100.0)

Source: Field survey.

Note: The figures in brackets indicate percentages of OSHG and NSHG members.

Chi-square ($\chi2$) = 76.904, d.f =3, p-value is 0.000, at 1 % significant level.

Social Empowerment Index

Table 7.15 Social Empowerment Index of Respondents

Level of Empowerment	SEI Score	OSHG	NSHG	All
Less Empowered	(0-0.25)	6 (3.0)	102 (51.0)	108 (27.0)
Medium Empowered	(0.25-0.50)	37 (18.5)	66 (33.0)	103 (25.8)
High Empowered	(0.50-0.75)	79 (39.5)	14 (7.0)	93 (23.2)
Very High Empowered	(0.75-1.0)	78 (39.0)	18 (9.0)	96 (24.0)
Total		200 (100.0)	200 (100.0)	400 (100.0)

Source: Field Survey.

Note: The figures in brackets indicate percentages of OSHG and NSH members.

Chi-square ($\chi2$) =176.428, d.f = 3, p-value 0.000, at 1 % significant level.

The twenty seven indicators of women empowerment discussed above are both quantitative as well as qualitative in nature. These indicators represent the social empowerment of women. In order to quantify the level of women empowerment a Social Empowerment Index (SEI) is prepared. The indicators influencing women empowerment are assigned arbitrary scores as shown in Appendix-7.1 and then the scores of these indicators are added together. The respondents who score between 0-0.25, 0.25-0.50, 0.50-0.75 and 0.75-1.0 are classified as less, medium, high and very high empowered respectively. The results of the SEI are exhibited in Table 7.15.

$$\text{Economic Empowerment Index (EEI)} = \frac{\text{Actual Score Obtained}}{\text{Maximum Score Obtained}}$$

The table provides that only 78.5 per cent of the OSHG members and 16 per cent of the NSHG members are found to be empowered. Only 18.5 per cent of the OSHG and 33 per cent of the NSHG fall in the medium empowered category. However, a very few per cent of OSHG members and as high 51 per cent of the NSHG members fall in the less empowered category.

SECTION-II
DETERMINANTS OF SOCIAL IMPACT ON WOMEN EMPOWERMENT

7.3 Determinants of Social Impact on Women Empowerment

The experiences of the field survey give an idea that amount of group loans used for income generating activities, age of the SHG members, their income, level of employment, assets, household income and level of mobility may be the significant determinants of social empowerment of the members. The present study finds out the impact of these variables on the level of social empowerment. The following tables explain how the change in these variables affects the level of women empowerment.

Age of the Member and Social Empowerment

Table 7.16 Age of the Members and Social Empowerment

Level of Empowerment	19-39	40-49	50-59	Above 60
		OSHG		
Less Empowered	2 (1.9)	3 (7.5)	1 (2.6)	0 (0.0)
Medium Empowered	16 (15.1)	9 (22.5)	9 (23.1)	3 (20.0)
High Empowered	44 (41.5)	15 (37.5)	14 (35.9)	6 (40.0)
Very High Empowered	44 (41.5)	13 (32.5	15 (38.5)	6 (40.0)
Total	106 (100.0)	40 (100.0	39 (100.0)	15 (100.0)
		NSHG		
Less Empowered	63 (50.8)	22 (53.7)	10 (43.5)	7 (58.3)
Medium Empowered	41 (33.1)	13 (31.7)	10 (43.5)	2 (16.7)
High Empowered	10 (8.1)	3 (7.3)	1 (4.3)	0 (0.0)
Very High Empowered	10 (8.1)	3 (7.3)	2 (8.7)	3 (25.0)
Total	124 (100.0)	41 (100.0)	23 (100.0)	12 (100.0)

Source: Field Survey.

Note: The figures in brackets indicate percentages of OSHG and NSHG membersemployedtheirrespective categories.

Table 7.16 shows the impact of age of the SHG members on the level of social empowerment. The table provides that 56.6 per cent and 60 per cent of the OSHG members and 41.2 per cênt and 39 per cent of the NSHG members in the age groups of 19-39 and 40-49 years are in the medium and high empowered categories respectively. In the age group of above 60 years, 80 per cent of the OSHG members are high and very high empowered but in case of NSHG members 75 per cent are less and medium empowered, and the remaining 25 per cent are high empowered. Therefore, there exists no particular relation between age and empowerment. In this way, it can be said that the age of members is not a significant determinant of women empowerment.

Educational Status and Social Empowerment:

Table 7.17 Educational status and Social Empowerment

Level of Empowerment	Illiterate	Primary	Secondary	Post-Secondary
		OSHG		
Less Empowered	19 (31.1)	1 (1.3)	1 (2.1)	1 (8.3)
Medium Empowered	26 (42.6)	15 (19.0)	7 (14.6)	2 (16.7)
High Empowered	13 (21.3)	34 (43.0)	17 (35.4)	2 (16.7)
Very High Empowered	3 (4.9)	29 (36.7)	23 (47.9)	7 (58.3)
Total	61 (100.0)	79 (100.0)	48 (100.0)	12 (100.0)
		NSHG		
Less Empowered	34 (46.6)	31 (46.3)	28 (68.3)	9 (47.4)
Medium Empowered	31 (42.5)	24 (35.8)	6 (14.6)	5 (26.3)
High Empowered	5 (6.8)	0 (0.0)	5 (12.2)	4 (21.1)
Very High Empowered	3 (4.1)	12 (17.9)	2 (4.9)	1 (5.3)
Total	73 (100.0)	67 (100.0)	41 (100.0)	19 (100.0)

Source: Field Survey.

Note: The figures in brackets indicate percentages of OSHG and NSHG members employed their respective categories.

Table 7.17 reflects the impact of educational status of the SHG members on their empowerment. It is revealed that an increase in the level of education results in increasing the level of empowerment and the members move from the less empowered category to medium, high and very high empowered categories. The table reveals that 79.7, 83.3 and 81.8 per cent of the OSHG members and 17.9, 17.1 and 26.4 per cent of the NSHG members educated up to primary, secondary and post-secondary level belongs to high and very high empowered category. In this way, it can be said that the educational status of members is not a significant determinant of women empowerment.

Employment Status and Social Empowerment

Table 7.18 Level of Employment and Social Empowerment (in days per annum)

Level of Empowerment	Un-employed	Below 80 Days	80-160 days	160-240 days	Above 240 days
OSHG					
Less Empowered	2 (10.5)	0 (0.0)	1 (2.4)	2 (2.1)	1 (3.4)
Medium Empowered	8 (42.1)	3 (20.0)	3 (7.1)	13 13.7)	10 (34.5)
High Empowered	6 (31.6)	10 (66.7)	14 (33.3)	37 (38.9)	12 (41.4)
Very High Empowered	3 (15.8)	2 (13.3)	24 (57.1)	43 (45.3)	6 (20.7)
Total	19 (100.0)	15 (100.0)	42 (100.0)	95 (100.0)	29 (100.0)
NSHG					
Less Empowered	19 (63.3)	10 (50.0)	23 (51.1)	35 (48.6)	15 (45.5)
Medium Empowered	7 (23.3)	7 (35.0)	15 (33.3)	24 (33.3)	13 (39.4)
High Empowered	1 (3.3)	0 (0.0)	1 (2.2)	8 (11.1)	4 (12.1)
Very High Empowered	3 (10.0)	3 (15.0)	6 (13.3)	5 (6.9)	1 (3.0)
Total	30 (100.0)	20 (100.0)	45 (100.0)	72 (100.0)	33 (100.0)

Source: Field Survey.

Note: The figures in brackets indicate percentages of OSHG and NSHG members employed their respective categories.

Table 7.18 reveals the impact of employment on the level of women empowerment. The table reflects that an increase in number of employment days results in increasing the level of empowerment in the SHG women. An increase in the employment days shifts the SHG members from the less and medium empowered categories to high and very high empowered categories. The table brings out that 52.6 and 75.9 per cent of the OSHG members and 44.4 and 51.5 per cent of the NSHG members employed for 160-240 and above 240 days per annum are medium and high empowered. In this way, the employment level of the SHG members is significantly influencing their level of empowerment.

Household Income and Social Empowerment:

Table 7.19 Household Income and Social Empowerment (Income in Rs. per month)

Level of Empowerment	Up to3000	3001-5000	5001-10000	Above 10000
		OSHG		
Less Empowered	2 (5.6)	2 (2.0)	1 (1.8)	1 (20.0)
Medium Empowered	6 (16.7)	15 (14.7)	16 (28.1)	0 (0.0)
High Empowered	14 (38.9)	38 (37.3)	23 (40.4)	4 (80.0)
Very High Empowered	14 (38.9)	47 (46.1)	17 (29.8)	0 (0.0)
Total	36 (100.0)	102 (100.0)	57 (100.0)	5 (100.0)
		NSHG		
Less Empowered	25 (54.3)	45 (48.4)	29 (52.7)	3 (50.0)
Medium Empowered	15 (32.6)	30 (32.3)	19 (34.5)	2 (33.3)
High Empowered	1 (2.2)	8 (8.6)	4 (7.3)	1 (16.7)
Very High Empowered	5 (10.9)	10 (10.8)	3 (5.5)	0 (0.0)
Total	46 (100.0)	93 (100.0)	55 (100.0)	6 (100.0)

Source: Field Survey.

Note: The figures in brackets indicate percentages of OSHG and NSHG members employed their respective categories.

Table 7.19 measures the impact of household income of the SHG members on their empowerment. The table shows that the SHG members with higher levels of family income are more empowered as compared to the members whose household income is comparatively less. The table provides that 68.5 and 80 per cent of the OSHG members and 41.8 and 50 per cent of the NSHG members with the respective household income Rs.5,000 – 10,000 and above 10,000 per month are medium and high empowered. The table provides that as the household income increases the level of empowerment also increases. In this way, household income is significantly influencing the level of women empowerment.

Loans used for Productive Purposes and Social Empowerment:

Table 7.20 Loans used for Productive Purposes and Social Empowerment (in Rupees)

Level of Empowerment	Nil	Up to 10000	10001 - 20000	20001-30000	Above 30000
OSHG					
Less Empowered	20 (45.5)	1 (25.0)	1 (3.1)	0 (0.0)	2 (2.5)
Medium Empowered	20 (45.5)	1 (25.0)	15 (46.9)	1 (1.9)	10 (14.5)
High Empowered	4 (9.0)	1 (25.0)	16 (50.0)	43 (84.3)	32 (46.8)
Very High Empowered	0 (0.0)	1 (25.0)	0 (0.00)	7 (13.8)	25 (36.2)
Total	44 (100.0)	4 (100.0)	32 (100.0)	51 (100.0)	69 (100.0)
NSHG					
Less Empowered	39 (36.4)	1 (3.7)	0 (0.0)	3 (9.1)	0 (0.0)
Medium Empowered	42 (39.2)	9 (33.3)	5 (20.8)	9 (27.3)	3 (33.3)
High Empowered	21 (19.6)	5 (18.5)	13 (54.2)	9 (27.3)	4 (44.5)
Very High Empowered	5 (4.8)	12 (44.5)	6 (25.0)	12 (36.3)	2 (22.2)
Total	107 (100.0)	27 (100.0)	24 (100.0)	33 (100.0)	9 (100.0)

Source: Field Survey.

Note: The figures in brackets indicate percentages of OSHG and NSHG members employed their respective categories.

Table 7.20 explains the level of empowerment of the SHG members who utilize different sums of group loans for income generating activities. The table provides that as the members utilize large amount of loans for productive purposes, they become more empowered. The table shows that more than half of the members who do not utilize loans for productive purposes are less and medium empowered. 83 per cent of the OSHG members and 66.7 per cent of the NSHG members who use above Rs. 30,000 for productive purposes belong to be high and very high categories of empowerment. In this way, the loans used for productive purposes also influence the women empowerment.

Level of Mobility and Social Empowerment:

Table 7.21 Level of Mobility and Social Empowerment

Level of Empowerment	Can't Go Outside	Can Visit Another Village	Can Visit Nearest Town	Can Visit City
		OSHG		
Less Empowered	2 (40.0)	0 (0.0)	1 (4.8)	0 (0.0)
Medium Empowered	2 (40.0)	8 (42.1)	1 (4.8)	3 (1.9)
High Empowered	1 (20.0)	3 (15.8)	6 (28.6)	98 (63.2)
Very High Empowered	0 (00.0)	8 (42.1)	13 (61.8)	54 (34.8)
Total	5 (100.0)	19 (100.0)	21 (100.0)	155 (100.0)
		NSHG		
Less Empowered	2 (25.0)	2 (6.9)	7 (7.6)	1 (1.4)
Medium Empowered	5 (62.5)	4 (13.8)	54 (58.7)	20 (28.2)
High Empowered	1 (12.5)	10 (34.5)	21 (22.8)	41 (57.7)
Very High Empowered	-	13 (44.8)	10 (10.9)	9 (12.7)
Total	8 (100.0)	29 (100.0)	92 (100.0)	71 (100.0)

Source: Field Survey.

Note: The figures in brackets indicate percentages of OSHG and NSHG members employed their respective categories.

Table 7.21 highlights the level of mobility of members on their empowerment. The table depicts that 40 and 40 per cent of the OSHG members and 25 and 62.5 per cent of the NSHG members who cannot go out of their houses independently fall in the less and medium empowered categories respectively. However, 57.9, 90.4 and 98 per cent of the OSHG members and 79.3, 33.7 and 70.4 per cent of the NSHG members having confidence to visit another village, nearest town and a city fall in the high empowered category. It establishes that women empowerment is directly influenced by their level of mobility.

Regression Analysis

A multiple linear regression is used to statistically measure the impact of all these determinants on the level of Social Empowerment Index (SEI). The following regression equation is used to measure the effect of key indicators on SEI.

$$SEI\ (Y) = b_0 + b_1 AGE + b_2 EDU + b_3 EMPL + b_4 HHINC + b_5 PROLOAN + b_6 ASSETS + b_7 MOBLITY + \ldots + \mu$$

Where:

SEI	= Social Empowerment Index (Dependent variable)
AGE	= Age of the members in years
EDU	= Education level of the members
EMPL	= Employment in person days in Post
SHG HHINC	= Household income of the members in rupees
PROLOAN	= Amount of loan used for productive purposes in rupees
ASSETS	= Assets (house + land +jewellery)
MOBLITY	= Level of mobility of the members

Table 7.22 Results of Regression Analysis

Variables	OSHG		NSHG	
	B	Sig.	B	Sig.
Constant	0.581* (14.009)	.000	0.604*	.000
AGE	0.000 (0.381)	.703	0.000	.577
EDU	0.003*** (1.798)	.074	0.001 (0.285)	.776
PROLOAN	0.012* (3.116)	.002	-0.003 (-0.793)	.429
EMPL	0.002 (0.287)	.774	0.010	.162
HHINC	-0.007 (-1.296)	.197	-0.003	.722
MOBLITY	0.014*** (1.882)	.061	-0.010	.325
ASSETS	0.009 (1.060)	.290	-0.028**	.026
Observations	200		200	
R^2	0.119		.037	
Adjusted R^2	0.087		.002	
F-value	3.711* (0.001)		1.046 (0.400)	

*Significant at 1 percent level. ** Significant at 5 percent level. ***Significant at 10 per cent level.
Note: The figures given in parentheses indicate t-values.

Table 7.22 highlights the coefficients of these variables. The regression results show that all the coefficients have positive values except variables viz., income in OSHG and amount of loans used for productive purposes, income, mobility and assets in NSHG. The coefficients of regression variables, e.g. amount of loans used for productive purposes, education and mobility of the OSHG members and only one coefficient of regression variable i.e., assets of the NSHG members are playing a significant role in women empowerment.

7.4 Summary

It can be noticed that the microfinance is helpful in empowering women socially. Education and training provided by microfinance lead to the development of the overall personality of the members. The SHG members have higher levels of employment, income and participation in household financial decision-making. It is also found that the members are more confident while travelling, visiting market and dealing with other members of the society. Members of the microfinance are able to raise their voice against various social exploitations more confidently. The regression results show that all the coefficients have positive values except variables viz., income in OSHG and amount of loans used for productive purposes, income, mobility and assets in NSHG. The coefficients of regression variables, e.g. amount of loans used for productive purposes and mobility of the OSHG members and only one coefficient of regression variable i.e., assets of the NSHG members are playing a significant role in women empowerment. Therefore, the microfinance has contributed a lot in empowering women socially.

8

Summary And Conclusions

Poverty is a major challenge to the South Asian country of India, the largest democracy in the world. With its accelerated economic growth since the last decade, India has emerged as a global player and as the world's fourth largest economy in terms of purchasing power parity and has advanced on most of the Millennium Development Goals. However, poverty remains as a major challenge. A focus on the poor assumes heightened salience especially in the face of criticism of the impact of globalization on labour sector of developing countries. While the employment opportunities for women have decreased in certain sectors it has improved in certain others. Yet, as they reiterate, gender based wage differentials cutting across sectors and occupations, coupled with increasing actualization and in formalization continue to haunt the employment scenario. In the wake of the precarious labor position in the context of globalization, a good portion of wealth generated by the recent growth of the country is invested to deliver services to poor.

Microcredit through Self Help Groups (SHGs) is one such attempt directed at different social groups of people who fall under the broad rubric of "the poor". Initiatives by both the state and non-state actors have actively promoted the mobilization of the poor, especially poor women, into SHGs as an attempt at a countervailing force against actualization and exclusion from the formal sectors of the economy. The small loans (microcredit) given to poor women empower them in several ways. Apart from aiding in extricating themselves from loans sharks, microcredit empowers poor women financially to meet certain emergencies without relying on others or even their own men folk. The microcredit by itself does not rescue a woman from chronic poverty unless it is backed up by a remunerative activity.

Further, the microcredit by itself is not the appropriate instrument for poverty alleviation of the most vulnerable segments among the category "poor" and that they need more structural solutions to the problem of their vulnerability and sense of insecurity. An attempt to review those studies that examine the impact of microcredit on women empowerment and gender relations has been limited. The effect of microcredit intervention through SHG concept on employment, income and poverty to understand the benefits of group lending to small borrowers is important. Further, certain issues like loan repayment performance of poor to formal, informal and microcredit sources have not received wide attention. The present study therefore, contributes to the debate on how microcredit influences women empowerment and gender relations.

Objectives:

i. To analyze the overview of rural indebtedness

ii. To examine the effect of microcredit on employment, income and poverty iii. To identify the factors influencing borrowing and repayment of loans

iv. To study the economic and social impact of microfinance in empowering women

v. To suggest policy initiatives for empowering women.

Organization of the Study

This study has been organized into Eight Chapters. The Introductory Chapter deals with problem, objectives and organization of the Study. The Second Chapter focused on the review of literature on credit market with special reference to microfinance. In the Third Chapter, an attempt is made to present the methods used in the Study. The Forth Chapter examined the effect of microcredit on employment, income and poverty. The Fifth Chapter presented the indebtedness of households and the factors influencing borrowing and repayment of loans. The economic impact of microfinance in empowering women and gender relations has been presented in the Sixth Chapter. The social impact of microfinance in empowering women has been presented in the Seventh Chapter. The last Chapter provides conclusions of the Study.

Sampling Design

In this Study, multi stage sampling technique is used in the selection of units. Accordingly, at the first stage, Visakhapatnam District is selected purposively. The second stage of sampling is the selection of Mandal. Chodavaram Mandal is selected keeping in view that it should satisfy the two criteria viz., (i) cover the maximum number of rural poor households and (ii) cover the maximum number of Self-Help Group (SHG)

households. The Third stage of sampling is the selection of villages. As Chodavaram village is a big village it is selected for the study, in order to cover the required number of sample households. (See Appendix 3.1 A, B, C). The Fourth stage of sampling involved the selection of households. In all, 400 SHG households were selected for the Study. While 200 members are from Old Self Help Groups (OSHG) and 200 members are from New Self Help Groups (NSHG). For selecting OSHG, the SHGs who have completed more than 5 years membership and for selecting NSHG, the SHGs having a membership of less than 5 years is considered. These two groups of households have been chosen keeping in view the probability proportion to their actual number in the total SHG households in the study area i.e., 10 per cent of the households.

Methodology

Techniques of Analysis

In analyzing the data, different statistical techniques are used. To study the employment among the sample households Worker Population Ratio (WPR), Labour Force Participation Rate (LFPR) and Unemployment Rate (UR) are used. To judge the income variation among the households, Co-efficient of Quartile Deviation amd Co- efficient of Variation techniques are used. The significance of difference between average incomes of OSHG and NSHG households is tested with the help of Z-test and F

– distribution measures the ratio of the variance between groups to the variance within groups. To examine the poverty levels, the Head Count Ratio (HCR) is used. Since all the sample households are poor, to measure shortfall and severity of poverty, Poverty Gap Ratio (PGR), Sen's Index and Modified Sen's Index of poverty are used. To find out whether the microfinance programme participation has led to empower the members, Chai-square test is used and the empowerment is measured with indices.

Regression Analysis: Determinants of Income:

Multiple regression analysis is used to identify the factors that determine the level of income of poor households.

Where:

$$PCIH\ (Y) = b_1 + b_2 SH, + b_3 PWH + b_4 WRag + b_5 WRnag + b_6 SLHH + b_7 PCIOS + b_8 PCILS + b_9 LH + b_{10} AH + b_{11} SAH + \ldots\ldots + \mu$$

PCIH = Annual per capita income of the household (Dependent Variable)
SH = Size of the household

PWH = percentage of workers in the household

WRag = wage rate of agricultural labour wage rate of non-agricultural
WRnag = labour
SLHH = size of the landholding of the household

PCIOS = per capita income from other source (self-employment)

PCILS = per capita income from livestock

LH = literacy level of the head of the household

AH = Age of the head of the household

SAH = Age squared of the head of the household.

Regression Analysis:

Determinants of Borrowings and Repayments:

Multiple regression analysis is used to identify the factors that determine the borrowings and repayment of loans of poor households.

Borrowings (Y) = $Y = a + b_1x_1 + b_2x_2 + b_3x_3 + b_4x_4 + b_5x_5 + \ldots + b_nx_n + \mu$ ---*Model-I*

Repayments (Y) = $Y = a + b_1x_1 + b_2x_2 + b_3x_3 + b_4x_4 + b_5x_5 + \ldots + b_nx_n + \mu$ ---*Model-II*

Where Borrowings = Different types of borrowings from different sources by the rural respondents of the selected area

Where Repayments = The repayment of loans borrowed by the rural respondents of the selected area.

Borrowings	=	Total loan amount borrowed (Dependent Variable)
Repayment	=	Total Repayment of loan amount taken (Dependent Variable)

Age (x_1)	=	Age of the respondent
Head (x_2)	=	Dummy variable, whether the respondent is head of Household
Literacy Level (x_3)	=	Number of Years of Education of the respondent
Earner (x_4)	=	Dummy variable, whether the respondent is working or not
Occupational Pattern (x_5)	=	Dummy variable, whether the respondent is employee
Size of the family (x_6)	=	Family size of the household
Asset holdings (x_7)	=	Value of the Assets owned by the household
Income (x_8)	=	Annual income of the household
Dependency ratio (x_9)	=	Dependency ratio of the household
Recurring Expenditure (x_{10})	=	Food and non-food Expenditure of Household
Non-Recurring Expenditure (x_{11})	=	Sickness of family members, ceremonies, etc.

Regression Analysis

Determinants of Empowerment

A multiple linear regression is used to statistically measure the impact of all these determinants on the level of empowerment. In this model we have estimated two regression models taking Economic Empowerment Index (EEI) and Social Empowerment Index (SEI) of the sample households where EEI and SEI of the respondents has taken as dependent variables and other relative variables are taken as independent variables. The independent variables are like Age, Literacy Level, Employment Days, Income, Loan Amount, Asset Holding and Mobility.

$$EEI\ (Y) = b_0 + b_1AGE + b_2EDU + b_3EMPL + b_4HHINC + b_5PROLOAN + b_6ASSETS + b_7MOBLITY + \ldots + u \text{---Model-I}$$

$$SEI\ (Y) = b_0 + b_1AGE + b_2EDU + b_3EMPL + b_4HHINC + b_5PROLOAN + b_6ASSETS + b_7MOBLITY + \ldots + u \text{---Model-II}$$

Where:

EEI	=	Economic Empowerment Index (Dependent variable)
SEI	=	Social Empowerment Index (Dependent variable)
AGE	=	Age of the members in years
EDU	=	Education level of the members
EMPL	=	Employment in person days in Post SHG
HHINC	=	Household income of the members in rupees
PROLOAN	=	Amount of loan used for productive purposes in rupees
ASSETS	=	Assets (house + land +jewellery)
MOBLITY	=	Level of mobility of the members

SOCIO-ECONOMIC PROFILE OF THE SAMPLE HOUSEHOLDS:

The socio-economic profile of the sample households shows that almost half of the heads are in the age group of 18-39 for both the OSHG and NSHG. The family size is less than four members in majority of the households. Regarding literacy levels of the head of households, the proportion of illiterate heads are high in both the households. Around 50 per cent of households are in the assets range of above Rs. 2,00,000/- in both the groups. More than half of the total members in both the households are earners. The dependency ratio is lower in both the households. To sum up, but for literacy the performance is satisfactory.

EMPLOYMENT, INCOME AND POVERTY AMONG POOR HOUSEHOLDS:

The proportion of persons employed in the UPS and UPSS is higher among the OSHG and NSHG households indicating the positive effect on employment pattern of the micro credit. Apart from the magnitude of employment, the analysis on the occupational pattern of the works showed that, the majority of the workers under the OSHG households are depending on household industry (29.6 per cent) followed by construction labour (29.4 per cent) etc. But in the case of NSHG households, majority of the workers are depending on construction labour (27.4 per cent) followed by salaried people (22.8 per cent) etc. This implies that there is an occupational shift towards non- farm or off-farm activities through micro credit.

The distribution of the households according to income range showed that 65 per cent of the OSHG households and 69.5 per cent of the NSHG households are in the income range of below Rs 75,000/- per year indicating that the microfinance has marginal impact on their income levels. The distribution of income by source shows that income from household industry (24.8 per cent) and income from wage (30.2 per cent) are the major sources in OSHG households and income from wage (30 per cent) and salaried income (25.4 per cent) in NSHG households. The average per capita income of the OSHG households is relatively higher than that of the NSHG. With the help of multiple regression the determinants of income of poor were analysed. The analysis shows that size of the household, percentage of workers in the household, wage rates of agricultural and non-agricultural labourers, size of landholding, per capita income from other sources like self-employment, age of the head of the household and age squared of the head of the household are the significant factors.

The per capita expenditure (recurring and non-recurring) for the OSHG households is greater compared to the NSHG households. This may be due to the fact that the OSHG households are having more access to formal institutions. In order to observe the income-expenditure relationship, the Eagle's law was tested. It was observed that there is a decline in the share of expenditure on food items as the income size increases. This decline is so sharp in the OSHG compared to the NSHG households.

The Planning Commission takes into consideration the monthly per capita expenditure norm to estimate the poverty. Having wide methodological differences in the methodology used for fixing the norm to identify the poverty line, all the estimates showed that the incidence of poverty is on a decline in India. In this study also monthly per capita expenditure as a measure of standard of living is used for the analysis of poverty. The official poverty line is adjusted to the year 2012-13 by using the consumer price Index for rural labourers. Accordingly the estimated poverty line of Ra. 997/- is taken for the rural areas in this Study. The empirical results show that the incidence of poverty is high in both the households. A lower Poverty Gap Ratio was found in the NSHG households compared to the OSHG. The Sen's Index reveals that the incidence and intensity of the poverty is high in OSHG comparably with NSHG and Modified Sen's Index of Poverty indicated that the distribution of poor is closer to the poverty line in both the households.

INDEBTDENESS OF RURAL POOR HOUSEHOLDS:

The analysis shows that, through microcredit intervention the formal credit can reach the rural poor. In both OSHG and NSHG households more than 60 per cent of the total borrowings were from microcredit sources. But the SHG households are still depends upon the informal sources for supplementing the productive activities which reflects the inadequacy of microcredit. An analysis of borrowings from microcredit shows that only 30 per cent of borrowings by rural households are used for productive purposes. An analysis of borrowings by rate of interest has clearly shown that microcredit is available for the members, at lower interest rates than formal and informal credit. An analysis of borrowings by nature of security has brought out that it is the personal security in the form of promissory note which replaced the collateral, in informal credit sector. In the case of microcredit, the personal security took another form as group security which replaced the collateral security. Therefore, the poor are getting access to formal credit through microcredit sources.

In microcredit borrowings the F-value of the regression model is 4.718 and indicates that the model is best fit and it is significant at 1percent level. The model explains 8.5 percentage of variation. In this model, four variables are found to be significant viz., literacy level, occupational pattern, size of the family and non-recurring expenditure. In this model the F value is 1.136. The model explains 1.6 percentage of variation. In this model, only one variable is found to be significant viz., non-recurring expenditure. In Informal credit borrowings too the regression model F-value is 4.817 which show that the model is best fit which is significant at 1 percent level. The model explains 13.4 percentage of variation. In this model two variables are found to be significant viz., recurring expenditure and non-recurring expenditure.

The analysis of repayment of loans has shown that repayment of microcredit is better (around 60 per cent) compared to informal credit (around 40 per cent) in OSHG and NSHG households. This may be due to the intimacy of the lender and the borrower in respect of microcredit. In case of microcredit, household industry and trade are found to be the major means of repayment while wage income, household industry and trade are the major means of repayment of informal credit in both the households. The repayment performance in respect of loans contracted from microcredit sources for all purposes is found to better where as in informal sources very poor repayment was reported in both the households. Repayments of loans by rate of interest show that in respect of microcredit, the repayment performance is better. However, in informal credit sources, there is no specific trend regarding the repayment performance of borrowers.

In the regression model for microcredit borrowings for OSHG, three variables are found to be significant viz., age, dependency ratio and non-recurring expenditure and for NSHG, three variables are viz., literacy level, occupational pattern and non-recurring expenditure are found to be significant. In formal credit borrowings for OSHG, three variables are found to be significant viz., Size of the Family, recurring expenditure and non-recurring expenditure, for NSHG two variables are found to be significant viz., occupational pattern and non-recurring expenditure. In informal credit borrowings for OSHG, two variables are found - income and non- recurring expenditure are significant and for NSHG, two variables are viz., asset holdings and non-recurring expenditure are found to be significant.

In the regression model for microcredit repayments for OSHG, three variables are found to be significant viz., literacy level, dependency ratio and income. For NSHG, non-recurring expenditure is significant. In formal credit repayments for OSHG, three variables are found to be significant viz., literacy level, earner and income, for NSHG two variables are found to be significant viz., occupational pattern and size of the family. In informal credit Repayments for OSHG, three variables are viz., income, recurring expenditure and non-recurring expenditure are significant and for NSHG, three variables are viz., asset holdings, recurring expenditure and non-recurring expenditure found to be significant.

In microcredit repayments the regression model is the F-value is 2.501 which show that the model is best fit and it is significant at 1 per cent level. The model explains 3.6 percentage of variation. In this model three variables are found to be significant viz., age, literacy level and non-recurring expenditure. The F-value 2.017 is significant at 5 per cent level and show that it is best fit. The model explains 15.6 percentage of variation. In this model three variables are found to be significant viz., Earner, Occupational pattern and Size of the family. In Informal credit repayments too the regression model is the F-value is 2.718 which show that the model is best fit and significant at 1 per cent level. The model explains 8.2 percentage of variation. In this model three variables are found to be significant viz., Income, Recurring Expenditure and Non-recurring Expenditure. Therefore, efforts should be made by the Government to provide gainful employment opportunities, which will help in improving the repayment performance of rural households.

THE ECONOMIC IMPACT ON SHG MEMBERS AND WOMEN'S EMPOWERMENT:

It can be concluded that microfinance is helpful in empowering women economically. The education, skill and training provided by microfinance lead to the development of the overall personality of the members. The SHG members have higher levels of employment, income and participation in household financial decision-making. It is also found that the members are more confident while travelling, visiting market for the purchase of household goods, and dealing with other members of the society. Members of the microfinance are able to raise their voice against various social exploitations more confidently. The regression results show that all the coefficients have positive values except variables viz., employment in OSHG and age, education and assets in NSHG. The coefficients of regression variables, e.g. age, amount of loans used for productive purposes, employment, spatial mobility and assets of the OSHG members and the coefficients of regression variables age, education, amount of loans used for productive purposes and mobility of the NSHG members are playing a significant role in women empowerment. In this way, microfinance has contributed a lot in the empowerment of women.

THE SOCIAL IMPACT ON SHG MEMBERS AND WOMEN'S EMPOWERMENT:

It can be noticed that the microfinance is helpful in empowering women socially. Education and training provided by microfinance lead to the development of the overall personality of the members. The SHG members have higher levels of employment, income and participation in household financial decision-making. It is also found that the members are more confident while travelling, visiting market and dealing with other members of the society. Members of the microfinance are able to raise their voice against various social exploitations more confidently. The regression results show that all the coefficients have positive values except variables viz., income in OSHG and amount of loans used for productive purposes, income, mobility and assets in NSHG. The coefficients of regression variables, e.g. education, amount of loans used for productive purposes and mobility of the OSHG members and only one coefficient of regression variable i.e., assets of the NSHG members are playing a significant role in women empowerment. Therefore, the microfinance has contributed a lot in empowering women socially.

To sum up the maturity of the SHGs is quite significantly contributing to the reduction of poverty, generating employment and empowering the women participants. It is also found that the mature group members are more empowered as compared to the young and middle age group members. The determinants of women empowerment show that as the members utilize the loans for productive purposes, they become more empowered. Therefore, the members must be motivated and assisted to utilize the group loans for productive purposes only. Some supervision on the loan utilization may also be introduced. Therefore, keeping the long-term objectives in mind, efforts should be made for the stabilization and sustainability of the group members. The problems faced by the members must be listened and resolved so that they can continue as group member for a longer period of time. The study brings out that microfinance in Andhra Pradesh is provided only through the SHG-bank linkage model and there is no role of NGOs in delivering the microfinance. But, it is evident that the success of microfinance programme largely depends upon the quality of groups. Therefore, the staff involved in the SHGs formation must be trained to form quality SHGs. The services of various NGOs can also be availed in order to achieve the programme objectives.

Appendix

APPENDIX-3.1A

Mandal wise Rural and Urban Population 2011 (Visakhapatnam)

Name of Madal or Sub-District	Rural Population	Urban population	Total population	% to Total Population	
				Rural	Urban
Anakapalle	95417	91520	186937	51.04	48.96
Anandapuram	60789	0	60789	100.00	0.00
Ananthagiri	49019	0	49019	100.00	0.00
Araku Valley	49960	6714	56674	88.15	11.85
Atchutapuram	66577	0	66577	100.00	0.00
Bheemunipatnam	56754	59595	116349	48.78	51.22
Butchayyapeta	66214	0	66214	100.00	0.00
Cheedikada	46643	0	46643	100.00	0.00
Chintapalle	63752	7888	71640	88.99	11.01
Chodavaram	**68242**	**20251**	**88493**	**77.12**	**22.88**
Devarapalle	58312	0	58312	100.00	0.00
Dumbriguda	49029	0	49029	100.00	0.00
G.Madugula	53884	0	53884	100.00	0.00
Gajuwaka	0	250423	250423	0.00	100.00
Golugonda	52852	0	52852	100.00	0.00
Gudem Kotha Veedhi	58542	4632	63174	92.67	7.33
Hukumpeta	51697	0	51697	100.00	0.00
K.Kotapadu	60498	0	60498	100.00	0.00
Kasimkota	67262	0	67262	100.00	0.00
Kotauratla	54510	0	54510	100.00	0.00
Koyyuru	50639	0	50639	100.00	0.00
Madugula	72006	0	72006	100.00	0.00
Makavarapalem	57568	0	57568	100.00	0.00
Munagapaka	55520	0	55520	100.00	0.00
Munchingi Puttu	47418	0	47418	100.00	0.00
Nakkapalle	73476	7603	81079	90.62	9.38
Narsipatnam	45074	46538	91612	49.20	50.80
Nathavaram	64607	0	64607	100.00	0.00
Paderu	50196	8787	58983	85.10	14.90
Padmanabham	52079	0	52079	100.00	0.00

(Contd...)

Paravada	52605	25560	78165	67.30	32.70
Payakaraopeta	66092	27001	93093	71.00	29.00
Peda Bayalu	51890	0	51890	100.00	0.00
Pedagantyada	0	95291	95291	0.00	100.00
Pendurthi	32380	114270	146650	22.08	77.92
Rambilli	53913	0	53913	100.00	0.00
Ravikamatham	70761	0	70761	100.00	0.00
Rolugunta	48388	0	48388	100.00	0.00
S.Rayavaram	74101	0	74101	100.00	0.00
Sabbavaram	62713	4621	67334	93.14	6.86
Visakhapatnam (Rural)	0	260192	260192	0.00	100.00
Visakhapatnam (Urban)	0	977771	977771	0.00	100.00
Yelamanchili	43288	27265	70553	61.36	38.64
Grand Total	2254667	2035922	4290589	52.55	47.45

Source: Director of Census Operations, Hyderabad.

APPENDIX-3.1B

Mandal wise SHG Details as on February 2010 (Visakhapatnam)

Mandal	No. of SHG Groups	No. of SHG Members
Anakapalli	1,676	18,921
Anandapuram	966	11,146
Ananthagiri	563	6,136
Araku valley	702	6,747
Atchutapuram	1,112	12,138
Bheemunipatnam	896	10,599
Butchayyapeta	1,100	10,963
Cheedikada	928	9,577
Chintapalle	865	9,056
Chodavaram	**1,602**	**16,845**
Devarapalle	1,110	12,452
Dumbriguda	693	7,704
Gangaraju madugula	826	9,111
Golugonda	913	10,339
Gudem kothaveedhi	766	8,823
Hukumpeta	901	9,879
K kotapadu	1,112	13,252
Kasimkota	1,080	12,325
Kotauratla	1,019	11,906
Koyyuru	801	8,872
Madugula	1,309	14,817
Makavarapalem	1,022	12,555
Munagapaka	1,115	12,109
Munchingiputtu	682	7,397

(Contd...)

Nakkapalli	1,585	17,033
Narsipatnam	1,452	17,112
Nathavaram	1,062	12,623
Paderu	838	9,303
Padmanabham	910	10,302
Paravada	834	10,355
Payakaraopeta	1,543	18,910
Pedabayalu	704	8,109
Pendurthi	519	6,688
Rambilli	1,032	11,413
Ravikamatham	1,194	13,941
Rolugunta	869	10,417
S Rayavaram	1,584	17,391
Sabbavaram	1,169	12,741
Yelamanchili	1,312	14,331

Source: SHG Federation Report, www.serp.ap.gov.in

APPENDIX-3.1C

Chodavaram Mandal Village Organization Details (Visakhapatnam District) (Rural) as on 2011-12

No	Vo Name	Total No Of Shgs Existing	Total No Of Members Existing
1	Adduru Grama Pedala Ikhya Sangham	39	405
2	Amberupuram Gramapedala Ikhyasangham	54	546
3	Amberupuram2	36	409
4	Ankupalem Grama Pedala Ikhya Sangham	24	204
5	**Annavaram Grama Pedala Ikhya Sangham**	**61**	**553**
6	Bangaramma Palem Grama Pedala Ikya Sangam	13	153
7	Bennavolu Grama Pedala Ikhya Sangham	39	423
8	Bhogapuram Grama Pedala Ikhaya Sangham	34	398
9	Butchayyapeta Grama Pedala Ikhya Sangham	13	140
10	Chakipalli Grama Pedala Ikhya Sangham	39	369
11	**Chodavaram 3 Grama Pedala Ikya Sangham**	**84**	**794**
12	**Chodavaram Grama Pedala Ikhya Sangham**	**32**	**331**
13	**Chodavaram2 Grama Pedala Ikhya Sangam**	**75**	**617**
14	**Chodavaram4 Grama Pedala Ikya Sangham**	**131**	**1019**
15	**Chodavaram5 Grama Pedala Ikhya Sangham**	**89**	**637**
16	**Chodavaram7 Gramapedalaikhysangam**	**38**	**329**
17	**Citizen Lic Colony**	**53**	**532**
18	Dhamunapalli Grama Pedala Ikhya Sangham	21	208
19	Duddupalem Grama Pedala Ikhya Sangham	30	360
20	Dwarakanagaram	41	301
21	G Jpuram Grama Pedala Ikhya Sangham	26	339

(Contd...)

22	Gajapathi Nagaram Grama Pedala Ikhya Sangham	39	423
23	Gandhavaram Grama Pedala Ikhya Sangham	37	387
24	Gandhigramam Grama Pedala Ikhya Sangham	28	230
25	Gavaravaram Grama Pedala Ikhya Sangham	55	524
26	Govada Grama Pedala Ikhya Sanhgam	71	743
27	Govindamma Colony Grama Pedla Ikhya Sangham	23	259
28	Gowripatnam Grama Pedala Ikhya Sangam	61	563
29	Jannavaram Grama Pedala Ikhya Sangham	21	231
30	Jannavaram Kothuru Grama Pedala Ikhya Sangham	6	57
31	Juthada Grama Pedala Ikhya Sangham	51	513
32	Kannampalem Grama Pedala Ikhya Sangham	21	246
33	Khandepalli Grama Pedala Ikhya Sangham	51	446
34	Lakkavaram Grama Pedala Ikhya Sangham	84	872
35	Laxmipuram Grama Pedala Ikhya Sangham	55	583
36	Mudrthy Grama Pedala Ikhya Sngham	31	361
37	Mycherlapalem Grma Pedala Ikhya Sangham	18	196
38	Narsapuram Grama Pedala Ikhya Sangham	29	324
39	Narsayyapeta Grama Pedala Ikhya Sangham	39	295
40	Pspeta	66	573
41	Rayapuraju Peta Grama Pedala Ikhya Sangham	24	259
42	Revallu Grama Pedala Ikhya Sangham	15	146
43	Seemunapalli Grama Pedala Ikhya Sangham	20	231
44	Sri Rampatnam Grama Pedala Ikhya Sangham	15	163
45	Thimmanapalem Gama Pedala Ikhya Sangham	10	119
46	Venkannapalem Grama Pedala Ikhya Sangham	65	528
47	Total	1907	18339

Source: SHG Federation Report, www.serp.ap.gov.in

APPENDIX 3.2: TECHNIQUES OF ANALYSIS

1. Employment measures

Worker Population Ratio (WPR):

WPR is defined as the number of persons/person-days employed per 1000 persons/ person-days (NSS 66th round, 2009-10).

$$WPR = \frac{\text{Number of employed persons}}{\text{Total population}} \times 1000$$

Labour Force Participation Rate (LFPR):

LFPR is defined as the number of persons/ person-days in the labour force per 1000 persons /person-days (NSS 66th round, 2009-10).

$$LEPR = \frac{\text{Number ofemployedpersons } + \text{Numberof unemployedpersons}}{\text{Total population}} \times 1000$$

Unemployment Rate (UR):

UR is defined as the number of persons/person-days unemployed per 1000 persons/person-days in the labour force (which includes both the employed and unemployed) (NSS 66th round, 2009-10).

$$UR = \frac{\text{Number ofunemployedpersons}}{\text{Number ofemployedpersons} + \text{Numberof unemployedpersons}} \times 1000$$

2. Income Variation Measures

In analyzing the data, different statistical techniques are used. To judge the income variation among the sample households, Co-efficient of Quartile Deviation, Co-efficient of Variation are calculated.

Co-efficient of Quartile deviation (Q.D):

$$Q.D = (Q3 - Q1) / (Q3 + Q1)$$

Where:

$Q1$ = lower Quartile value

$Q3$ = upper Quartile value

Co-efficient of variation (C.V):

$$C.V. = \sigma / \mu \times 100$$

Where:

Z-test:

σ = Standard Deviation

μ = Mean

In addition to the above, the significance of difference between average incomes of OSHG and NSHG households is tested with the help of Z-test.

$$Z = \frac{x_1 - x_2}{\sqrt{\frac{\sigma_1^2}{n_1} + \frac{\sigma_1^2}{n_2}}}$$

Where

F-test:

1	=	Mean of the first population
2	=	Mean of the second population
$\sigma 1$	=	variance of the first population
$\sigma 2$	=	variance of the second population
$n1$	=	size of the first population
$n2$	=	Size of the second population

The F – distribution measures the ratio of the variance between groups to the variance within groups. If there is no real difference from group to group, any sample difference will be explainable by random variation and the variance between groups should be close to the variance within groups. However, if there is a real difference between the groups, the variance between groups will be significantly larger than the variance within groups.

$$F = \frac{S_1^2}{S_2^2} \text{ or } \frac{S_2^2}{S_1^2}$$

S_1^2 = Sum of the squares between sample

S_2^2 = Sum of the squares with sample

3. Poverty Measures

To examine the poverty levels, the Head Count Ratio (HCR) is used. Since all the sample households are poor, to measure shortfall and severity of poverty, PGR, Sen's Index and Modified Sen's Inde of Poverty are used.

Head Count Ratio (HCR):

Where

$$HCR = \frac{q}{n}$$

q = Number of people below poverty line. n= Total population.

Poverty Gap Ratio (PGR):

Where

$$PGR = \frac{(z-m)}{z} \times HCR$$

z = Poverty line expressed in the monetary terms

m = Mean Per Capita Monthly Expenditure of the poor

Sen Index (Sp):

Amartya Sen (1976, 1981) applied to measures poverty index. In this way HCR measures incidence (proportion of poor), PGR measures intensity (depth of poverty or how poor the poor are?) and Gp measures severity (income concentration inequality).

$$Sp = HCR[PGR + (1-PGR)Gp]$$

Sen Index combines the three ratios. Where: HCR = Head Count Ratio

PGR = Income Poverty Gap Ratio

Gp = Gini coefficient

Modified Sen's Index of Poverty (P):

The Sen-Shorrocks-Thon (SST) index is an index of poverty intensity. It is also called the modified Sen Index of poverty intensity. This index is proposed by Shorrocks (1995)as an extension of the Sen (1976) index. The SST index measures poverty incidence, depth, and inequality jointly and hence is a comprehensive poverty measure. In addition, this index can be decomposed into its constituting parts transparently. Xu and Osberg (2002) also show that based on the Sen index and two of its constituting components (poverty rate and average poverty gap), one can always compute the SST index from the Sen index as follows:

$$\text{SST index} = (\text{poverty rate}) \times (\text{Sen index}) + 2 \times (\text{poverty rate}) \times (1 - \text{poverty rate}) \times (\text{average poverty gap})$$

4. Empowerment Index measures:

$$\text{Economic Empowerment Index (EEI)} = \frac{\text{Actual Score Obtained}}{\text{Maximum Score Obtained}}$$

$$\text{Social Empowerment Index(SEI)} = \frac{\text{Actual Score Obtained}}{\text{Maximum Score Obtained}}$$

Chi-square Test

It is a non-parametric test applied to find out the association among two or more attributes. The test is applied to find out whether the microfinance programme participation has led to increased level of confidence, physical mobility, household decision-making power etc. among the members. The value of Chi-square is calculated as follows:

$$\chi^2 = \sum \frac{(O-E)^2}{E}.$$

Where:

O = Observed frequencies

E = Expected frequencies

The calculated value of Chi-square is compared with the Table value for degree of freedom which is equal to: (No. of columns -1) × (No. of rows-1) at certain specified level of significance. If the calculated value is greater than the Table value the difference between observed and expected value is considered significant.

APPENDIX-4.1

OSGH

Coefficient Correlations[a]										
	SAH	**WRag**	**WRnag**	**PCILS**	**SH**	**LH**	**PCIOS**	**PHW**	**SLHH**	**AH**
SAH	1.000									
WRag	.165	1.000								
WRnag	.075	.150	1.000							
PCILS	-.090	-.089	-.040	1.000						
SH	.146	-.023	-.169	-.082	1.000					
LH	.056	.131	.213	-.017	.044	1.000				
PCIOS	.041	.066	.605	.108	.005	-.013	1.000			
PHW	.097	-.059	-.258	-.012	.669	.111	-.271	1.000		
SLHH	-.153	-.840	-.107	.072	.005	-.117	.022	.037	1.000	
AH	-.987	-.142	-.043	.055	-.186	-.005	-.036	-.178	.125	1.000
a. Dependent Variable: PCIH										

NSHG

Coefficient Correlations[a]										
	SAH	**SLHH**	**PCIOS**	**SH**	**LH**	**PCILS**	**WRnag**	**PHW**	**WRag**	**AH**
SAH	1.000									
SLHH	.055	1.000								
PCIOS	-.026	-.077	1.000							
SH	.231	.051	-.216	1.000						
LH	.075	.134	-.290	.080	1.000					
PCILS	-.103	-.188	.144	-.045	.000	1.000				
WRnag	.061	-.168	.656	-.352	.001	.196	1.000			
PHW	.234	.056	-.395	.573	.296	-.063	-.353	1.000		
WRag	.010	-.712	.040	-.140	-.095	-.316	.054	-.069	1.000	
AH	-.987	-.049	.024	-.233	-.059	.094	-.051	-.299	-.016	1.000
a. Dependent Variable: PCIH										

Coefficient Correlations[a]										
	SAH	**SLHH**	**WRnag**	**SH**	**LH**	**PCILS**	**PCIOS**	**PHW**	**WRag**	**AH**
SAH	1.000									
SLHH	-.004	1.000								
WRnag	.083	-.132	1.000							
SH	.196	.020	-.262	1.000						
LH	.053	.060	.120	.051	1.000					
PCILS	-.098	-.133	.088	-.067	.010	1.000				
PCIOS	.023	-.039	.609	-.087	-.140	.112	1.000			
PHW	.176	.020	-.297	.614	.201	-.032	-.318	1.000		
WRag	.051	-.779	.098	-.083	-.036	-.205	.050	-.062	1.000	
AH	-.988	.006	-.063	-.217	-.022	.078	-.022	-.245	-.048	1.000
a. Dependent Variable: PCIH										

APPENDIX-6.1

Economic Empowerment Indicators

Sl. No	Indicators	Response	Score
1	Education	Illiterate	0
		Primary	1
		Secondary	2
		Technical	4
2	Working Days	Unemployed	0
		Below 80	1
		80-160	2
		160-240	3
		Above 240	4
3	Income	Upto 1000	1
		1000-2000	2
		2000-3000	3
		3000-4000	4
		4000 abvoe	5
4	Assets	House	1
		House and Land	2
		House, Land and jewellery	3
5	Borrowing Amount	Upto 5000	1
		5000-10000	2
		10000-15000	3
		15000-20000	4
		20000-25000	5
		25000-30000	6
		30000-35000	7
		Above 35000	8

Sl. No	Indicators	Response	Score
6	Control over resources	No Change=0 Little Improvement =1 Moderate Improvement=2 Good Improvement=3	
7	Credit worthiness		
8	Freedom from Money lenders		
9	Bargaining power		
10	Self-employment		
11	Banking habits		
12	Aware of Property rights		
13	Marketing skills		
14	Production skills		
15	Household occupation		
16	Reduction in wasteful expenditure		
17	Food habits		
18	Minor repairs to house		
19	Reduction in Consumption Exp.		
20	Loan repayments		
21	Purchase of Household durables		

APPENDIX -6.2: ECONOMIC VARIABLES

Indicator	Category of SHG	0	1	2	3	Total	χ2
Control over Resources	OSHG	0(0.0)	20(10.0)	143(71.5)	37(18.5)	200(100.0)	93.608 (0.000)
	NSHG	10(5.0)	98(49.0)	82(41.0)	10(5.0)	200(100.0)	
	ALL	10(2.5)	118(29.5)	225(56.2)	47(11.8)	400(100.0)	
Credit worthiness	OSHG	0(0.0)	21(10.5)	97(48.5)	82(41.0)	200(100.0)	70.003 (0.000)
	NSHG	14(7.0)	31(15.5)	140(70.0)	15(7.5)	200(100.0)	
	ALL	14(3.5)	52(13.0)	237(59.2)	97(24.2)	400(100.0)	
Freedom from money lenders	OSHG	5(2.5)	23(11.5)	86(43.0)	86(43.0)	200(100.0)	40.600 (0.000)
	NSHG	19(9.5)	34(17.0)	116(58.0)	31(15.5)	200(100.0)	
	ALL	24(6.0)	57(14.2)	202(50.5)	117(29.2)	400(100.0)	
Bargaining power	OSHG	5(2.5)	12(6.0)	34(17.0)	149(74.5)	200(100.0)	65.195 (0.000)
	NSHG	5(2.5)	28(14.0)	97(48.5)	70(35.0)	200(100.0)	
	ALL	10(2.5)	40(10.0)	131(32.8)	219(54.8)	400(100.0)	
Self- employment potential	OSHG	0(0.0)	18(9.0)	75(37.5)	107(53.5)	200(100.0)	81.243 (0.000)
	NSHG	10(5.0)	52(26.0)	111(55.5)	27(13.5)	200(100.0)	
	ALL	10(2.5)	70(17.5)	186(46.5)	134(33.5)	400(100.0)	
Banking habits	OSHG	-	22(11.0)	70(35.0)	108(54.0)	200(100.0)	8.260 (0.000)
	NSHG	-	32(16.0)	89(44.5)	79(39.5)	200(100.0)	
	ALL	-	54(13.5)	159(39.8)	187(46.8)	400(100.0)	
Aware of property rights	OSHG	6(3.0)	43(21.5)	114(57.0)	37(18.5)	200(100.0)	96.670 (0.000)
	NSHG	16(8.0)	131(65.5)	43(21.5)	10(5.0)	200(100.0)	
	ALL	22(5.5)	174(43.5)	157(39.2)	47(11.8)	400(100.0)	
Marketing skills	OSHG	11(5.5)	14(7.0)	94(47.0)	81(40.5)	200(100.0)	62.070 (0.000)
	NSHG	20(10.0)	49(24.5)	112(56.0)	19(9.5)	200(100.0)	
	ALL	31(7.8)	63(15.8)	206(51.5)	100(25.0)	400(100.0)	
Production skills	OSHG	13(6.5)	25(12.5)	89(44.5)	73(36.5)	200(100.0)	24.465 (0.000)
	NSHG	15(7.5)	40(20.0)	113(56.5)	32(16.0)	200(100.0)	
	ALL	28(7.0)	65(16.2)	202(50.5)	105(26.2)	400(100.0)	
Household occupation	OSHG	10(5.0)	14(7.0)	148(74.0)	28(14.0)	200(100.0)	61.866 (0.000)
	NSHG	12(6.0)	79(39.5)	88(44.0)	21(10.5)	200(100.0)	
	ALL	22(5.5)	93(23.2)	236(59.0)	49(12.2)	400(100.0)	
Reduction in wasteful expenditure	OSHG	6(3.0)	48(24.0)	91(45.5)	55(27.5)	200(100.0)	48.415 (0.000)
	NSHG	12(6.0)	91(45.5)	88(44.0)	9(4.5)	200(100.0)	
	ALL	18(4.5)	139(34.8)	179(44.8)	64(16.0)	400(100.0)	
Food habits	OSHG	2(1.0)	6(3.0)	57(28.5)	135(67.5)	200(100.0)	103.298 (0.000)
	NSHG	9(4.5)	10(5.0)	146(73.0)	35(17.5)	200(100.0)	
	ALL	11(2.8)	16(4.0)	203(50.8)	170(42.5)	400(100.0)	
Minor repairs to house	OSHG	16(8.0)	12(6.0)	97(48.5)	75(37.5)	200(100.0)	89.899 (0.000)
	NSHG	18(9.0)	82(41.0)	83(41.5)	17 (8.5)	200(100.0)	
	ALL	34(8.5)	94(23.5)	180(45.0)	92(23.0)	400(100.0)	

(Contd...)

Reduction in consumption Expenditure	OSHG	1(0.5)	20 (10.0)	72(36.0)	107(53.5)	200(100.0)	95.949 (0.000)
	NSHG	14(7.0)	76(38.0)	85(42.5)	25(12.5)	200(100.0)	
	ALL	15(3.8)	96(24.0)	157(39.2)	132(33.0)	400(100.0)	
Loan repayments	OSHG	4(2.0)	4(2.0)	18(9.0)	174(87.0)	200(100.0)	55.823 (0.000)
	NSHG	5(2.5)	20(10.0)	68(34.0)	107(53.5)	200(100.0)	
	ALL	9(2.2)	24(6.0)	86(21.5)	281(70.2)	400(100.0)	
Purchase of household durables	OSHG	12(6.0)	11(5.5)	91(45.5)	86(43.0)	200(100.0)	163.767 (0.000)
	NSHG	50(25.0)	87(43.5)	59(29.5)	4(2.0)	200(100.0)	
	ALL	62(15.5)	98(24.5)	150(37.5)	90(22.5)	400(100.0)	

Note: No Change = 0, Little Improvement =1, Moderate Improvement = 2, Good Improvement = 3.

APPENDIX-7.1

Social Empowerment Index Indicators

Sl. No	Indicators	Response	Score
1	Education	Illiterate	0
		Primary	1
		Secondary	2
		Technical	4
2	Working Days	Unemployed	0
		Below 80	1
		80-160	2
		160-240	3
		Above 240	4
3	Income	Upto 1000	1
		1000-2000	2
		2000-3000	3
		3000-4000	4
		4000 abvoe	5
4	Assets	House	1
		House and Land	2
		House, Land and jewellery	3
5	Borrowing Amount	Upto 5000	1
		5000-10000	2
		10000-15000	3
		15000-20000	4
		20000-25000	5
		25000-30000	6
		30000-35000	7
		Above 35000	8

Sl. No	Indicators	Response	Score
6	Self confidence		
7	Reduction in alcoholic habits		
8	Education of daughters		
9	Education of sons		
10	Mobility		
11	Access to markets		
12	Adaption of small family norms		
13	Discontinuation of early marriages		
14	Reduction in domestic violence		
15	Decision making in the family		
16	Decision making in the group		
17	Child labour discontinuation		
18	Status in the family	No Change=0 Little Improvement =1 Moderate Improvement=2 Good Improvement=3	
19	Status in the society		
20	Clothing		
21	Social functions/marrages		
22	Aware of rights of women		
23	Access to public participation		
24	Access to information on Government Programmes		
25	Participation in development programes		
26	Ability to meet Government officials		
27	Ability to meet non-officials		
28	Communication skills		
29	Sanitation status		
30	Personal hygiene		
31	Nutritional status		
32	Visiting hospitals		

APPENDIX -7.2

Social Variables

Indicator	Category of SHG	0	1	2	3	Total	χ2
Self-confidence	OSHG	2(1.0)	4(2.0)	92(46.0)	102(51.0)	200(100.0)	53.378 (0.000)
	NSHG	8(4.0)	50(25.0)	80(40.0)	62(31.0)	200(100.0)	
	ALL	10(2.5)	54(13.5)	172(43.0)	164(41.0)	400(100.0)	
Reduction in alcoholic habits	OSHG	10(5.0)	96(48.0)	65(32.5)	29(14.5)	200(100.0)	22.085 (0.000)
	NSHG	39(19.5)	95(47.5)	45(22.5)	21(10.5)	200(100.0)	
	ALL	49(12.2)	191(47.8)	110(27.5)	50(12.5)	400(100.0)	
Attitude towards the education of daughters	OSHG	4(2.0)	8(4.0)	101(50.5)	87(43.5)	200(100.0)	14.093 (0.000)
	NSHG	7(3.5)	27(13.5)	78(39.0)	88(44.0)	200(100.0)	
	ALL	11(2.8)	35(8.8)	179(44.8)	175(43.8)	400(100.0)	
Attitude towards the education of sons	OSHG	9 (4.5)	12(6.0)	62(31.0)	117(58.5)	200(100.0)	99.821 (0.000)
	NSHG	33(16.5)	80(40.0)	42(21.0)	45(22.5)	200(100.0)	
	ALL	42(10.5)	92(23.0)	104(26.0)	162(40.5)	400(100.0)	
Mobility	OSHG	5(2.5)	19(9.5)	57(28.5)	119(59.5)	200(100.0)	20.591 (0.000)
	NSHG	2(1.0)	29(14.5)	92(46.0)	77(38.5)	200(100.0)	
	ALL	7(1.8)	48(12.0)	149(37.2)	196(49.0)	400(100.0)	
Access to markets	OSHG	0(0.0)	9(4.5)	127(63.5)	64(32.0)	200(100.0)	92.260 (0.000)
	NSHG	5(2.5)	90(45.0)	70(35.0)	35(17.5)	200(100.0)	
	ALL	5(1.2)	99(24.8)	197(49.2)	99(24.8)	400(100.0)	
Adoption ofsmall family norm	OSHG	3(1.5)	20(10.0)	83(41.5)	94(47.0)	200(100.0)	28.189 (0.000)
	NSHG	6(3.0)	47(23.5)	99(49.5)	48(24.0)	200(100.0)	
	ALL	9(2.2)	67(16.8)	182(45.5)	142(35.5)	400(100.0)	
Discontinuation of early marriages	OSHG	12(6.0)	35(17.5)	70(35.0)	83(41.5)	200(100.0)	12.062 (0.000)
	NSHG	6(3.0)	51(25.5)	87(43.5)	56(28.0)	200(100.0)	
	ALL	18(4.5)	86(21.5)	157(39.2)	139(34.8)	400(100.0)	
Reduction in domestic violence	OSHG	3(1.5)	12(6.0)	118(59.0)	67(33.5)	200(100.0)	136.787 (0.00)
	NSHG	22(11.0)	103(51.5)	37(18.5)	38(19.0)	200(100.0)	
	ALL	25(6.2)	115(28.8)	155(38.8)	105(26.2)	400(100.0)	
Decision making in the family	OSHG	15(7.5)	20(10.0)	64(32.0)	101(50.5)	200(100.0)	66.728 (0.000)
	NSHG	27(13.5)	79(39.5)	55(27.5)	39(19.5)	200(100.0)	
	ALL	42(10.5)	99(24.8)	119(29.8)	140(35.0)	400(100.0)	
Decision making in the group	OSHG	9(4.5)	13(6.5)	80(40.0)	98(49.0)	200(100.0)	79.015 (0.000)
	NSHG	18(9.0)	84(42.0)	50(25.0)	48(24.0)	200(100.0)	
	ALL	27(6.8)	97(24.2)	130(32.5)	146(36.5)	400(100.0)	
Child labour discontinuation	OSHG	8(4.0)	16(8.0)	72(36.0)	104(52.0)	200(100.0)	28.787 (0.000)
	NSHG	28(14.0)	40(20.0)	62(31.0)	70(35.0)	200(100.0)	
	ALL	36(9.0)	56(14.0)	134(33.5)	174(43.5)	400(100.0)	
Status in the family	OSHG	7(3.5)	10(5.0)	143(71.5)	40(20.0)	200(100.0)	117.167 (0.000)
	NSHG	27(13.5)	91(45.5)	57(28.5)	25(12.5)	200(100.0)	
	ALL	34(8.5)	101(25.2)	200(50.0)	65(16.2)	400(100.0)	
Status in the society	OSHG	18(9.0)	21(10.5)	139(69.5)	22(11.0)	200(100.0)	78.742 (0.000)
	NSHG	20(10.0)	98(49.0)	63(31.5)	19(9.5)	200(100.0)	
	ALL	38(9.5)	119(29.8)	202(50.5)	41(10.2)	400(100.0)	

(Contd...)

Clothing	OSHG	9(4.5)	17(8.5)	132(66.0)	42(21.0)	200(100.0)	93.300 (0.000)
	NSHG	21(10.5)	96(48.0)	68(34.0)	15(7.5)	200(100.0)	
	ALL	30(7.5)	113(28.2)	200(50.0)	57(14.2)	400(100.0)	
Social function/ marriages	OSHG	17(8.5)	49(24.5)	106(53.0)	28 (14.0)	200(100.0)	69.759 (0.000)
	NSHG	15(7.5)	109(54.5)	30(15.0)	46(23.0)	200(100.0)	
	ALL	32(8.0)	158(39.5)	136(34.0)	74(18.5)	400(100.0)	
Aware of rights of women	OSHG	1(0.5)	22(11.0)	123(61.5)	54(27.0)	200(100.0)	107.910 (0.000)
	NSHG	23(11.5)	96(48.0)	43(21.5)	38(19.0)	200(100.0)	
	ALL	24(6.0)	118(29.5)	166(41.5)	92(23.0)	400(100.0)	
Access to public participation	OSHG	2(1.0)	11(5.5)	116(58.0)	71(35.5)	200(100.0)	80.994 (0.000)
	NSHG	12(6.0)	80(40.0)	71(35.5)	37 (18.5)	200(100.0)	
	ALL	14(3.5)	91(22.8)	187(46.8)	108(27.0)	400(100.0)	
Access to information on Government programmes	OSHG	4(2.0)	19(9.5)	134(67.0)	43(21.5)	200(100.0)	70.937 (0.000)
	NSHG	11(5.5)	79(39.5)	58(29.0)	52(26.0)	200(100.0)	
	ALL	15(3.8)	98(24.5)	192(48.0)	95(23.8)	400(100.0)	
Participation in Development programmes	OSHG	4(2.0)	30(15.0)	134(67.0)	32(16.0)	200 (100.0)	63.297 (0.000)
	NSHG	23(11.5)	71(35.5)	58(29.0)	48(24.0)	200(100.0)	
	ALL	27(6.8)	101(25.2)	192(48.0)	80(20.0)	400(100.0)	
Able to meet Government officials	OSHG	0(0.0)	39(19.5)	128(64.0)	33(16.5)	200(100.0)	63.158 (0.000)
	NSHG	22(11.0)	69(34.5)	56(28.0)	53(26.5)	200(100.0)	
	ALL	22(5.5)	108(27.0)	184(46.0)	86(21.5)	400(100.0)	
Able to meet Non-officials	OSHG	4(2.0)	70(35.0)	105(52.5)	21(10.5)	200(100.0)	92.649 (0.000)
	NSHG	43(21.5)	81(40.5)	26(13.0)	50(25.0)	200(100.0)	
	ALL	47(11.8)	151(37.8)	131(32.8)	71(17.8)	400(100.0)	
Communication skills	OSHG	1(0.5)	7(3.5)	117(58.5)	75(37.5)	200(100.0)	141.342 (0.000)
	NSHG	26(13.0)	92(46.0)	44(22.0)	38(19.0)	200(100.0)	
	ALL	27 (6.8)	99(24.8)	161(40.2)	113(28.2)	400(100.0)	
Sanitation status	OSHG	2(1.0)	54(27.0)	83(41.5)	61(30.5)	200(100.0)	46.841 (0.000)
	NSHG	19(9.5)	97(48.5)	35(17.5)	49(24.5)	200(100.0)	
	ALL	21(5.2)	151(37.8)	118(29.5)	110(27.5)	400(100.0)	
Personal hygiene	OSHG	2 (1.0)	21(10.5)	114(57.0)	63(31.5)	200(100.0)	98.440 (0.000)
	NSHG	24(12.0)	93(46.5)	50(25.0)	33(16.5)	200(100.0)	
	ALL	26(6.5)	114(28.5)	164(41.0)	96(24.0)	400(100.0)	
Nutritional status	OSHG	5(2.5)	16(8.0)	136(68.0)	43(21.5)	200(100.0)	76.904 (0.000)
	NSHG	19(9.5)	55(27.5)	51(25.5)	75(37.5)	200(100.0)	
	ALL	24(6.0)	71(17.8)	187(46.8)	118(29.5)	400(100.0)	
Visiting hospitals	OSHG	11(5.5)	27(13.5)	132(66.0)	30 (15.0)	200(100.0)	78.285 (0.000)
	NSHG	24(12.0)	100(50.0)	59(29.5)	17(8.5)	200(100.0)	
	ALL	35(8.8)	127(31.8)	191(47.8)	47(11.8)	400(100.0)	

Note: No Change = 0, Little Improvement =1, Moderate Improvement = 2, Good Improvement = 3.

Bibliography

Adams, D. W., Graham, D. H., & Pischke, J. V. (1984), *Undermining Rural Development with Cheap Credit,* Boulder and London: West view Press.

Agarwal, B. (1992), "The Gender and Environment Debate: Lessons from India", *Feminist Studies*, 18(1): 119-58.

Agarwal, B. (1994), "Gender and Command Over Property: A Critical Gap in Economic Analysis and Policy in South Asia", *World Development,* 22(10): 1455-78.

Agarwal, B. (1997), "Environmental Action, Gender Equity and Women's participation", *Development and Change*, 28(1): 1-44.

Ahluwalia, M. S. (1978), "Rural poverty and agricultural performance in India", *The Journal of Development Studies,* 14(3): 298-323.

Axelrod, R. (1981), *The Evolution of Cooperation*, Basic Books, New York.

Baland, J. M., & Platteau, J. P. (1996), "Halting Degradation of Natural Resources: Is there a Role for Rural Communities?", *Food and Agriculture Organisation of the United Nations*, Clarendon Press, Oxford.

Bansal, D. (2010), "Impact of Microfinance on Poverty, Employment and Women Empowerment in Rural Punjab", unpublished thesis, Punjabi University, Bathinda.

Bardhan, P. K. (1974), "On life and death questions", *Economic and Political Weekly*, 9(32/34):1293-1304.

Bennett, L., Goldberg, M., & Hunte, P. (1996), "Ownership and sustainability: Lessons on group-based financial services from South Asia", *Journal of International Development*, *8*(2):271-288.

Besley, T. & Coate S. (1995), "Group Lending, Repayment Incentives and Social Collateral", *Journal of Development Economics*, 46(1): 1-18.

Besley. T. (1994), "How Do Market Failures Justify Interventions in Rural Credit Markets?", The *World Bank Research Observer*, 9(1): 27-47.

Bhatt, N., & Tang, S. Y. (1998), "The Problem of Transaction Costs in Group Based Micro Lending: An Institutional Perspective" *World Development*, 26(4): 623-38.

Bhatt, V.V. (1987), "Financial Innovations and Credit Market Evolution", *Economic and Political Weekly*, 22(22): M45-M54.

Bhowmick. (2007), *Economics of poverty*, New Delhi: Deep and Deep Publications.

Boserup, E. (1970), *Women's Role in Economic Development.* Earthscan, London.

Bouman, F. J. A. (1984), "Informal Saving and credit Arrangement in Developing countries: Observations from Sri Lanka", In Adams D.W et al. (eds.), *Undermining Rural Development with Cheap Credit*, West view Press, Boulder and London.

Bratton, M. (1986), "Financing Small Holder Production: A Comparison of Individual and Group Credit Schemes in Zimbabwe", *Public Administration and Development*, 6 (2): 115-32.

Braverman, A., & Guasch, J. L. (1986), "Rural credit markets and institutions in developing countries: Lessons for policy analysis from practice and modern theory", *World Development*, 14(10): 1253-1267.

Braverman, A., & Guasch, J. L. (1993), Administrative Failures in Government Credit

Programs, *The Economics of Rural Organization: Theory, Practice, and Policy*, 53-69.

Buchanan, J.B. & Gorden, T. (1965), *The Calculus of Consent*, University of Michigan, Michigan.

Campbell, R., & Snowden, L. (Eds.), (1985), Paradoxes of Rationality and Cooperation: Prisoners Dilemma and Newcomb's Problem, University of British Columbia Press.

Chari-Wagh, A. (2009), "Raising Citizenship Rights for Women through Microcredit Programs: An Analysis of MASUM, Maharashtra, India", *Community Development Journal,* 44(3): 403-414.

Chavan, P., & Ramakumar, R. (2002), "Micro-Credit and Rural Poverty", *Economic and*

Political Weekly, 37(10): 955-965.

Coleman, J. S. (1988), "Social Capital in the Creation of Human Capital", *American*

Journal of Sociology, S95-S120.

Cuevas, C. E., & Graham, D. H. (1984), "Agricultural Lending Costs in Honduras" In Adams, Dale W. Douglas H. Graham and J. D. Von Pischke (eds.), *Undermining Rural Development with Cheap Credit*. Westview Press, Boulder.

Dandekar, V. M., & Rath, N. (1971), "Poverty in India-I: Dimensions and Trends", *Economic and Political Weekly*, 6(1): 25-48.

Dasgupta, R. (2001), "An Informal Journey through Self-Help Groups", *Indian Journal of Agricultural Economics*, 56(3): 370-386.

Datt, G., Ravallion, M., & Mundial, B. (1990), Regional disparities, targeting, and poverty in India, *Agriculture and Rural Development Department*, World Bank, W.P.S. 375.p.37.

Desai, B.M. (1983), "Group Lending in Rural Areas", In Von J.D. Pischke, Dale W. Adams and Gordon Donald (eds.), *Rural Financial Markets in Developing Countries*, Johns Hopkins University Press, Baltimore.

Dessing, M. (1990), "Support for micoenterprises: lessons for sub-Saharan Africa", Vol. 122, World Bank, Washington D.C.

Dev, S. M. (1988), "Regional disparities in agricultural labour productivity and rural poverty in India", *Indian Economic Review*, 23(2): 167-205.

Devereux, J., & Fishe, R. P. (1993), "An Economic Analysis of Group Lending Programs in Developing Countries", *The Developing Economics*, 31 (1): 102-121.

Dutta, I. (2002), "Knowledge and Skills in a Global Economy: A Dialectic of Inclusion and Exclusion", *Indian Journal of Lobour Economics,* 45(4): 1121-28.

Ebrahim, A. (2001), "NGO Behaviour and Development Discourse: Cases from Western India", *International Journal of Voluntary and Nonprofit Organizations*, 12(2): 79-101.

Fernandes, L. (2006), *India's New Middle Class: Democratic Politics in an Era of Economics Reform*, U of Minnesota Press.

Floro, S. L., & Yotopoulos, P. A. (1991), *Informal Credit Markets and the New Institutional Economics: The Case of Philippine Agriculture,* Westview Press, Boulder.

Gaiha, R., Imai, K., & Kaushik, P. D. (2001), "On Targeting and Cost Effectiveness of Anti-Poverty Programmes in Rural India", *Development and Change,* 32 (2): 309-342.

Galab, S., & Rao, N. C. (2003), "Women's self-help groups, poverty alleviation and empowerment", *Economic and Political weekly*, 38 (12/13): 1274-1283.

Gaurav, D. (1996): „*Poverty in India (1951-52): Trends and Decompositions'*, Mimeo, World Bank.

Ghatak, M. (1999), "Group lending, local information and peer selection", *Journal of development economics*, 60 (1): 27-50.

Ghatak, M., & Guinnane, T. W. (1999), "The Economics of Lending with Joint Liability: Theory and Practice", *Journal of Development Economics*, 60 (1): 195-228.

Godquin, M. (2004), "Micro-Finance and Repayment Performance in Bangladesh: How to Improve the Allocation of Loans by MFIs", *World Development*, 32 (11): 1909- 1926.

Goetz, A. M., & Gupta, R. S. (1996), "Who takes the Credit? Gender, Power, and Control over Loan Use in Rural Credit Programs in Bangladesh", *World Development*, 24(1): 45-63.

GOI, (2012), Annual Report 2011-12, Consumer Price Index Numbers for Agricultural and Rural Labourers, Government of India. BASE: 1986-87=100, table no: 2.02.

GOI, (2013), All-India Consumer Price Index Numbers for Agricultural and Rural Labourers on Base 1986-87=100, November, 2013, http://labourbureau.nic.in/.

Gonzalez-Vega, C. (1982), "Credit Rationing Behaviour of Agricultural Lenders: The Iron Law of Interest rate Restrictions", In Adams D.W et al. (eds.), *Undermining Rural Development with Cheap Credit,* Boulder and London: Westview Press.

Gothoskar, S. P. (1988), On some estimates of rural indebtedness, *Reserve Bank of India Occasional Papers*, 9(4), 299-325.

Government, A.P. (2011), Handbook of Statistics, Visakhapatnam District.

Gupta S.P. (1995), "Recent Economic Reform and its Impact on Poor", Paper presented at the National Conference on poverty and Employment, New Delhi, pp. 8-9, March 27-29.

Gupta, S. P. (1995), "Economic reform and its impact on poor", *Economic and Political Weekly*, 30(22):1295-1313.

Hashemi, S. (2001), Including the poorest: linking microfinance and safety net programs, CGAP, Occasional Paper no: 20.

Hashemi, S. M., Schuler, S. R., & Riley, A. P. (1996), "Rural Credit Programs and Women's Empowerment in Bangladesh", *World Development*, 24 (4): 635-653.

Hashemi, Syed M. (1997), "Those Left Behind: A Note on Targeting the Hardcore Poor", In Wood Geoffrey D and Sharif, Iffath A (Eds), *Who Needs Credit; Poverty and Finance in Bangladesh*, Zed Books, London and New York.

Himanshu (2007), "Recent Trends in Poverty and Inequality: Some Preliminary Results", *Economic and Political Weekly*, 42(6): 497-508.

Hoff, K., & Stiglitz, J. E. (1990), "Introduction: Imperfect information and rural credit markets-puzzles, policy perspectives." *The World Bank Economic Review*, 4(3): 235-250.

Hossain, M. (1988), "Credit for alleviation of rural poverty: The Grameen Bank in Bangladesh", working paper No. 65, *Intl Food Policy Res Inst.*

Hulme, D., & Mosley, P. (1996), *Finance against poverty, Vol. 1*, Routledge Publication, New York.

Huppi, M., & Feder, G. (1990), "The Role of Groups and Credit Cooperatives in Rural Lending", *The World Bank Research Observer*, 5 (2): 187-204.

Jacka, T. (2010), "Women"s Activism, Overseas Funded Participatory Development, and Governance: A Case Study from China", *Women's Studies International Forum*, 33 (2): 99-112.

Jain, S., & Mansuri, G. (2003), "A Little at a Time: The Use of Regularly Scheduled Repayments in Micro-Finance Programs", *Journal of Development Economics*, 72 (1): 253-79.

Jhabvala, R., & Sinha, S. (2002), "Liberalization and the Woman Worker", *Economic and Political Weekly*, 37(21): 2037-2044.

Kabeer, N. (1999), "The Conditions and Consequences of Choice: Reflections on the Measurement of Women"s Empowerment", Discussion Paper, No. 108, *United Nations Research Institute for Social Development,* Geneva.

Kabeer, N. (2001), "Conflict over Credit: Re-evaluating the Empowerment Potential of Loans to Women in Rural Bangladesh", *World Development*, 29(1): 63-84.

Kakwani, N., & Subbarao, K. (1990), *Rural poverty in India, 1973-86*, Population and Human Resources Department, World Bank.

Karim, L. (2008), "Demystifying Microcredit: The Grameen Bank, NGOs, and Neoliberalism in Bangladesh", *Cultural Dynamics*, 20(1): 5-29.

Karnakar K.G. (1988), *Rural Credit and Self-Help Groups-Microfinance needs and Concepts in India*, Sage publications, New Delhi, pp.234-236

Kelkar, G., Nathan, D., & Jahan, R. (2004), "Redefining Women"s „Samman": Microcredit and Gender Relations in Rural Bangladesh", *Economic and Political Weekly,* 39(32): 3627-3640.

Khandker, S. (2001), "Does micro-finance really benefit the poor? Evidence from Bangladesh", *In ponencia presentada a Asia and Pacific Forum on Poverty: Reforming Policies and Institutions for Poverty Reduction*, The Asian Development Bank, Manila (pp. 5-9).

Khandker, S. R. (1998), "Micro-Credit Programme Evaluation: A Critical Review1", *IDS bulletin*, 29(4): 11-20.

Khandker, S. R. (1998), *Fighting poverty with microcredit: experience in Bangladesh*, Oxford University Press.

Khandker, S.R. & Khalily, B. & Khan, Z. (1995), Grameen Bank Performance and Sustainability, *World Bank, Discussion Paper 306*,Washington D.C.

Kumaran, K. P. (2001), "Changing Role of Grass Root Level Organisations in the Context of Participatory Rural Development", *Social Action-New Delhi, 51*(1): 74-82.

Kumari, K. B. V. (2011), *Microcredit as a poverty alleviation strategy, women's empowerment and gender relations* (Doctoral dissertation, Rutgers University-Graduate School-New Brunswick). See also at http://rucore.libraries.rutgers.edu/rutgers-lib/33894/PDF/1/

Llanto G. M. (1990), "Asymmetric Information in Rural Financial Markets and interlinking of Transactions through Self-help Groups", *Saving and Development*, 14(2): 137-52.

Longwe, S. H.; and Clarke, R. (1994), "Women in Development, Culture and Youth: Workshop Readings", *Longwe Clarke and Associates*, Lusaka, Zambia.

Madheswaran, S. & Dharmadhikari, A. (2001), "Empowering Rural Women through Self-Help Groups", *Indian Journal of Agricultural Economics*, 56 (3): 427-43.

Malhotra, A.; Schuler, S.R.; and Boender, C. (2002), Measuring Women"s Empowerment as a Variable in International Development, World Bank, Washington, DC.

Malik M.S. (2000), "Economic Reforms and Effect on Poverty", *Yojana,* 44 (7): 10-18. Marchand, M. H. (2009), "The Future of gender and Development After 9/11: Insights from Postcolonial Feminism and Transnationalism", *Third World Quarterly*, 30(5): 921-935.

Mayoux, L. (1998), "Participatory Learning for Women's Empowerment in Micro-Finance Programmes: Negotiating Complexity, Conflict and Change", *IDS Bulletin*, 29 (4): 39-50.

Mayoux, L. (2001), "Tackling the Down Side: Social Capital, Women's Empowerment and Micro-Finance in Cameroon" *Development and Change*, 32 (3): 435-64.

Mayoux, L. (2002), "Micro Finance and Women"s Empowerment: Rethinking "best practice", *Development Bulletin*, 57: 76-81.

McCulloch, N., & Baulch, B. (2000), "Simulating the Impact of Policy upon Chronic and Transitory Poverty in Rural Pakistan" *Journal of Development Studies*, 36(6): 100-130.

Mearns, R. (1999), Access to land in rural India: policy issues and options, Working paper no: 2123, World Bank.

Mearns, R., & Sinha, S. (1999), Social exclusion and land administration in Orissa, India, Working paper no: 2124, World Bank.

Mehta, R. & Bhandari, S. (2005), "Poverty in Asia: Trends Issues and Polices in Poverty in India", in Nageswar Rao (ed.), *Global and Regional Dimensions*, Deep and Deep Publications, New Delhi, pp. 50-66.

Minhas, B. S., Jain, L. R., & Tendulkar, S. D. (1991), "Declining incidence of poverty in the 1980s: Evidence versus artefacts", *Economic and Political Weekly*, 26 (27/28): 1673-1682.

Mishra, V.N. and M. Rao (2003), "Trade Policy, Agricultural Growth and Rural Poor", *Economic and Political Weekly,* 38 (43): 4588-4603.

Mizan, A.N. (1994), *In Quest of Empowerment: The Grameen Bank Impact on Women's Power and Status*, University Press Limited, Dhaka.

Montgomery, R., Bhattacharya, D., Hulme, D., & Mosley, P. (1996), Credit for the poor in Bangladesh, The BRAC Rural Development Programme and the Government Thana Resource Development and Employment Programme, *Finance against poverty*, 2: 94-176.

Morduch, J. (1999), "The Micro-Finance Promise", *Journal of Economic Literature*, 37(4): 1569-1614.

Morduch, J. (1999), "The Roles of Subsidies in Micro-Finance: Evidence from the Grameen Bank", *Journal of Development Economics*, 60 (1): 229-48.

Mosley, P. (1996), "Metamorphosis from NGO to Commercial Bank: The Case of BancoSol in Bolivia", in Hulme, D. & Mosley, P. (ed.), *Finance against Poverty*, Vol. 2, Routledge Publications, London.

Mosley, P., & Dahal, R. P. (1985), "Lending to the Poorest: Early Lessons from the Small Farmers' Development Programme, Nepal", *Development Policy Review*, 3(2): 193-207.

Mukherjee, M. N. Bhattacharya and GS Chatterjee,(1972), "Poverty in India: Measurement and Amelioration," *Commerce*, 125(3198): 19.

Nayyar, R. (1991), *Rural poverty in India: an analysis of inter-state differences*, Oxford University Press, Mumbai, pp.27-61.

NSSO (2003), Debt & Investment: NSS 59th Round, Government of India.

NSSO (2003), Situation Assessment Survey of Formers: NSS 59th Round, Government of India.

NSSO (2006), Household Borrowings and Repayments in India: NSS 59th Round, Government of India.

NSSO (2010), *NSS KI: Key Indicators of Employment and Unemployment in India*, 2009-10.

Nussbaum, Martha C. (2000), *Women and Human Development: The Capabilities Approach,* Vol. 3, Cambridge University Press, Cambridge.

Oakerson, R. J. (1986), "A Model for the Analysis of Common Property Problems", *In proceedings of the Conference on Common Property Resource Management,* Washington: National Academic Press.

Okin, S. M. (2008), *Justice, gender, and the family,* Basic books, USA.

Olson, M. (1965), *The Logic of Collective Action,* Oxford: Oxford University Press. Papola, T.S. & Sahu, P.P. (2012), "Growth and Structure of Employment in India Long-Term and Post-Reform Performance and the Emerging Challenge", *Institute for Studies in Industrial Development*, ICSSR, New Delhi. Available at http://isidev.nic.in/pdf/ICSSR_TSP_PPS.pdf

Parker, J. and Pearce, D. (2001), Microfinance, Grants, and Non-Financial Responses to Poverty Reduction: Where does Microcredit fit? Consultative Group Focus Note number 20, Washington D.C, See also at http://ntl.ids.ac.uk/cgap/wnewlib.htm.

Parpart, J. L., Connelly, P., & Barriteau, V. E. (Eds.), (2000), *Theoretical perspectives on gender and development*, IDRC.

Pateman, C. (1987), "Feminist Critiques of the Public/Private Dichotomy", In Anne Phillips (ed.) *Feminism and equality*, Basil Blackwell, Oxford.

Pitt, M. M., Khandker, S. R., Chowdhury, O. H., & Millimet, D. L.(2003), "Credit Programs for the Poor and the Health Status of Children in Rural Bangladesh", *International Economic Review,* 44 (1): 87-118.

Pitt, M., Khandker, S., & Cartwright, J. (2004), "Does micro-credit empower women? Evidence from Bangladesh", Evidence *from Bangladesh), World Bank Policy Research Working Papers*, No: 2998.

Poteete, A. R., & Ostrom, E. (2004), "Heterogeneity, Group Size and Collective Action: The Role of Institutions in Forest Management", *Development and Change*, 35(3): 435-461.

Prabhu, K. S., Nadkarni, A., & Achuthan, C. V. (1988), "Rural credit: mystery of the missing households", *Economic and Political Weekly*, 23(50): 2642-2646.

Puhazhendhi V. & Satyasai K. J. S. (2000), "Micro Credit for the Rural People: An Impact Evaluation", *National Bank for Agriculture and Rural Development*, Mumbai. Also see http://www.nabard.org/mcid/impactstudy.htm.

Putnam, R. D., Leonardi, R., & Nanetti, R. Y. (1994), *Making democracy work: Civic traditions in modern Italy*, Princeton university press.

Radhakrishna, R. (2007), Report, Expert Group on Agricultural Indebtedness, Department of Economic Affairs, Ministry of Finance, Government of India.

Rahman, A. (1999), "Micro-credit Initiatives for Equitable and Sustainable Development: Who Pays?", *World development*, 27(1): 67-82.

Rahman, A. (1999), "Micro-Credit Initiatives for Equitable and Sustainable Development: Who Pays?", *World Development*, 27(1): 67-82.

Rahman, H. Z., & Hossain, M. (1995), *Rethinking rural poverty: Bangladesh as a case study*, Sage Publications Pvt. Ltd, India.

Rai, S. M. (2002), *Gender and the political economy of development,* Polity Press, UK. Rajan, R. S. (2002), "Trade Liberalisation and Poverty; Revisiting the Age Old Debate", *Economic and Political Weekly,* 37 (49): 4941-4946.

Rajasekhar, D. (1996), "Problems and Prospects of Group Lending in NGO Credit Programmes in India", *Savings and Development*, 20 (1): 79-104.

Ravallion, M., & Datt, G. (1996), "How important to India's poor is the sectoral composition of economic growth?", *The World Bank Economic Review*, 10(1): 1-25.

Reinke, J. (1998), "Does Solidarity Pay? The Case of the Small Enterprise Foundation, South Africa", *Development and Change*, 29(3): 553-576.

Rutherford, S. (2001), *The Poor and Their Money*, New Delhi, Oxford University Press (Oxford India Paperbacks).

Sahu, G. B., & Rajasekhar, D. (2005), "Banking Sector Reforms and Credit Flow to Indian Agriculture", *Economic and Political Weekly*, 40(53): 5550-5559.

Schaefer-Kehnert, W. (1980), "Success with group lending in Malawi", *Quarterly Journal of International Agriculture*, *19*(4): 331-337.

Schneider, H. (Ed.) (1997), *Microfinance for the Poor?,* OECD Publishing.

Schuler, S. R., & Hashemi, S. M. (1994), "Credit programs, women's empowerment, and contraceptive use in rural Bangladesh", *Studies in family planning*, 65-76.

Sen, A. (1981), *Poverty and Famines: An Essay on Entitlement and Deprivation*, Oxford University, Press.

Sen, A. (1999), *Development as freedom*. Oxford University Press, Oxford.

Sharma, M., & Zeller, M. (1997), "Repayment Performance in Group Based Credit Programs in Bangladesh: An Empirical Analysis", *World Development*, 25 (10): 1731-1742.

Shetty, S. (2003), Gender, Poverty, Empowerment and the Promise of Microcredit in India and the United States, *Dissertation Abstracts International, Section A: Humanities and Social Sciences,* 63(10): 3758.

Shiva, V. (1988), *Staying Alive, Women, Ecology and Survival in India*, Kali, New Delhi.

Shorrocks, A. F. (1995), "Revisiting the Sen Poverty index", *Econometrica: Journal of the Econometric Society*, 63(5): 1225-1230.

Stiglitz, E. Joseph (1990), "Peer Monitoring and Credit Markets" *The World Bank Economic Review*, 4 (3): 351-66.

Stiglitz, J. E., & Weiss, A. (1981), "Credit Rationing in Markets with Imperfect Information", *American Economic Review*, 71 (3): 393-410.

Sundaram, K. (2001), "Employment and Poverty in 1990s", *Economic and Political Weekly,* 36 (32): 3039-3049.

Sundaram, K., & Tendulkar, S. D. (2004), "The Poor in India Labour Force", *Economic and Political Weekly,* 39(48): 5121-32.

Sundaram, K., & Tendulkar, S. D. (2003), "Poverty in India in the 1990s: An analysis of changes in 15 major states", *Economic and Political Weekly*, 38 (14): 1385-1393.

Thakur, R. (2010), "Poverty-Progeny of Progress", in N.S Iyengar (ed.), *Poverty and Sustainable Development*, Deep and Deep Publications, New Delhi, pp. 90-112. Todd, Helen (1996), *Women at the Center*. Westview Press. New York.

UNDP (1995), Human Development Report, Oxford University Press, New York.

UNICEF (1997), Give us credit, *Division of Evaluation, Policy and Planning, Available online: http://www. unicef. org/credit/-credit. pdf*

Van Bastelaer, T. (2000), "Imperfect information, social capital and the poor's access to credit", *Center for Institutional Reform and the Informal Sector (IRIS), University of Maryland.*

Varian, H. (1990), "Monitoring Agents with Other Agents", *Journal of Institutional and Theoretical Economics*, 146(1): 153-174.

Verma, V. (2004), "Engendering Development: Limits of Ferminist Theories and Justice", *Economics and Political Weekly*, 39(49): 5246-5252.

Vogel, R. C. (1984), "The effect of subsidised Agricultural Credit on Income Distribution in Costa Rica", In Adams D.W et al. (eds.), *Undermining Rural Development with Cheap Credit*, Boulder and London: Westview Press.

Vonderlack-Navarro, R. (2010), "Targeting women versus addressing gender in microcredit: Lessons from Honduras". *Affilia*, 25(2): 123-134.

Woolcock, M. J. (1999), "Learning from failures in microfinance", *American Journal of Economics and Sociology*, 58(1): 17-42.

World Bank (1996), "Bangladesh: Poverty Alleviation Microfinance Project" Staff Appraisal Report South Asia Region, Country Department-1, Private Sector Development and Finance Division, Washington

World Bank (2001), *Engendering Development: Through Gender Equality in Rights, Resources and Voice*, World Bank Policy Research Report, Oxford University Press, Oxford.

World Bank (2010), World Development Report 2002, Oxford University Press, Oxford. Wright, G. A. (2000), *Microfinance systems: Designing quality financial services for the poor*, Zed books, London.

Wydick, B. (1999), "Can Social Cohesion be Harnessed to Repair Market Failures?

Evidence from Group Lending in Guatemala*", The Economic Journal*, 109 (457): 463-475.

Xu, K., & Osberg, L. (2002), "The social welfare implications, decomposability and geometry of the Sen Family of poverty indices", *Canadian Journal of Economics,* 35(1): 138-152.

Yaron, J. (1992), Assessing Development Finance Institutions. *World Bank, Discussion Paper 174*, Washington D.C., p.12.

Yifu Lin, J., & Nugent, J. B. (1995), "Institutions and Economic Development", *Handbook of Development Economics*, 3: 2301-2370.

Young, H. P. (2001*), Individual strategy and social structure: An evolutionary theory of institutions,* Princeton University Press.

Zaman, H. (1997), "Micro-credit Programs: Who Participated and to What Extent?", In Wood Geoffrey D and Sharif, Fifth A (Eds.*), Who Needs Credit; Poverty and Finance in Bangladesh,* Zed Books London.

Zeller, M. (1994), "Determinants of credit rationing: A study of informal lenders and formal credit groups in Madagascar", *World Development*, 22(12): 1895-1907.